Lecture Notes in Computer Science 4745

Commenced Publication in 1973
Founding and Former Series Editors:
Gerhard Goos, Juris Hartmanis, and Jan van Leeuwen

Editorial Board

Emmanuel Gaudin   Elie Najm   Rick Reed (Eds.)

SDL 2007: Design for Dependable Systems

13th International SDL Forum
Paris, France, September 18-21, 2007
Proceedings

Springer

Volume Editors

Emmanuel Gaudin
PragmaDev SARL
18, rue des Tournelles, 75004 Paris, France
E-mail: emmanuel.gaudin@pragmadev.com

Elie Najm
ENST
Département Informatique et Réseaux
46, rue Barrault, 75634 Paris Cedex 13, France
E-mail: Elie.Najm@ENST.fr

Rick Reed
Telecommunications Software Engineering Limited
The Laurels, Victoria Road, Windermere, Cumbria LA23 2DL, United Kingdom
E-mail: rickreed@tseng.co.uk

Library of Congress Control Number: 2007934912

CR Subject Classification (1998): C.2, D.2, D.3, F.3, C.3, H.4

LNCS Sublibrary: SL 5 – Computer Communication Networks and
Telecommunications

ISSN   0302-9743
ISBN-10   3-540-74983-7 Springer Berlin Heidelberg New York
ISBN-13   978-3-540-74983-7 Springer Berlin Heidelberg New York

Springer is a part of Springer Science+Business Media

springer.com

© Springer-Verlag Berlin Heidelberg 2007
Printed in Germany

Typesetting: Camera-ready by author, data conversion by Scientific Publishing Services, Chennai, India
Printed on acid-free paper   SPIN: 12161393   06/3180   5 4 3 2 1 0

Preface

This volume contains the papers presented at the 13th SDL Forum, Paris, France entitled "Design for Dependable Systems" and reflects the intent to have a balance between experience reports and research papers related to System Design Languages.

The language that was at the heart of the first few SDL Forums was the ITU-T Specification and Description Language defined in Z.100, and the application domain was almost entirely fixed-line telephone communication. Mobile telephony was for the super-rich and electronics in cars was just for radios.

Ever since its inception, 30 years ago, the Z.100 language has been used for model-driven development in the telecommunication industry. Nowadays, model-driven engineering is a must for all industries and has been generalized by OMG to all application domains as covered by a paper on an automotive case study in this volume. What has been happening over the past few years is that the infrastructure has been put in place providing good support for the model-driven paradigm, so that the economic benefit of the approach makes it more of a necessity than a choice for designing dependable systems. The experience report from Motorola in this volume underlines this trend.

Although the SDL Forum Society that organizes these SDL Forums has it roots in telecommunications, the System Design Languages needed for modeling in that industry are applied in other real-time engineering domains such as aerospace, the ubiquitous Bluetooth devices, and railways. For the last few years all modeling languages and technologies have had a tendency to converge towards UML, and since UML 2.0 and its profile definition capability came out, there is now an amazing number of diverging profile proposals based on older technologies. This was reflected in the conference programme with tutorials on SysML, SDL-RT, MARTE, and Z.109 covering different aspects of system modeling. An example in this volume is the paper that utilizes the UML 2.0 Testing Profile.

This latter paper is one of a number that shows the continuing interest and developments in the ITU-T Testing and Test Control Notation (TTCN). Although much of the evolution of TTCN has been through the work of ETSI, it is still largely seen as an ITU-T standard. In some ways this makes sense as ITU-T re-publishes the ETSI revisions of TTCN as a truly international standard (Z.140 series). TTCN is widely used with the ITU-T Message Sequence Chart (Z.120) and Specification and Description Language (Z.100 series). These are also used with another ITU-T product, Abstract Syntax Notation One (X.680 series), which is used to define protocol data units with their associated encoding rules (X.690 series). However, these languages are not thought to be adequate to capture requirements. A new language for User Requirements Notation (Z.150 series) is in progress, which includes Use Case Maps — covered by another paper in this volume.

So with all these ITU-T languages for system design, what is the role of UML?

UML is seen, as its name implies, as a unifying concept between languages. Because UML leaves a number a semantic issues open and even states frequently that there is *no specific notation* for a particular concept, it is in reality largely a framework that has to be populated with specific semantics and notations before it can be used to completely develop products. One route is to choose a particular UML tool, whose implementation (such as writing actions in C or Java) will have fixed certain issues, but at the cost of potentially being locked into that tool. Another route is to provide UML profiles for existing languages, thus not only binding UML to the semantics and notation of the language, but also providing some glue between different notations. It is the latter route that the ITU-T is taking (albeit rather slowly), with Z.109 being approved in 2007 as the UML profile for Z.100. Other profiles are in the ITU-T work plan for X.680, Z.120, Z.140 and Z.150. A related path is presented in the first paper in the volume, providing a meta-model for (a subset of) Z.100.

UML also has another role. If you ask someone who claims to be using UML which diagrams they use, often the reply will be that they mainly use Class Diagrams and Object Diagrams. The other 11 types of UML diagrams are used less frequently and some quite rarely (if at all). This is partly because the Class Diagrams and Object Diagrams meet a need that is not well met by other notations. Even the ITU-T in its 1996 Z.100 SDL+ methodology supplement suggested using diagrams in the Object-Modeling Technique notation (a forerunner of UML subsumed into UML in the unifying process). This is why it is natural to use these diagrams with the ITU-T languages: UML is frequently used for class and object modeling with Z.100 and other state machine languages in this volume and elsewhere. UML therefore not only provides the glue, but itself provides an important member of a set of System Design Languages.

Although the original Z.100 of 30 years ago was a paper and pencil language, none of this engineering today would be practical without computer-based tools because the systems in question are much more complex. This is evident from most of papers. As well as tools to directly support System Design Languages, included in this volume are papers on a real-time operating system and the use of probability modeling to analyze realistic-size networks without encountering state space explosion. At first glance, it may seem that these papers are not relevant, but you will probably change your mind when you read the papers, as a key issue in both cases is performance. There are many factors involved in the design for dependable real-time systems, so it is hard to predict what might be relevant for a future SDL Forum.

Thanks

A volume such as this could not, of course, exist without the contributions of the authors, who are thanked for their work.

The Programme Committee were also the reviewers of the papers, and are thanked for their work selecting the papers and the programme.

Irfan Hamid of ENST is thanked for his editorial assistance in preparing this volume.

The organization was greatly assisted by the various sponsors that provided valuable support. SDL 2007 was sponsored by:

- Centre National de la Recherche Scientifique
- Cinderella
- France Telecom
- PragmaDev
- Télécom Paris - École Nationale Supérieure des Télécommunications (ENST)
- Telelogic

July 2007   Emmanuel Gaudin
                                                                       Elie Najm
                                                                       Rick Reed

Organization

Each SDL Forum is organized by the SDL Forum Society with the help of local organizers. The Organizing Committee consists of the Board of the SDL Forum Society plus the local organizers and others as needed depending on the actual event. For SDL 2007 the local organizers from PragmaDev and ENST need to be thanked for their effort to ensure that everything was in place for the presentation of the papers in this volume.

Organizing Committee

Chairman, SDL Forum Society	Rick Reed (TSE Ltd.)
Treasurer, SDL Forum Society	Martin von Löwis (Hasso-Plattner-Institut)
Secretary, SDL Forum Society	Andreas Prinz (Agder University College)
Conference Chair	Emmanuel Gaudin (PragmaDev)
Programme Committee Chair	Elie Najm (ENST)

Programme Committee

Daniel Amyot (Université d'Ottawa, Canada)
Reibert Arbring (Ericsson, Sweden)
Rolv Bræk (NTNU, Norway)
Eric Brunel (PragmaDev, France)
Pierre Combes (France Telecom, France)
Philippe Desfray (Objecteering Software, France)
Laurent Doldi (Isoscope, France)
Anders Ek (Telelogic, Sweden)
Jaqueline Floch (SINTEF, Norway)
Birgit Geppert (Avaya Labs Research, USA)
Reinhard Gotzhein (Universität Kaiserslautern, Germany)
Jens Grabowski (University of Göttingen, Germany)
Susanne Graf (Verimag, France)
Peter Graubmann (Siemens, Germany)
Loïc Hélouët (INRIA Rennes, France)
Paul Herber (Sandrila, UK)
Dieter Hogrefe (ETSI - MTS, Germany)
Eckhardt Holz (University of Potsdam, Germany)
Ferhat Khendek (Concordia University, Canada)
Tae-Hyong, Kim, KIT, Korea)
Shashi Kumar (Jönköping University, Sweden)
Philippe Leblanc (Telelogic, France)

Vesa Luukkala (Nokia, Finland)
Anna Medve (University of Pannonia, Hungary)
Pedro Merino Gómez (University of Malaga, Spain)
François Michaillat (Alcatel, France)
Birger Møller-Pedersen (University of Oslo, Norway)
Elie Najm (ENST Paris, France)
Patrik Nandorf (Ericsson, Sweden)
Ian Oliver (Nokia, Finland)
Anders Olsen (Cinderella, Denmark)
Benoit Parreaux (France Telecom, France)
Javier Poncela González (University of Malaga, Spain)
Andreas Prinz (Agder University College, Norway)
Rick Reed (TSE, UK)
Manuel Rodríguez Cayetano (University of Valladolid, Spain)
Eldor Rødseth (SystemSoft, Norway)
Alain Rossignol (Astrium, France)
Richard Sanders (SINTEF, Norway)
Amardeo Sarma (NEC, Germany)
Ina Schieferdecker (Fraunhofer FOKUS, Germany)
Bran Selic (IBM Rational, Canada)
Edel Sherratt (University of Wales Aberystwyth, UK)
Martin von Löwis (Hasso-Plattner-Institut Potsdam, Germany)
Thomas Weigert (Motorola, USA)

SDL Forum Society

The SDL Forum Society is a not-for-profit organization that in addition to running the SDL Forum:

- Runs the SAM (System Analysis and Modeling) workshop every 2 years between SDL Forum years.
- Is a body recognized by ITU-T as co-developing the Z.100 to Z.109 and Z.120 to Z.129 and other language standards;
- Promotes the ITU-T System Design Languages.

For more information on the SDL Forum Society, see `www.sdl-forum.org`.

Table of Contents

Model Driven Engineering

Testing

Language Extensions

Implementation

Modeling Experience and Extensions

A Model-Based Standard for SDL

Andreas Prinz[1], Markus Scheidgen[2], and Merete S. Tveit[1]

[1] Faculty of Engineering, Agder University College
Grooseveien 36, N-4876 Grimstad, Norway
{andreas.prinz,merete.s.tveit}@hia.no
[2] Department of Computer Science, Humboldt Universität zu Berlin
Unter den Linden 6, 10099 Berlin, Germany
scheidge@informatik.hu-berlin.de

Abstract. Language descriptions have much information captured in plain (English) text, and even the formalised parts are often informally connected with the overall language definition. These imprecise descriptions are hardly usable to automatically generate language tool environments out of the language standard. SDL has already managed to define syntax and semantics in a quite formal way. Currently, this formality is connected by using different types of grammars. Meta-models, however, have proven to be a good way of expressing complex facts and relations. Moreover, there are tools and technologies available realising all language aspects based on completely formal and still easily understandable meta-model-based descriptions. This paper is about an experiment of combining all these existing techniques to create a definition of (a subset of) SDL. This allows to have immediate tool support for the language. This experiment includes the language aspects concrete syntax representation, static semantic constraints, and language behaviour. It turns out that this is almost possible.

1 Introduction

Model Driven Development (MDD) uses models to describe systems on a higher level of abstraction. This abstraction, i.e. hiding of much detail, is possible because models are instances of more and more complex modelling languages, which provide more and more specific concepts. Therefore, there is a need for more complex and (domain) specific modelling languages. Furthermore languages in an MDD environment are only meaningful if they come with a comprehensive tool environment. So there are two challenges: creating a human readable language standard and providing tool support for the language.

It is obvious that it is necessary to have a description of the language first. We will call such a description a meta-model. Today, there are several language description techniques and meta-tools that allow to describe and realise single language aspects like concrete syntax, static semantic analysis, model execution, or code generation. Tooling can be achieved by manually building language tools or by creating modelling tools automatically from the language description. In the latter case, the language description has to be completely formal.

E. Gaudin, E. Najm, and R. Reed (Eds.): SDL 2007, LNCS 4745, pp. 1–18, 2007.

The contribution of this paper is a combination of existing and new techniques forming one cohesive language description with the possibility to create a complete tool environment from it. We start with a representative sub-set of SDL (this sub-set provides all features necessary for the well-known camera example), and create meta-model-based descriptions that can function as a human-readable standard and an SDL tool environment including textual and graphical editors, static semantic checker, and model simulator.

The current SDL standard [8] with its formal semantics specification [7] already showed that most language aspects can be described formally without ambiguities. In [3], Prinz et. al. showed that even aspects that are usually described informally, like language behaviour, can be described formally allowing tools to be created from such formal descriptions in an at least semi-automated way. In [4] we discussed the possibility to use meta-modelling as the basis for integrating different languages and tools with each other. We already successfully evaluated the possibilities for automated tool support based on meta-models in the context of domain specific languages in [10,14].

In this paper we explain how different meta-modelling techniques work together. We focus on the two main purposes given above: how to present the language description in a user-friendly way and how to use the description for generating tools. Although in an ideal world, these two purposes would coincide, we could not achieve a complete match in this experiment.

The paper is structured as follows. In Sect. 2 we will introduce the different language aspects that we used in this experiment together with their relation to each other. The subsequent sections will present the approaches and technologies that we used to describe the different aspects one by one, namely structure (Sect. 3), constraints (Sect. 4), representation (Sect. 5), and behaviour (Sect. 6). Each section contains parts of the SDL language as examples. In the concluding Sect. 7, we discuss our results and suggest further work.

2   Basics

In [9] meta-modelling is defined as: *The construction of an object-oriented model of the abstract syntax of a language.* However, in our article we use the term meta-model in a wider sense: *A meta-model is a model that defines a language completely including the concrete syntax, abstract syntax and semantics.*

As a language description, meta-models can have several aspects that we have already identified in [10]. Figure 1 shows these aspects. Even though there is no complete agreement about what parts a language description consists of, these or similar parts can be identified in most contexts. The picture shows the following parts.

Structural information for the meta-model includes all the information about which concepts exist in the domain and how they are related. An example of this would be a MOF (Meta Object Facility) class diagram. In our understanding, this part does just include very simple structural properties and not more advanced concepts that rely on the use of constraints.

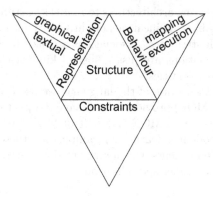

Fig. 1. Structure of a Meta-model

Constraints give additional information about the structure in that they identify the allowed structure according to additional logical constraints. This will include first-order logic constraints (e.g. written in Object Constraint Language (OCL)) as well as multiplicity constraints. In classical compiler theory these are collected under the name of static semantics and in a meta-model context they are called well-formedness rules.

Representation describes model serialization syntax and information about how the models are to be (re)presented to the user. The textual grammars (concrete textual syntax) are well understood in terms of compiler theory. When it comes to graphical grammar (concrete visual syntax), there is less agreement and there are some open research topics.

Behaviour describes how the model is used. This item includes execution of the model as well as mappings. By mapping we understand a relation between the model itself and another representation, e.g. in another language. A typical example would be a compiler from Java to JVM, or a mapping from a platform independent model to a platform specific model. An execution is the real run of the model, which is of course only possible if the model is executable. A typical example here would be a run of a Petri net.

In Fig. 1, the structure is the central aspect and all the other parts relate to the structure. The constraints have to be connected to the structural elements that they constrain. The representation parts describe the representation of elements in the structure, whereas the behaviour parts describe a behaviour for the elements defined in structure.

3   Structure

The structure part of a language description defines an abstract data structure for models, programs, or specifications written in that language. Like in model-driven development, object-oriented models in the form of class diagrams, are used in most meta-modelling architectures to model structures. These type models use classes as refinable classifications of entities by means of shared characteristics, modelled with attributes. Associations are used to classify the relations between entities. Associations are just a special kind of classifiers and actual links are a special kind of entities.

For a user-friendly description of the language, we use CMOF from MOF 2.0 [11]. CMOF (complete MOF) provides additional concepts to model abstractions compared to EMOF (essential MOF also part of MOF 2.0), which only defines a set of basic meta-modelling features. Examples for these additional CMOF features are property refinements, which allow to relate attributes or association ends in the context of classifier specialisation.

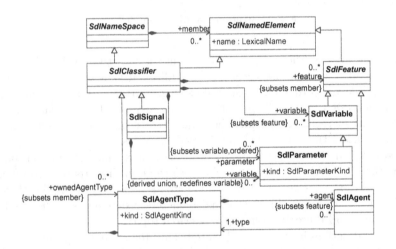

Fig. 2. Classifier concepts in SDL

In terms of languages, classes classify model elements based on the language concept that they instantiate. For example, all the agent types in all the existing SDL specifications are instances of the agent type concept. The first sample meta-model part in Fig. 2 describes the language concept *agent type* as a meta-model class. Attributes and associations are used to define the structural characteristics of agent types: an agent type can contain other agent types, it can contain type-based agents, it has parameters and variables. The example also shows how characteristics of more abstract language concepts can be reused. Agent types and signals for example, are just special SDL classifiers. SDL classifiers have features, like variables or parameters, as general characteristics. Variables are just one special form of features, and parameters just one special form of variables. Agent types inherit containment of variables and parameters and extend their set of features, containing variables and parameters already, with agents as just another type of feature. Signals inherit ownership of parameters. Signals also inherit ownership of variables and features, but only allow parameters as possible variables or features. The redefinition of the property variable in signal as a derived union ensures that parameters are the only possible subset of variables.

Using all the CMOF features to express abstractions, enabled us to compose a meta-model for SDL from a predefined library of abstract language concepts. We re-used the UML infrastructure library accordingly to create the SDL meta-model. The UML infrastructure library was used to define the UML, so this approach makes sure that the two languages UML and SDL have a common base in their underlying language infrastructure.

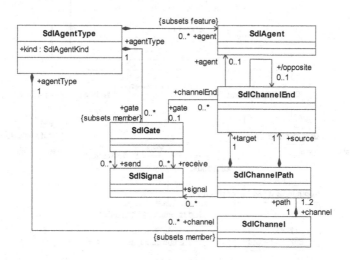

Fig. 3. Concepts for communication structures in SDL

Figure 3 shows another part of the SDL structure meta-model. This meta-model part covers the concepts of the sample specification in Fig. 4, which shows a block type definition (the entire example can be found in [15]). This block type definition is shown twice: in SDL syntax and as an object diagram, instantiating the SDL structure meta-model.

After having defined the structural meta-model in MOF 2.0, we had to find a proper tool supporting such descriptions. Although it is possible to find tools for MOF 2.0 (e.g. [13]), we decided to take a simpler tool which allows better integration with the other aspects as described in the next sections.

For the language tooling, we use Ecore (the meta-modelling language of EMF [1]). Ecore is a simple language allowing to express structures with just a few basic concepts. It is similar to EMOF. In Ecore the expressive power of the CMOF additional concepts has to be implemented manually, for example with OCL-expressions. Because of its simplicity, Ecore has the advantage of a clearer mapping to programming languages and more extensive tool support.

Compared with the SDL standard, the MOF-based structure definition yields almost the same object structure of a specification. The advantage is that it has much richer classification of the language concepts.

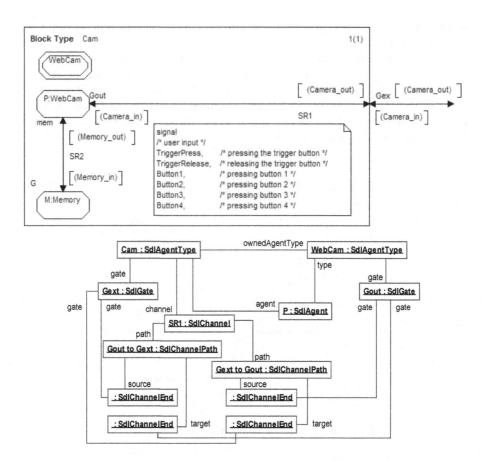

Fig. 4. Part of an example SDL specification and its model representation

4   Constraints

Structure models are designed to define valid graphs of objects and links, by defining classes and associations. To complement these concepts of constructive modelling, we use boolean expressions to constrain the possible instances of a meta-model.

To define such static semantic rules for SDL, we use the Object Constraint Language (OCL) [12]. OCL is specifically designed as an expression language for object-oriented structures. It allows to define expressions based on types defined in a meta-model. These expressions, defined at meta-level, can then be evaluated on models. OCL is a statically typed language. Each formula is defined in the context of a meta-model type. Based on this context type an expression can use the features of the corresponding meta-element to navigate through models. OCL uses several predefined operators and functions to combine feature values into a value for an OCL expression. Predefined functions and operators are derived from first order predicate logic.

We will illustrate the use of OCL with a sample constraint as given in the SDL standard. The text in Z.100 [8] is as follows:

> The contained *Agent-definitions* of an *Agent-definition* with the *Agent-kind* **PROCESS** shall all have the the *Agent-kind* **PROCESS**.

In the formal SDL semantics [7], this is formalised using first-order predicate logic to define expressions over abstract syntax as follows:

$$\forall d \in \textit{Agent-type-definition} : (d.agentKind_1 = \texttt{process}) \Rightarrow$$
$$(d' \in \textit{Agent-type-definition} \cup \textit{Agent-definition} : d'.parentAS1 = d \Rightarrow$$
$$d'.agentKind_1 = \texttt{process})$$

In the meta-model, the same constraint is part of the context of *SdlAgentType* as follows:

```
context  SdlAgentType
inv: (self.agentKind = #PROCESS) implies
        (self.ownedAgentType->union(self.agent.type)->forAll(
            agentKind = #PROCESS))
```

In our approach the meta-model reflects the SDL structures as defined with grammars in the SDL standard. Therefore, we can use the same conditions from the SDL standard as a formal basis for corresponding OCL expressions. It is obvious that the two descriptions above match. The only difference is that in the meta-model-based OCL we navigated along object structures, instead of sets and nodes obtained from the abstract syntax tree in the grammar-based SDL standard. It should also be noted that the grammar-based SDL standard uses a complete view on all objects and uses logic to narrow onto the objects of interest. OCL, in contrast, starts with the object of interest and collects all other information from there.

Another sample constraint ensures compatibility of the two gates in bidirectional channels. It exemplifies the navigation through the more complex communication structures given in Fig. 3:

```
context  SdlChannel
inv: self.path->size = 2 implies
    self.path->forAll(p1, p2 | p1 <> p2 implies
        (p1.source.gate = p2.target.gate and
        p1.target.gate = p2.source.gate))
```

For defining all the constraints in the current SDL standard, it was necessary to define auxiliary functions. Fortunately, OCL allows arbitrary typed expressions and is thus also suitable as a query language, even though the name Object Constraint Language suggests that it can only be used for constraints (boolean expressions). This allows to define derived and behavioural query features in meta-models based on OCL, as long as these features do not change the model. With derived properties and query operations, meta-modelling allows to define utility functions on the static SDL models based on simple OCL expressions. These utilities can be used in the realisation of other language aspects, such as the language behaviour. The following sample expression implements the association end *attribute* of *SdlChannelEnd*, which calculates the opposite *channel end* of the context *channel end* (*self*):

```
context SdlChannelEnd::opposite:SdlChannelEnd
body: let otherChannelPath: SdlChannelPath =
            self.channel.channel.path->select(c|
                c <> self.channel)->first() in
        if channel.target = self then otherChannelPath.source
        else otherChannelPath.target endif
```

Finally, OCL can be used to express constraints that realise enhanced meta-modelling features.In Sect. 3 we argued that the simple meta-modelling language Ecore cannot be used to define the refinement of features. But those refinement expressions, provided by MOF 2, can be realised via OCL constraints. For example, for each redefined property there has to be an OCL expression that states that the redefined property always has the same values as the redefining property.

In summary, the OCL-based constraint definition is similar to the SDL standard regarding constraints and auxiliary functions. The main difference is that OCL is object-oriented.

5   Representation

In general, models are abstractions and do not have concrete appearance. But we need a concrete model representation to communicate them. Models in our minds need to be transformed into a concrete representation of the same model on a piece of paper or computer screen. Since model representations are the basis to exchange them with others, these representations need to be written in well defined model notations. All language users have to know the same notation in order to allow reasoning and exchange of models.

A notation is the definition of a model representation based on the structure meta-model. Hence, notations are defined at the meta-level. A notation defines a set of possible representations. Each representation represents a model of a corresponding meta-model. For describing a representation, we distinguish between three kinds of meta-models: the language *structure meta-model*; a model that describes the entities of our notation, the *notation model*; and a *mapping model* that connects these two models, mapping notation concepts to language concepts. All three models together provide all information necessary to provide model representations in a concrete notation. Of course, in simple situations it would be preferable with just one representation description. In Sect. 5.1 we give more reasons why it is necessary to consider an explicit mapping.

By separating notation model and structure meta-model, we allow to define multiple notations for the same language. In the following we describe textual and graphical representations for SDL models based on our SDL structural meta-model.

5.1   Textual Representation

SDL is a language that has two syntax forms, a textual and a graphical. Although the textual syntax is moved out of the standard into a separate attachment, it is still an important format for tools and information exchange.

The textual syntax is not directly related to the meta-model of a language, which is more like an abstract syntax. Firstly, the textual representation contains information that is abstracted in the meta-model, such as indentation, comments or keywords. If this was the only difference, we could generate a unique concrete representation from a meta-model instance given some formatting instructions. However, SDL does also allow several representations for the same model construct. In fact, most programming languages allow this kind of flexibility, often referred to as *syntactic sugar*.

An example of this is given in Fig. 5 which shows the structure on the left-hand side and the representations on the right-hand side. All three representations have the same internal structure, with differences being in the graphical or the textual appearance or both. The solid arrows from the right-hand side to the left-hand side represent the semantic mapping from the representation alternatives to the same structure elements.

Please note that in the SDL standard, the mapping to the abstract syntax (i.e. the structure), is given by two mappings. The first mapping is called transformation and describes an in-place replacement within the concrete syntax. In Fig. 5, this is illustrated with a dashed line arrow. We might call this mapping a syntactic mapping. The second step in the SDL standard is an almost 1:1-mapping between the transformed concrete syntax and the abstract syntax.

Conceptually, the structure meta-model acts as the common core of all language elements. The concrete notation describes additions like keywords, comments, or

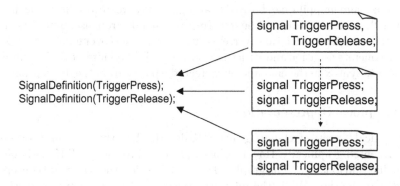

Fig. 5. Two concrete representations for an SDL construct

different syntactic forms. In order to capture this situation best, we use a direct mapping from the notation model to the structure meta-model. For textual representations, the notation model is given by a context-free grammar. The mapping model describes which concrete syntax elements refer to which meta-model elements.

As Fig. 5 illustrates, there might be several mappings from representation to model elements, as in the case of the signal definitions. We give the mapping for the signal definition below. We start with the concrete syntax description.

```
<signal definition>::=
   signal <signal definition item>
   { <comma> <signal definition item> }* <end> .
<signal definition item> ::= <signal name> [<sort list>] .
<sort list> ::=
   <left parenthesis> <sort> { <comma> <sort>}*
   <right parenthesis> .
```

This definition is mapped to the meta-model using the following (uni-directional) transformation.

```
<signal definition>(items) ==>
   { SignalDefinition(name=i.name, sorts=i.sorts)
   | with i in items }
```

A typical pattern in textual languages is the definition-use pattern. At some place an element is defined, and at some other place or even several other places the element is used. One may think of methods, variables, types or similar things. This situation is represented by an identifier in grammars, but by a direct link in a meta-model according to the type property in the type of association. This way identifiers only live in the textual representation and are almost useless for the meta-model.

Identifier resolution is formalised in the meta-model by a function *resolve* which does the resolution for an identifier given the complete SDL specification. This is done by defining an auxiliary function as detailed at the end of Sect. 4. The current SDL semantics has chosen the same approach by defining an auxiliary function *idToNodeAS1*.

Grammar and mapping can be used to automatically create an editor, which creates an SDL model according to the structure meta-model from user input based on the textual notation model. However, existing tools do only cover for a 1:1 mapping between concrete notation and structure meta-model. Therefore we did not pursue the concrete syntax to the end, and only created a parser from the description.

5.2   Graphical Representation

The graphical aspects of a language like SDL describe how the structural concepts are represented graphically. How is a block presented to the user? How should a system diagram look like? The graphical concepts are, like the structural concepts, related to each other. While the relations between the concepts in the structure describe how the language concepts are related to each other in a structural way, the

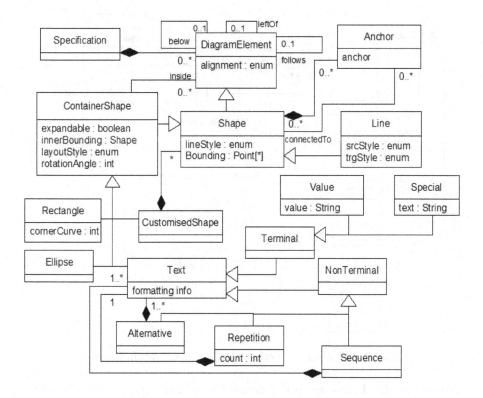

Fig. 6. Meta-Meta-Model for Graphical Representation

relations between the graphical concepts say something about how the concepts are related to each other graphically. The relations specify how the graphical concepts is related to each other to form valid diagrams in that language.

To be able to specify some kind of representation by structural meta-model (notation model), it is necessary to have a meta-meta-model for that. The meta-meta-model specifies the concepts and relations that are necessary to define the language graphics, in the same way that MOF or Ecore specify which concepts and which relations are allowed when defining a structure model (see Sect. 3). Figure 6 presents how the meta-meta-model for graphical notations looks according to our approach. This model defines the concepts that can be used to define a graphical notation.

The top-level element is the graphical *Specification* that consists of a number of *Diagram Elements*. These diagram elements are related to each other in one way or the other. A *Shape* is a diagram element, and there exist two main categories of Shapes - *Container Shape* and *Line*. A Container Shape is, as the name tells, a shape that can have other Diagram Elements *inside* itself. There are four different kinds of Container Shapes: *Rectangle*, *Ellipse*, *Customised Shape* and *Text*. One or more *Anchors* belonging to a *Shape* are used to specify where the *Shape* could be connected to another *Shape*. The *Anchor* is specified based on the property *Bounding* in Shape.

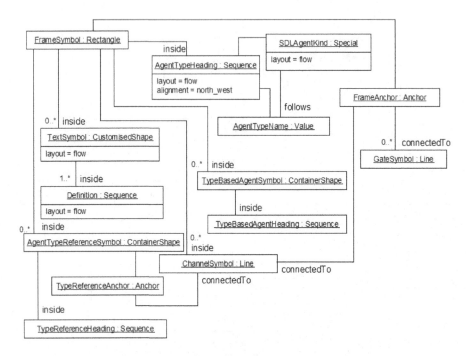

Fig. 7. SDL graphical meta-model for the concepts in Fig. 3

Most graphical languages do also include textual concepts, and how these textual concepts are handled must also be included in the meta-meta-model. Inspired by traditional grammar approaches for text handling, a *Text* element is either a *Terminal* or a *NonTerminal*. A terminal represents "words" in the language, and examples of a value from SDL are e.g. the name of an agent type, or an attribute. A *Special* textual element is another kind of terminal which models both keywords (e.g. **signal**, **use**) and special signs (e.g. ";", ":") which are all predefined. An example of a non-terminal is a text *Sequence*. A text sequence is in turn a composition of a number of other text elements (both terminals and non-terminals).

The meta-meta-model for graphical representation in Fig. 6 is at the same level as the MOF meta-meta-model in the OMG four level hierarchy. It makes it possible to specify the SDL graphical representation. To illustrate this, a small excerpt of the SDL graphical meta-model is shown in Fig. 7. The graphical concepts we see in this model, are some of the concepts that are necessary to model a block type diagram. They correspond to the concepts in the structure meta-model in Fig. 3.

The graphical model for SDL is mapped to the meta-model that specifies the structure. Since there should be a clear separation between these two language concepts, no direct references exist in the meta-models. This separation allows the exchangeability of different language notations. The mapping is a simple horizontal mapping from the graphical representation to the structure starting with the relation between the top elements.

```
FrameSymbol ==> SDLAgentType
```

The value of the SDLAgentKind in the heading of the diagram (from the graphics) is then mapped to the value of the AgentKind in the structure:

```
FrameSymbol.AgentTypeHeading.SDLAgentKind ==>
SDLAgentType.kind
```

This way, the mapping integrates the language aspects, and instances from the two meta-models are related in a correct way.

Unfortunately, there is no tool yet being able to handle such a graphics description. The best tool available in connection with Ecore is GMF (Graphical Modeling Framework)[6]. GMF is a framework that provides a platform for building graphical editors, and it acts as a bridging technology between the GEF platform [5] and the EMF modelling platform. GMF consists of two parts: the generative and the runtime part. The runtime part could be seen as a set of plug-ins extending the already existing EMF and GEF functionality. The generative part, on the other hand, is mainly covering the parts that make it possible for the user to define diagram editors using specially designed EMF meta-models and to generate code based on this information.

When defining the graphical representation in GMF, all the graphical concepts that are in the language and their appearance are specified in the *graphical definition model* (the notation model). The *tooling definition model* is an additional model that defines an editor toolbar and additional menu items, pop-up menus etc. These items can be used to modify instances of the graphical definition model. The graphical definition, the tooling definition and the structure definition (the .ecore file defined by EMF) are then bound together by using the *mapping model*. This mapping specification is then transformed into a *generator model*, which in turn is used to generate all the code necessary to run a diagram editor.

That far, the GMF approach maps nicely to our description. However, in practice GMF is only able to handle very simple specifications, in particular very simple relations in the mapping model. This means that we had to map the graphical model manually onto GMF, thereby losing much of its content. Of course, we gained also something as the tooling definition model is going beyond our description. The current graphical tool is adapted to fit the camera example as defined in [15].

Finally, we want again to compare our work with the existing standard. In the standard, both graphical and textual syntax are very loosely connected to the abstract syntax. Moreover, the notation to define the graphical syntax is not very formal. Our new definition solves all these deficiencies. However, still we do not have proper tool support.

6   Behaviour

In terms of behaviour (see again Fig. 1), for an SDL standard only the execution semantics is relevant. Mappings are interesting for SDL compiler tools, but not necessary to define the SDL behaviour.

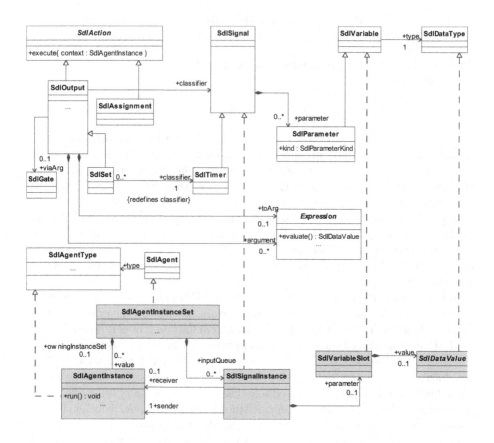

Fig. 8. Runtime elements for state automatons

To define the execution semantics we have to distinguish between two different kinds of structure elements, as detailed in [14]. The first kind describes abstract syntax elements; the structure model of SDL consists of such elements. The other kind of structure elements describes data that is needed at runtime. These runtime data include variable assignments, process instances, input buffers, etc. We therefore have to augment the regular structure description for SDL with descriptions for runtime data. The runtime elements are usually related to corresponding syntax elements, e.g. an *agent instance* at runtime level represents an *agent type* defined at syntax level. In a way, when creating instances of syntax elements, the related runtime representations are instantiated. This way the syntax elements function as factories producing related runtime elements. Figure 8 shows the syntax and runtime structure needed to describe the *signal output* action in SDL; syntax elements (white) are related to runtime elements (grey) by dashed arrows.

A similar distinction was also used for the SDL-2000 semantics [7]. Structural SDL elements were related to runtime elements defined as Abstract State Machines (ASM) [2]. Both were connected by an initialisation, i.e. an instantiation.

```
rule execute(o: Output, Self: SDLAgentInstance) =
  let values = [evaluate(a,Self) | a in arguments(o)] in
  SignalOutput(o, values, toArg(o))
  currentStatement(Self) := continueStatement(o)

rule SignalOutput(s,vSeq,toArg) =
  let invReference = (toArg memberof PId) and
     (resolve(s) notin Signalset(Interface(toArg)))
  in
    if not invReference then
      choose g in ingates(Self) with Applicable(s, toArg, g) do
        extend SdlSignalInstance with si do
          SdlSignal(si) := s
          forall idx in Indices(vSeq) do
           value(parameterValue(si)[idx]):= vSeq[idx]
          receiver(si) := toArg; sender(si) := Self
          Insert(si, now, g)
      endchoose
    endif
```

Fig. 9. Execution of output in ASM

Behavioural elements were translated to ASM runtime behaviour using a compilation function. This way, structural SDL elements relate to runtime elements with their corresponding abstract syntax counterpart. Behavioural SDL elements are just abstract syntax elements which do not need a separate runtime representation. The current SDL standard moves the behavioural elements into the runtime (ASM) domain using the compilation function. This is not necessary for the new approach, because all elements already live in the same domain. For our meta-model-based approach, we replaced the compilation function by a direct use of the syntax elements. Instead of translating the SDL syntax tree elements into ASM elements, we use an ASM interpretation of the SDL elements, as it is done already now for the structural SDL elements. The ASM execution functions that shall run the model are attached to the corresponding syntax elements. Fig. 8 shows an example, where output is a syntax element with an execution function. The ASM execution function for the concrete SDL action *signal output* is given in Fig. 9. It might be interesting to note that the current ASM semantics takes a global view, i.e. all ASM agents can see everything (at least in principle). The new version is object-oriented in that it attaches the ASM code to the syntax or runtime objects. This is easily achieved starting from the current semantics, because it is now already formulated such that it refers to an executing object. The only thing we have to find out, is the context where the rule has to be placed.

In ASM, the context is shown by the parameters of the rules. As already stated in [14], the runtime elements have to have one context, whereas the syntax elements need two contexts: a runtime context and a syntax context. In the code in Fig. 9, *Self* denotes the runtime context, i.e. the actual *agent instance*. The syntax context

```
rule Run(Self:SdlAgentInstance) = // AgentProgram
 if (agentMode1(Self) = initialisation) then
  InitAgent
 else if (agentMode1(Self) = execution) then
  if ExecRightPresent(Self) then
   ExecAgent
  else
   GetExecRight
  endif
 endif
endif
```

Fig. 10. Run of an agent instance in ASM

(the *signal output* statement) is given by the first parameter in the rule. In terms of object-orientation this first parameter resembles the *this* parameter.

In a similar style, the behaviour for the runtime elements is given. One example here is a process instance as shown in Fig. 10. In the object-oriented model, this function is associated to a runtime object of type *SDLAgentInstance*, which is referred to in the ASM using the *Self* variable.

For the new dynamic description, we reused the existing ASM description many times. In order to achieve object-orientation, all semantic functions had to be attached to syntax elements or runtime elements. Moreover, the compilation function was not necessary any longer because the runtime actions were directly attached to the abstract syntax elements.

7   Conclusions

In this article, we combined different technologies to create a description of SDL that covers the language aspects *structure*, *constraints*, *representation*, and *behaviour*. The resulting artifact can be used as a human readable standard, as well as a basis for the automated generation of SDL reference tools. A complete tools suite can be generated automatically: you can write an SDL specification in a generated SDL editor, check this specification, and execute it. We did this for the basic part of SDL. This restricted SDL was extensive enough to realise the camera example with the generated tools.

The resulting meta-model for SDL has some limitations and there are issues that couldn't be solved satisfactorily. The different language aspects, especially representation, require extensions and modifications of the language's structure model. This creates the additional burden of aligning different similar models with each other. Examples for this are representations that often provide different notations for the same language concepts; behaviour operations and constraints that have to be put into the structure model, even though the structure model is independent from these aspects. The presentation of the language description is another problem, because meta-models used for tooling are cluttered with technical information which is either not relevant for a standard or that a standard should abstract from.

Therefore, you need to describe more than necessary for a language standard to allow automatic tooling.

Compared to the SDL standard, our approach allows to utilize meta-model-based technologies that are more and more replacing grammar-based language development tools. The object-oriented meta-models allow for better reuse of abstract language concepts, and eventually lead to more coherent and compact language descriptions. The techniques used are mostly graphical and allow therefore easier human comprehension. Meta-modelling in combination with proper tooling, allows to display the language definition at different abstraction levels by omitting details thereby enhancing human understanding.

All this leads to a language standard that is a model. Of course, we can also have a printable document out of this model, but this is just another representation.

Future work will include further enhancements of language tools. Because those tools are generic tools parametrized through language descriptions, all languages immediately profit from further enhancements in this generic language tooling. Another important point is support for evolving languages. A language, as software, yields requirements that may change over time and therefore a language, its tools, and all the programs and specifications in a language may be subject to changes. Through the unification principle *everything is a model*, also meta-models profit from agile modelling techniques. General techniques like model transformations, or meta-model specific techniques like meta-model/model co-adaptation might be used to either evolve a language or to tailor a language to domain specific needs (profiling).

References

1. Budinsky, F., Steinberg, D., Merks, E., Ellersick, R., Grose, T.J.: Eclipse Modeling Framework (The Eclipse Series). Addison-Wesley Professional, Reading (2003)
2. Börger, E., Stärk, R.: Abstract State Machines. In: A Method for High-Level Design and Analysis. Springer, Berlin (2003)
3. Eschbach, R., Glässer, U., Gotzhein, R., von Löwis, M., Prinz, A.: Formal definition of SDL-2000: Compiling and running SDL specifications as ASM models. In: Abstract State Machines 2001: New Developments and Applications, J.UCS Special issue, vol. 7(11) (2001)
4. Fischer, J., Holz, E., Prinz, A., Scheidgen, M.: Tool-based language development. Comput. Networks 49(5), 676–688 (2005)
5. Eclipse Graphical Editing Framework, See http://www.eclipse.org/gef
6. Eclipse Graphical Modeling Framework, See http://www.eclipse.org/gmf
7. ITU-T. SDL - ITU-T Specification and Description Language, Formal Semantics. ITU-T Recommendation Z.100, Annex F (November 2000)
8. ITU-T. SDL - ITU-T Specification and Description Language (SDL-2000). ITU-T Recommendation Z.100 (August 2002)
9. Greenfield, J., Short, K., Cook, S., Kent, S.: Software Factories: Assembling Applications with Patterns, Frameworks, Models & Tools. John Wiley & Sons, Chichester (2004)
10. Nytun, J.P., Prinz, A., Tveit, M.S.: Automatic generation of modelling tools. In: Rensink, A., Warmer, J. (eds.) ECMDA-FA 2006. LNCS, vol. 4066, pp. 268–283. Springer, Heidelberg (2006)

11. OMG. Meta Object Facility (MOF) 2.0 Core Specification. Object Management Group, formal/2006-01-01 (January 2006)
12. OMG. OCL 2.0 Specification. Object Management Group, formal/2006-05-01 (May 2006)
13. Scheidgen, M.: A MOF 2.0 for Java. Humboldt-Universität zu Berlin, http://www.informatik.hu-berlin.de/sam/meta-tools/aMOF2.0forJava
14. Scheidgen, M., Fischer, J.: Human comprehensible and machine processable specifications of operational semantics. In: Akehurst, D.H., Vogel, R., Paige, R.F. (eds.) ECMDA-FA. LNCS, vol. 4530, pp. 157–171. Springer, Heidelberg (2007)
15. Tveit, M.S.: A Cinderella-based prototype of a digital camera– a contribution to the SDL'05 design contest. Telektronikk 2.2006 (2006), See also http://www.telenor.com/telektronikk/volumes/pdf/2.2006/ Page_121-130.pdf

Model Driven Development and Code Generation: An Automotive Case Study[*]

Michele Banci[1], Alessandro Fantechi[1,2], Stefania Gnesi[1], and Giovanni Lombardi[1]

[1] ISTI-CNR, Via G. Moruzzi 1, 56124 Pisa, Italy
{michele.banci,stefania.gnesi,giovanni_lombardi}@isti.cnr.it
[2] DSI - Università degli Studi di Firenze, Via S. Marta, 3, 50139 Firenze, Italy
fantechi@dsi.unifi.it

Abstract. Describing an application as a simple composition of services allows advanced features that exploit different platforms to be conceived and to be formalized at a high abstraction level. Several languages and formalisms have been proposed to this aim; UML diagrams are also used to this purpose. Starting from such an abstract description, still much work is needed to derive a working application, with a model-driven development process that needs to introduce and formalize many details. In this paper we report an experience in deriving an executable formal model from a high level specifications, originally given following a mainly architectural UML approach. The development process is illustrated on an automotive case study. A state of the art code generation tool is then applied to produce a prototype implementation of the analyzed system.

Keywords: Service-Oriented applications, formal modeling, automatic code generation, formal verification, formal validation.

1 Introduction

Service-oriented computing is emerging as an interesting paradigm to describe, at various levels of abstraction, systems composed by dynamic assembly of classic computational entities, each of which provides a service to other entities, and which can be distributed over different platforms and communication networks.

Describing an application as a simple composition of services allows advanced features that exploit different platforms to be conceived and to be formalized at a high abstraction level. Several languages and formalisms have been proposed to this aim; the different languages adopted in the SENSORIA project [6] constitute an example of this variety.

In the very same project, UML diagrams have also been used to this purpose, and in particular have been used to give a first formalization to an automotive case study. This case study defines several services given to the future car user by application of mostly already available technology.

---

[*] This work has been partially supported by the project SENSORIA, IST-2005-016004.

E. Gaudin, E. Najm, and R. Reed (Eds.): SDL 2007, LNCS 4745, pp. 19–34, 2007.

UML deployment diagrams, which give a static view of the architecture, have been used for a first formalization of the composition of services. A representation showing the evolution of the architecture was then required: for this purpose, UML sequence diagrams were used to represent the evolving connections within the service oriented architecture of the vehicle and its environment, and the interactions among services. Such an abstract description may serve as the starting point of a refinement process, that, by introducing implementation details, aims to produce a working prototype.

In this paper we report an experience aimed at producing an early prototype from such an abstract specification, through a first refinement step (from UML Sequence Diagrams to UML State Diagrams) and using an industrial strength, state of the art, modeling tool capable of automatic code generation. This requires a second refinement step, aimed at a more precise formalization of state machines. The tool used in this experience was SCADE. The method described in [2] to bridge the semantic gap between UML state diagrams and SCADE statecharts (SSM) has inspired the work we have done on the SENSORIA automotive case study. Formal verification has been used during the process to maintain consistency of the transformation between UML state diagrams and SSM.

The paper is organized as follows: In Sect. 2 we present the SENSORIA case study, by using both a natural language description and a first formal specification by UML sequence diagrams. In Sect. 3 we briefly introduce the SCADE tool and its formalisms, while in Sect. 4 we present the rules followed in order to translate the UML model into a SCADE model, and a description of the obtained SCADE model. Section 5 concludes the paper showing the prototype implementation, obtained by automatically generated code for the business logic wrapped in a communication interface to provide the implemented services.

2   SENSORIA Case Study

Today's embedded computers in cars can access communication networks like the Internet and thereby provide a variety of new services for cars and drivers. A set of possible scenarios of the automotive domain have been examined within the scope of the SENSORIA project, among which we select a car repair scenario low oil level for illustrating the different techniques presented in this article.

Some of the functionality described in the scenario are already integrated in modern vehicles; other functionality might be available to drivers in the near future.

We have chosen this scenario because of its complexity, in which all aspects of service interaction can be studied.

The actors and their interaction with the system in the scenario are the following:

- **Sensor systems:** cause low oil level alert
- **Discovery engine:** discovers services needed (towing, repair)
- **Driver:** communicates with towing and repair service
- **Tow truck:** receives GPS co-ordinates of stranded vehicle
- **Repair shop:** receives diagnostic data from stranded vehicle

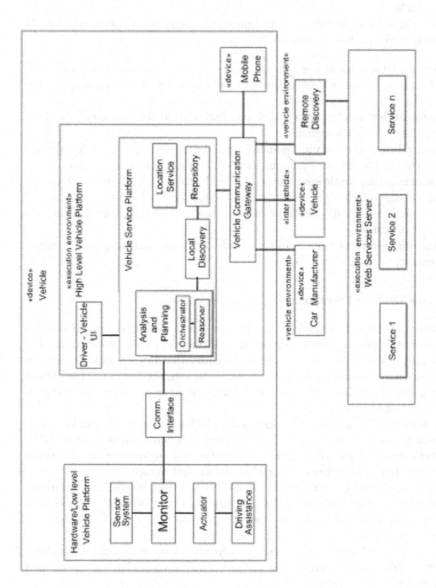

Fig. 1. Modules of simplified automotive service architecture

The sensor systems cause an in-vehicle diagnostic system to check why the oil level has reached a minimum. The result of the diagnostic system is passed on to the discovery engine, which then locates the appropriate services needed (adequate repair shop, tow truck) based on the diagnostics, the driver's preferences and the location of the vehicle.

The main components of the overall car system architecture (as seen in Fig. 1) that are involved in this scenario are:

1. **Service Planning**: is a specific software vehicle component, it manages some events (e.g. anomalous sensor data) and reacts to dedicated enabling services (e.g. In-car diagnostic service).
2. **Communication System**: enables communication between internal and external services of the vehicle.
3. **In-car diagnostic service**: is an In-Vehicle integrated service, analyses events reported by the Service Planning, and produces a problem description.
4. **External diagnostic service**: is provided by the vehicle producer. Data sensors and the vehicle state are sent to a dedicated server where they are analyzed and compared to a diagnostic errors database; this server's answers provide a correct diagnosis.
5. **On road repair service**: is an external service that performs an automatic repair service reservation.

2.1   Low Oil Level Scenario by UML Specification

The structure of a service oriented architecture can be visualized by UML deployment and composite structure diagrams. A deployment diagram is used to represent the (usually nested) nodes of the architecture such as hardware devices or software execution environments. Figure 3 shows a UML deployment diagram of the car and its environment as a first approximation of an architecture model related to architecture of the low oil level scenario.

In addition to UML deployment diagrams, which give a static view of the architecture, a representation showing the evolution of an architecture is required. UML sequence diagrams have been used to represent the evolving connections within the service oriented architecture of the vehicle and its environment.

Several scenarios of evolution have been described using sequence diagrams. In the following we show some of them; the so called "success" scenario, that refers to the normal way of operation, is presented in Fig. 4, while Fig. 5 and Fig. 6 represent alternative scenarios.

The two alternative scenarios presented here are related to two error situations: other error situations concerning special cases have been considered and have been singularly modeled by sequence diagrams.

1. *Time Out error*: The Communication System tries to connect to the External Diagnostic Service, which is unable to answer (connection error); after a predefined time interval the communication system retries to connect; this procedure is repeated until a connection is established.

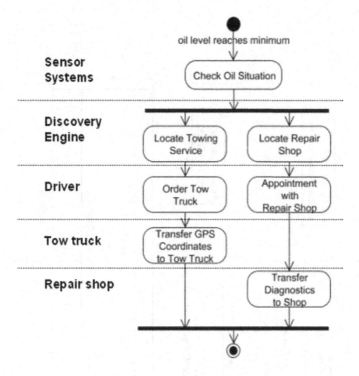

Fig. 2. System Flowchart

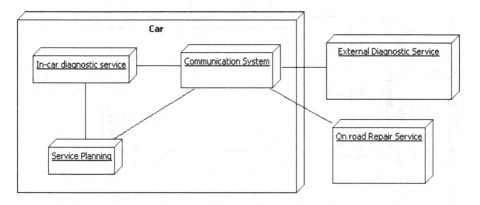

Fig. 3. Low Oil Level Deployment Diagram

2. *Send & Receive data error*: After establishing a connection with the External Diagnostic Service, the vehicle GPS coordinates and diagnostics data are automatically sent to the External Diagnostic Service at regular intervals by the communication system; if the communication system obtains no answers by the External Diagnostic Service, then the vehicles data will be automatically sent to the External Diagnostic Service at regular intervals by the communication system until the service provides an answer.

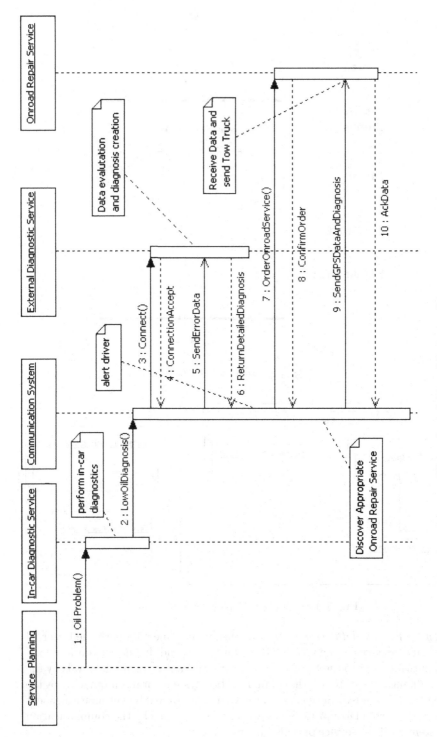

Fig. 4. Low Oil Level Sequence Diagram

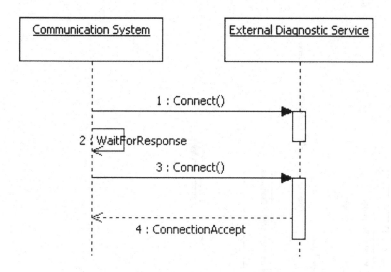

Fig. 5. - Time Out error - Low Oil Sequence Diagram

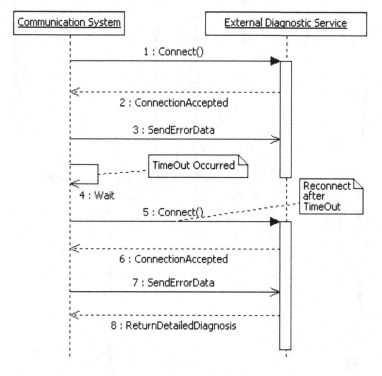

Fig. 6. Send & Receive error - Low Oil Sequence Diagram

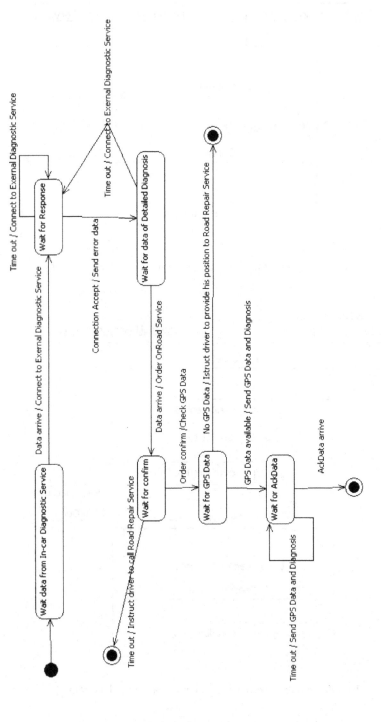

Fig. 7. Communication System

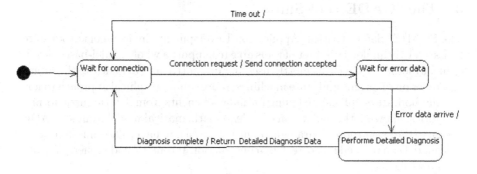

Fig. 8. External Diagnostic Service

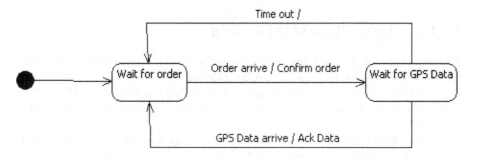

Fig. 9. On Road Repair Service

2.2 Sequence Diagram

The synthesis of State Diagrams from Sequence Diagrams has been extensively studied in the literature: [9] presents a survey of these works, while the first application to UML Sequence and State Diagrams can be found in [7].

The UML state diagrams related to the main classes involved in the low oil level scenario are given in Fig. 7, Fig. 8 and Fig. 9.

The State Diagram in Fig. 7 represents the behavior of the in-car communication system that have been implemented merging the above mentioned sequence diagrams. The State Diagrams in Fig. 8 and Fig. 9 represent two other external actors that provide the services.

A formal verification over the obtained state diagrams can be done in order to check that the synthesis process has not violated some desired safety or liveness properties, by means of model checking. The model checker UMC for UML state diagrams and the UCTL state-action based temporal logic has been used for this purpose (see [1,8] for a description of UCTL and UMC).

A typical property of interest in this case is for example: "If a low oil level alarm is raised, then if no time-outs of any sort occur, a towing truck is eventually called" that can be expressed using UCTL as:

$$AG[OilProblem](< TimeOut > true | AF < OrderOnRepair service > true)$$

3   The SCADE Tool-Suite

The SCADE (Safety Critical Application Development Environment) tool-suite by Esterel Technologies is a set of tools able to support a whole model-based development method. SCADE is mostly used in automotive and avionics applications, and relies on diagrams and state machines, represents a graphical approach to formal method. Its graphical modeling formalism benefits from deterministic formal semantics, allowing the derivation of a clean mathematical model from a SCADE design to the synchronous paradigm of the Lustre [4] language. The same deterministic model can be used for correct-by-construction automatic code generation and formal verification [5].

SCADE provides a verification technique based on formal verification tools over the model as well.

4   From UML SD to SCADE SSM

The process we have followed in transforming the UML state diagrams to SCADE Safe State Machines is inspired to that described in [2].

In particular, each UML State Diagram is directly mapped to a SCADE SSM, due to the similarity of their internal structure. This step has been carried out manually.

However SCADE is based on the synchronous data-flow paradigm. Inputs and outputs of a SCADE block are typed data-flows. The type of a data-flow can be simple (bool, int, real) or structured (a structure or tuple made of a set of typed fields).

A SSM is a particular kind of block, so the messages and stored variables that are used in UML to synchronize two State Diagrams have to be transformed into data flow between blocks.

In the special case when the first field of a structured input data-flow is of type bool (or when the input data-flow's type itself is bool), this boolean value can be used as a "signal presence status" in triggers of transitions in SCADE Safe State Machines. Symmetrically, when the first field of a structured output data-flow is of type bool (or when the output data-flow's type itself is bool), this boolean value represents the "signal presence status" of the output signal, set to true if and only if the signal is emitted during the execution of a SCADE node. Input or output flows associated with such a Boolean presence status can be used to represent sporadic or transient signals which are considered only for some specific executions of the SCADE node.

4.1   The SCADE Model

The SCADE formal model of the Low-Oil-System uses SSMs (Safe State Machines) encapsulated into block diagrams as illustrated in Fig. 10, Fig. 11 and Fig. 12. The global system named Low-oil scenario has been sliced in three different models: the in-car subsystem and two out-car subsystems representing the diagnostic system and the car repair shop.

The modeling methodology used is the same for each subsystem, so we will illustrate only the in-car subsystem model. The main object of this subsystem is a generic high level data-flow block (Fig. 10). This main block includes three interconnected SSMs (Fig. 11). To this block input data flows from the in car sensors system and from a gateway connected to external services arrive. From this in-car system several signals are sent to the out-car services.

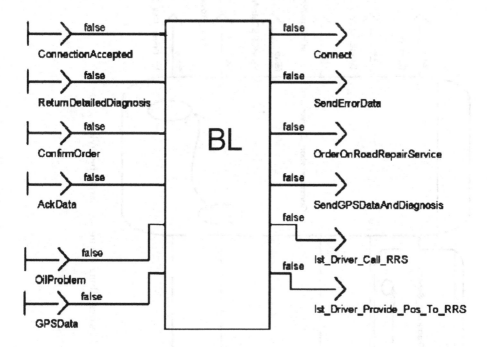

Fig. 10. Main in-car block

Although SCADE provides several kinds of data flow blocks we have modeled our system using state machines only, for a direct correspondence to the UML State Diagrams.

Figure 12 shows the main state machine, namely the Communication System, which is actually similar to the corresponding UML one of Fig. 7.

4.2   Formal Verification of Safety Requirements

In order to validate the performed transformation on the models developed using the SCADE tool, several functional test scenario have been verified using the SCADE simulator.

Moreover, the same properties that have been verified over the UML state diagram model have also been verified over the SCADE state machines by means of the native model checker Design Verifier tool, in order to check that the transformation to SCADE has not introduced violations to the desired properties.

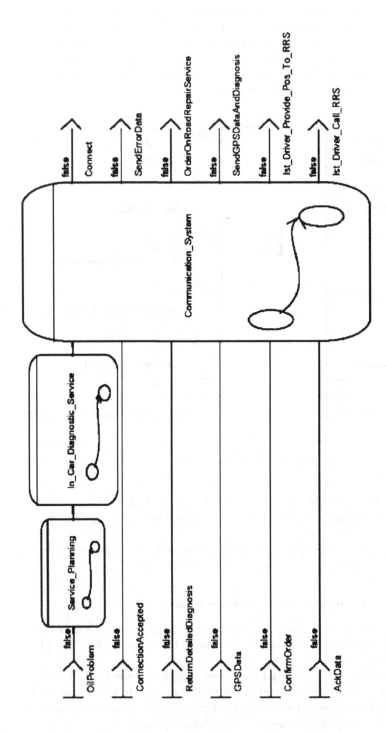

Fig. 11. SSMs describing the in-car system behaviour

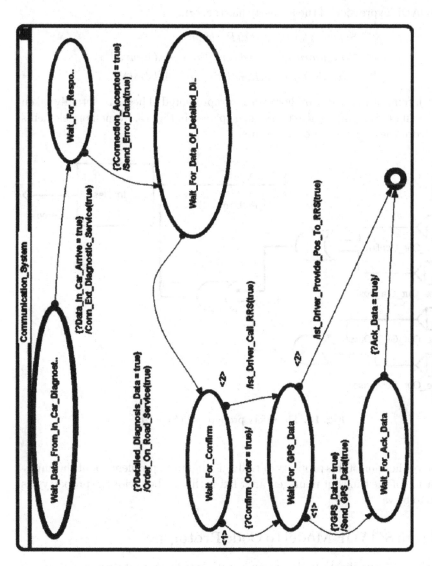

Fig. 12. The Communication System SSM

The property defined above for the UML model can be expressed on the variables of the SCADE model as:

When the low oil sensor has become true and there are no time out errors then the repair shop has to acknowledge the request sent to it (see Fig. 4).

The SCADE expression of the property has the form:

$$ServicePlanning(OilProblem)$$
$$\wedge\neg\ CommunicationSystem(\text{``}TimeOutOccured\text{''})$$
$$\Rightarrow OrderOnRoadRepairService(AckData)$$

in which temporal aspects are however not represented. These are actually taken into account in the graphical expression, displayed in Fig. 13, by memory elements that record the occurrences of the events.

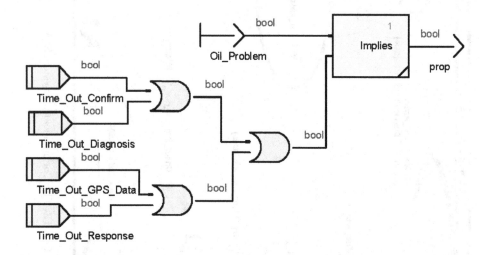

Fig. 13. The safety properties in SCADE

The verification of this property initially highlighted a problem about the implementation of the time out manager: after fixing this misbehavior the property has shown to be valid.

5   From SCADE Model to Code Prototype

After the model verification, the system constituted by three state models has also been implemented using the capabilities of the automatic code generator.

To perform the simulation, some user interfaces have been implemented and mapped to the model using a gateway provided by the SCADE tool. After the environment supported simulation these user interfaces have been reused to stimulate the automatically generated code.

At the end of the whole development process we have obtained three independent systems, communicating by TCP/IP sockets, each of them exposing one or more services. The simulated stimuli from the in-car side have been sent by the above cited user interfaces.

The final structure is similar to that illustrated in the deployment diagram of Fig. 3.

The complete prototype consists of some generic parts (the user interfaces and the TCP/IP communication modules) and some specific parts (what is often called "business logic"), that have been automatically generated in C language directly from the models. At the end of the development phase we have obtained:

1. C code automatically generated by the SCADE tool and representing the model behavior.
2. Generic wrap code to build a dll containing the business logic C code above .
3. A generic TCP/IP module, to communicate with the environment (the other two models: on road repair shop, external diagnostic services) that provide services and vice versa.
4. An On Board Console (see Fig. 14) that is the user interface to simulate the in-car sensor layer.

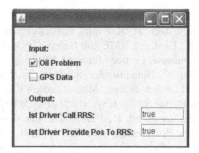

Fig. 14. On Board Console

The different parts have then been integrated in order to build an application able to simulate the scenarios from which we have started the development process, with all the concerned interactions.

6   Conclusions

We have reported an experience in deriving an executable prototype from a high level specification of a service oriented application related to an automotive case study. The experience has been made inside a research effort aiming at defining a complete model-driven development process from high level specifications to executable code, based on industrial-strength tools.

In particular the purpose of the experience was to evaluate the adoption of a tool like SCADE, which allows for code generation, formal verification and test case generation, to refine the partly formalized UML state diagrams of the original specifications, with state machines having a formal semantics.

The followed development process, starting from a UML sequence diagram description of typical usage scenarios of the automotive case study, has included first the synthesis of UML state diagrams from the sequence diagrams and then a refinement step mainly based on the translation of the state diagram model into an executable SCADE model. Despite some semantic differences between the two formalisms, this translation has proved straightforward. Formal verification by model checking has helped to check the semantic consistency of the transformation.

The obtained SCADE model has allowed to exploit automatic code generation. The generated code has then been embedded in a communication framework that in the end has made it possible to produce an executable prototype of the initial specification. The proposed development process, despite the usage of different formalisms, has resulted to be effective in producing in a short time a working prototype from the original concept, thanks to the supporting tools (model checkers, simulators and code generators) used at the various steps.

References

1. Model Checker for UML Statechart Diagrams, `fmt.isti.cnr.it/umc/`
2. Le Guennec, A., Dion, B.: Bridging UML and Safety-Critical Software Development Environments, ERTS, Toulouse, France (January 2006)
3. Brooks, C., Lee, E.A., Liu, X., Neuendorffer, S., Zhao, Y., Zheng, H.: Heterogeneous Concurrent Modeling and Design in Java. Memorandum UCB/ERL M04/27, EECS, University of California, Berkeley, CA USA 94720 (July 2004)
4. Halbwachs, N., Caspi, P., Raymond, P., Pilaud, D.: The synchronous dataflow programming language lustre. Proceedings of the IEEE 79(9), 1305–1320 (1991)
5. Raymond, P.: Compilation efficace d'un langage d'eclaratif synchrone: le generateur de code Lustre-v3. PhD thesis, Institut National Polytechnique de Grenoble (1991)
6. Wirsing, M., Clark, A., Gilmore, S., Hölzl, M.M., Knapp, A., Koch, N., Schroeder, A.: Semantic-Based Development of Service-Oriented Systems. In: Najm, E., Pradat-Peyre, J.F., Donzeau-Gouge, V.V. (eds.) FORTE 2006. LNCS, vol. 4229, Springer, Heidelberg (2006)
7. Whittle, J., Schumann, J.: Generating statechart designs from scenarios. In: ICSE 2000. Proceedings of the 22nd International Conference on on Software Engineering, Limerick Ireland, June 4-11, 2000, pp. 314–323. ACM, New York (2000)
8. ter Beek, M.H., Fantechi, A., Gnesi, S., Mazzanti, F.: An action/state-based model-checking approach for the analysis of an asynchronous protocol for Service-Oriented Applications. In: Brim, L., Haverkort, B., Leucker, M., van de Pol, J. (eds.) FMICS 2006 and PDMC 2006. LNCS, vol. 4346, Springer, Heidelberg (2007)
9. Liang, H., Dingel, J., Diskin, Z.: A comparative survey of scenario-based to state-based model synthesis approaches. In: SCESM '06. Proceedings of the 2006 international workshop on Scenarios and state machines: models, algorithms, and tools, Shanghai, China, pp. 5–12. ACM, New York (2006)

Experiences in Deploying Model-Driven Engineering

Thomas Weigert, Frank Weil, Kevin Marth, Paul Baker, Clive Jervis,
Paul Dietz, Yexuan Gui, Aswin van den Berg, Kim Fleer, David Nelson,
Michael Wells, and Brian Mastenbrook

Motorola
Schaumburg, Illinois, USA
thomas.weigert@motorola.com

Abstract. In this paper, we describe how Motorola has deployed model-driven engineering in product development, in particular for the development of highly reliable telecommunications systems, and outline the benefits obtained. Model-driven engineering has dramatically increased both the quality and the reliability of software developed in our organization, as well as the productivity of our software engineers. Our experience demonstrates that model-driven engineering significantly improves the development process for telecommunications systems. We discuss the elements we found most important for deployment of model-driven engineering in a large product development organization: An appropriate modeling language, a powerful domain-specific code generator, and a deployment support team.

1 Introduction

Motorola has more than 15 years of history deploying model-driven engineering techniques to develop highly reliable network elements for large-scale telecommunication systems. Model-driven engineering has dramatically increased the quality and reliability of the developed software as well as the productivity of the software engineers [1].

This paper describes the model-driven engineering approach Motorola has been deploying. Model-driven engineering relies on capturing an application design in domain-specific languages; in Motorola, specifications are expressed using UML profiles [2,3] such as the SDL Profile [4], using ASN.1 [5], or using customized protocol-specification languages [6]. In the telecommunications domain, the basic domain abstractions are asynchronous, communicating processes based on finite-state machines and protocol data units. The specifications are subject to validation by operationally interpreting the specification and through executing formally defined test cases (written at the level of the design model in a test-specific notation, typically, but not exclusively, TTCN [7]) against this specification. Domain-specific programming knowledge is captured in code generators that transform the high-level designs into optimized product software targeted to the chosen platform.

E. Gaudin, E. Najm, and R. Reed (Eds.): SDL 2007, LNCS 4745, pp. 35–53, 2007.

We will summarize the productivity and quality gains observed and estimate how widely these techniques are applicable to the development of telecommunications applications. We will also discuss the elements we found most important for deployment of model-driven engineering in a large product development organization: An appropriate modeling language, a powerful domain-specific code generator, and a deployment support team. This information should enable the readers to decide if model-driven engineering will be beneficial to their respective organizations.

2   Model-Driven Engineering

The conventional software development process begins with capturing product requirements in design models, characterized by informal diagrams and pseudocode. Even if modern specification languages, such as UML or SDL, are being used to capture the designs, these languages are typically used to develop informal diagrams with unclear or imprecise semantics. These diagrams are then hand-translated by a team of software developers into product code in the target language. The hand-written code undergoes inspection and testing and is finally deployed at the target. A workflow following these lines is still the norm in most software development organizations and is subject to several problems that contribute to the often-tainted reputation of software engineering.

Firstly, the informality and imprecision of the notations used to capture product designs tends to lead to misunderstandings between developers, in particular, when development is conducted in a globally distributed manner. More often than not, it is more luck than planning when the design diagrams are interpreted consistently across geographically dispersed organizations. What one usually observes instead is that when separately developed components are assembled into the final product, they do not work fully together. In particular, misunderstandings due to the informality of the designs in error situations or exception scenarios lead to the introduction of defects that cause product failures.

Secondly, the translation of design documents into code by hand is error-prone and slow. The resultant artifacts are difficult to reuse in similar applications since much of the implementation detail of the product is intertwined with the code derived from the designs.

Finally, defects are repaired at the level of the hand-written code resulting in design documents that become hopelessly out of synch with the code and become incomplete or, worse, misleading. If testing reveals serious misunderstandings of requirements, it may be more efficient to abandon the outdated design model and the current version of the hand code than it is to try to patch the hand code in place, even given the accompanying loss of productivity.

In contrast, model-driven engineering proposes a software development process that starting from product requirements aims to capture designs in standardized high-level notations with well-defined semantics. A precisely defined semantics of the design model allows verification techniques to be applied to the model. For example, state-space exploration can reveal concurrency pathologies or other hard-to-find defects in the design. If, in addition, one is able to operationally interpret the product designs, the correctness of these designs can be established through simulation. Ideally, test cases are derived from the requirements and the designs are verified against these test cases. The designs are then translated into product code by a code generator. Finally, the resultant code is subjected to tests (again derived from the requirements) and is deployed on the target platform.

Viewed in more detail, we divide model-driven engineering into two sets of activities: In application engineering, we execute the model-driven engineering process to develop products based on their software requirements. In addition, model-driven engineering supplements application development with the development of domain-specific capabilities.

In domain engineering, we first try to find a notation that is as close to the application domain as possible. The closer the concepts of the design notation are to the concepts of the application domain, the easier it will be to capture the designs, and the more likely it will be that the designs are correct.

Secondly, we need to identify techniques to verify that the design documents are correct, that is, that they reflect the application that we intend to build. This may involve the development of simulation tools or of mathematical techniques such as model checking.

Finally, we need tools to translate the design documents into product code executing on the chosen target platforms.

Domain engineering generates a set of assets that can be drawn upon in application development. Rather than code, following a model-driven engineering process, the assets are the capabilities to produce software in a selected application domain, including the domain-specific notations, verification tools, and code generators. In application engineering, these capabilities are then deployed to produce a particular product.

The model-driven engineering vision has been realized in a number of Motorola business units in small steps: In 1989, a design simulation environment for a proprietary design notation was developed and piloted in development projects. When later, in 1991, the first commercial simulation tools became available for a standardized notation (SDL), development teams began migrating to SDL [8]. In 1992, for the first time the complete software for a real-time embedded Motorola product (a pager) was generated from high-level designs, without relying on any hand-written code. It was not until 1994 that the first commercial code generation tools with similar capabilities became available. Subsequently, several Motorola business units adopted design simulation as a new development paradigm. In 1998, the first shipping Motorola products were automatically derived from high-level design specifications: a base station for the TETRA radio communication system and a base site controller (BSC) for a telecommunications network. The subsequent years saw a steady increase in the penetration of model-driven engineering, as legacy products were gradually replaced by newly developed network elements.

3   Benefits

The benefits afforded by model-driven engineering are productivity and quality improvements. These benefits come from various sources:

- Design models are easier and faster to produce and test
- Labor-intensive and error-prone development tasks are automated
- Design effort is focused on applications, not on platform details
- Reuse of designs and tests between platforms or releases is enabled
- Design models can be verified through simulation and testing
- Design models are more stable, complete, and testable
- Standardized common notations avoid retraining of engineers
- The learning curve for new engineers is shortened

3.1   Productivity

Pushing much of the development detail into the code generator allows designs to be more abstract, which results in designs that are easier to produce and easier to show correct.

There are fewer inspections required to ensure product quality than when using conventional development. On average, developers rely on three inspection cycles of the model instead of four cycles of the source code when compared to following the conventional process. In addition, inspection rates are higher and have increased from 100 source lines of code per hour to in between 300 and 1000 "source lines" of models per hour. Thus, not only are fewer inspections required, but also the remaining inspections are much more efficient and at a level of abstraction more amenable to inspection by developers.

Code automation on average results in a five-fold increase in the number of source lines of code produced per staff months over the development life cycle. The effort spent in the design phase increases (from a traditional waterfall point of view), but this is more than made up by the dramatic reduction in coding effort. While the overall effort improvement is straightforward to measure, the improvement in each development phase is difficult to quantify due to a fundamental change in the process itself. The design phase changes from a loosely defined and rarely revisited step to a central aspect of the development that is not only kept up to date, but is also typically used for multiple product versions as part of a product-line architecture [9].

Code generators have reached a level of maturity such that effectively no errors are being introduced into the resultant code. For example, over the last several years, only one field failure was logged against the code generator itself, which has produced many millions of lines of code deployed in the field. Subsequently, no effort has to be expended to correct coding defects.

Figure 1 shows the productivity improvements (as measured in assembly equivalent lines of code produced per staff month) in the development of several features (labeled F1 through F5) on a BSC. The chart compares the productivity rates achieved using the conventional life cycle with those using model-driven

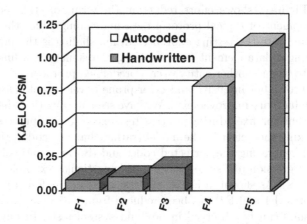

Fig. 1. Productivity improvement for network element applications

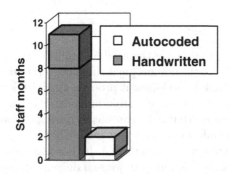

Fig. 2. Effort reduction for data marshaling (bars with thick outline indicated test)

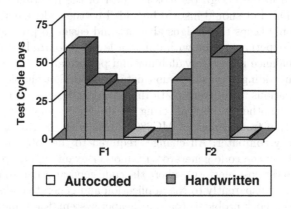

Fig. 3. Effort reduction in test cycle

engineering. Figure 2 shows effort reduction (in terms of staff months) during the development of typical protocol data marshaling code (the areas with thick outline indicate the testing effort). Data marshaling is the process of encoding/decoding a data element (e.g., an integer, a structure, a linked list) for transmission to/from another entity over a predefined protocol.

Automation of labor-intensive and error-prone development tasks results in additional productivity improvements. We have seen a dramatic reduction in the turn-around time for fixes during process test execution. A process test cycle involves: (i) fixing the defect in the model (rather than the code), (ii) writing a test case, (iii) generating the corrected code, and (iv) automatically executing the complete regression test suite (which in this particular example consisted of over 10,000 tests). As shown in Fig. 3, the test cycle across four releases of two network features (F1 and F2) has been reduced from 25-70 days to 24 hours.

Similar results can be observed in box and system tests. In many systems, over 90% of the tests are automated using TTCN scripts, which has led to a 30% reduction in box-test cycle time.

3.2   Platform Targeting

Model-driven engineering removes the need for embedding platform characteristics and domain detail into the designs (again impacting productivity and quality). Following the conventional development process, much irrelevant information—irrelevant from the point of view of system functionality—had to be kept in the design document to ensure that it be considered during coding. This extraneous information negatively affects productivity and quality.

For example, an important feature of a high-availability middleware layer developed by Motorola is the ability to journal ongoing transactions, allowing a computing node to recover from failure and continue execution at the point where a run-time fault occurs. The code necessary to perform the journaling should not be captured in the design (as it is not part of the functional requirements of the application) but should instead be added by the code generator. Such an approach not only keeps the designs abstract and easier to produce and verify, but also allows experimentation with different levels of journaling granularity to find the right balance between availability and performance.

Avoiding embedding implementation detail into design enables rapid retargeting of applications to different platforms. A given design can be moved from one platform to another without affecting the design. As an example, we moved a BSC application from a rack of MC6809 cards with distributed memory to a shared-memory computer. All changes required to the software architecture were performed by the code generator. In another example, an application was migrated to a lower-cost platform, where the code generator had to provide SysV message queues transparently to the application and generate code in a manner so as to avoid deadlock problems (on the cheaper system, the same thread could not acquire the same mutex repeatedly). The effort was 10 staff days to capture these differences in the code generator as compared to an estimated 80 days for hand porting the code.

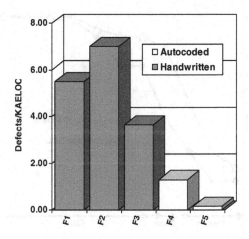

Fig. 4. Quality improvement for network element application

Incorporating platform specifics into the code through a code generator also enables engineers to experiment at a low cost with alternative implementation strategies, software architectures, or hardware choices.

Finally, the separation between platform-specific information and application information supports more efficient team structures. Platform experts capture their knowledge in code generators, and the application development teams can focus exclusively on the design and testing of new applications.

3.3   Quality

The models required as input for code generation are more complete and can be verified through simulation (or other techniques), resulting in significant quality improvements. The quality impact of model-driven engineering is dramatic and almost guaranteed. It is largely a consequence of the increased phase containment effectiveness enabled by semantically precise and operationally interpretable specifications.

Motorola data shows that simulation is about 30% more effective in catching defects than the most rigorous Fagan inspections. This is true for both overall faults and serious faults. Based on this fact alone (assuming that the code generator does not introduce additional defects), we can expect a 3X reduction in defects, which is also borne out by the data: In Fig. 4, from the development of five features (F1 through F5) on a network element, we see defect reduction rates well beyond that number. Applications have recently been developed with zero design defects.

Approximately 50% of defects are requirements errors. These are typically the hardest errors to find, and thus also the costliest. Working with models of requirements enables mathematical techniques to be applied to these models, which enables detection of these hard-to-find defects. In the telecommunications

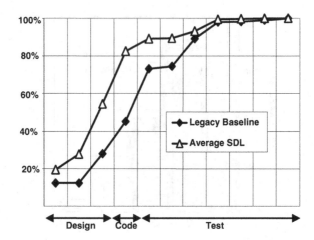

Fig. 5. Cumulative fault discovery rate across the development life cycle

domain, many such errors are due to concurrency pathologies, i.e., they result from unforeseen interactions of concurrently executing system components. We have developed techniques based on theorem proving and realized these in tools that detect such situations [10]. Each project that has leveraged these techniques has demonstrated that a substantial number of requirements defects that had previously escaped to later development phases can be discovered early.

Figure 5, which shows percentage of total defects found over time, illustrates that faults are found much earlier following model-driven engineering than with the conventional process. Finding defects sooner is significant, since it is much cheaper to fix defects earlier. Our internal data confirms Boehm's observation that the cost of fixing defects increases exponentially with the distance between where a defect is sourced and where it is discovered [11]. Finding double the errors in the design phases as shown in Fig. 5 translates into large cost savings.

The availability of tools operating on design notations encourages convergence on standard common notations with the associated benefits of sharing expertise and projects between different development teams. The learning curve for new engineers to get familiar with a product has been substantially shortened. When a new engineer studies the application models, domain knowledge is exposed rather than obfuscated in the product code. Consequentially, the time required for a new developer to acquire sufficient domain knowledge to become productive has been shortened by 2-3X.

4   Penetration and Applicability

Deployment of model-driven engineering varies substantially between product teams. Figure 6 shows the penetration across the components of a release of a telecommunications system, as of 2002. The size of each chart indicates the relative amount of effort that went into producing the corresponding component.

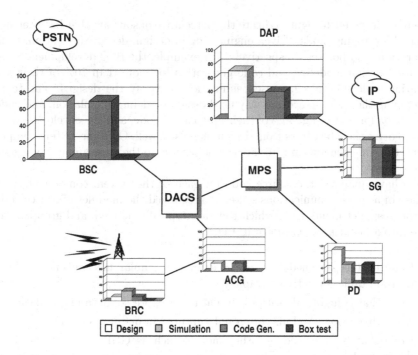

Fig. 6. Deployment of model-driven engineering across network element development

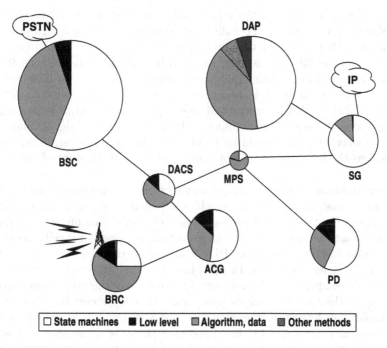

Fig. 7. Automation potential across network element development

The bars, from left to right, indicate the percentage of software that has been developed leveraging model-driven engineering in design, design verification, code generation, and box test, respectively. For example, the BSC development team has used design modeling and code generation for more than 70% of their application code, but has not used simulation to verify the designs. The team developing the surveillance gateway used design modeling, simulation, and code generation for more than 80% of their application code, and the developers were able to drive their box tests from design models as well. On some system components, the code generation rates are still lower due to the large amount of legacy code present.

We have analyzed the source code for each of the system components of a release of a telecommunications system, categorized the modules of source code by the design elements from which they are typically derived, and grouped the code into four buckets, as shown in Fig. 7:

- Code that is specified by state machines or similar mechanisms (such as decision tables or activity graphs)
- Code that is highly algorithmic in nature or expresses data manipulations
- Code that is low level and often not captured in detail in designs
- Code that is described by other means, such as GUI layout or database design tools.

The size of each pie reflects the relative effort that went into developing the particular network element; the individual sections reflect the design elements characterizing that portion of the developed network element. For example, 56% of the code on the BSC can be characterized by state machines. This software is the main control logic of the application, routing calls between base stations (similar to cells in a mobile telephony system) and the mobile switching system. About 39% of the code is characterized by computation, comprising the packing and unpacking of protocol data units and the evaluation of signal quality to determine whether a call should be handed over between base stations. About 5% concerns the interface to the transcoders and is usually stubbed out in the designs.

The distribution of the four categories varies between network elements. Our experience is that all of the state-machine oriented code can be derived from designs as can most or all of the algorithmic code, depending on the availability of a suitable action language in the design notation or domain-specific notations such as those described earlier for PDU marshaling code. The low-level code is unlikely to be generated automatically. Mileage in the "other" categories varies, but this code comprises a relatively small percentage of the overall application.

Rolling up the data for various telecommunication systems reveals that the potential for model-driven engineering is at least 73%, but may go as high as 96%. The individual percentages are less important than the message: a significant portion of a telecommunication system is amenable to code generation from high-level designs.

5   Representation of Models

The fundamental assumption of model-driven engineering is that the model is the central element of the development process and that all activities in the development process are aimed at creating the model or deriving other artifacts from the model. It is, therefore, not surprising that a critical aspect of the successful use of model-driven engineering is how to represent a model.

When Motorola embarked on deploying model-driven engineering, the dominant modeling language for real-time telecommunication applications was SDL [8], while UML [12] had emerged as the dominant modeling language for general-purpose computing applications.

While UML aims to be applicable to a wide range of application domains, SDL has focused on the modeling of reactive, state/event driven systems typically found in telecom applications. In order to subsume the possible variances of application domains, UML does not define all language concepts (such as its concurrency semantics) to the level of detail necessary to allow unambiguous interpretation. SDL, on the other hand, gives precise, formal semantics for all its concepts. In addition, UML relies on implementation languages for executable specifications; SDL is a language for specifying executable models independently of an implementation language.

After the emergence of UML, a typical SDL usage scenario was that UML is used for describing the entities of a system and the relationships these entities bear to each other during analysis modeling, while SDL is used for detailed design. Our experience revealed that these design notations had shortcomings that limited the applicability of code generation, and the combined usage model proved awkward [13,14]. In response, an enhanced version of SDL was adopted in 1999, supporting language elements required by our engineering teams. In 2003, the latest release of UML was adopted, integrating the lessons learned from SDL deployment.

A smoother integration of these notations was provided by the ITU Recommendation Z.109 which defines the SDL UML Profile [4]. Thanks to this profile, users can easily transition from the more abstract UML analysis models to the unambiguous and executable SDL design models. The SDL UML profile allows users to treat an SDL model as a specialization of the generic UML model thus giving more specific meaning to entities in the application domain (blocks, processes, services, gates, channels, etc.). A number of features have been introduced in SDL which directly support SDL and UML convergence:

- UML-style class symbols provide both partial type specifications and references to type diagrams containing the definition of that type;
- UML-style graphics for SDL concepts such as types, packages, inheritance, and dependencies;
- Composite states that combine the hierarchical organization of Statecharts with the transition-oriented view of SDL finite state machines;
- Interfaces that define the encapsulation boundary of active objects; and
- Associations between class symbols.

While UML has its focus and strength on object oriented data modeling, SDL has its strength in the modeling of concurrent active objects, of the hierarchical structure of active objects, and of their connection by means of well-defined interfaces. As a response to user requirements for more design level concepts as well as for better support of object-oriented modeling of active objects, the SDL heritage provides the following concepts:

- A complete action language that makes SDL independent of implementation languages. In line with the rest of SDL, behavior is specified in an imperative style and may be mixed with graphical SDL.
- Object oriented data based on single inheritance and with both polymorphic references (objects) and values, even in the same inheritance hierarchy. Type safety is preserved in the presence of covariance through multiple dispatch.
- Composite states that are defined by separate state diagrams (for scalability); entry/exit points are used instead of state boundary crossing (for encapsulation), any composite state can be of a state type (for reuse), and state types can be parameterized (for even more reuse).
- Object-orientation applied to active objects including inheritance of behavior specified through state machines and inheritance of the (hierarchical) structure and connection of active objects.
- Virtual types that allow the redefinition of inherited types.
- Constraints on redefinitions in subclasses and on actual parameters in parameterization that afford strong error checking at modeling time.

In the latest revisions of UML [15] it has been recognized that UML greatly benefits from inclusion of above concepts. The SDL UML profile provides identifies a subset of UML organizations can focus on when modeling.

6   Code Generation

The most crucial component in the deployment of model-driven engineering proved to be a code generator that is able to translate high-level design specifications into product-quality code [16]. Code generators are the most crucial not only because they dramatically decrease the effort spent on translating specifications into code and make this process quickly repeatable, but also because users did not want to spend the necessary effort to make design models executable if they later had to translate those models into code manually (users did not want to "code twice", as they tended to put it). This was the case independent of that design simulation alone had a dramatic impact on the quality of the developed product.

Commercial tools supporting code generation in the embedded system domain have become available. While these tools do generate code corresponding to a complete application (rather than merely header files or code templates as was the case in the past), by necessity the resultant software is generic and does not include any code that is imposed by specifics of the application domain. Unfortunately, such generic code is rarely sufficient to ship a product. Even in the most successful deployments of commercial tools in our organization, engineers had to add a significant amount of hand-written code linking the generic application to the specific platform. In addition, these tools usually do not generate code that marshals a PDU in and out of the generated application.

The downside of adding hand-written code into the code that has been generated by the tool is apparent: The necessary integration as well as any domain-specific optimizations or data realizations are difficult to write and require intricate understanding of the code generators, as they have to be fit into code that the engineers did not write and should not have to understand. Architectural assumptions may have to be retrofitted into the generated code. The resultant product becomes much harder to maintain and cannot easily be ported to new target platforms. Even if a tool maintains any changes applied to the generated code across design modifications (a process usually referred to as "round-trip" engineering), these shortcomings still apply.

In certain application domains, producing code in a generic manner may not even work. In particular, in highly constrained domains such as subscriber applications, when commercial code generators have failed it is more often than not due to unacceptable memory usage.

To work around these difficulties in developing code generators, we tried to understand how an engineer develops code starting from high-level designs. Engineers are usually very skilled and know a lot about the process of translating product designs into efficient product code that will satisfy the constraints of their application domains. We identified several different "kinds" of knowledge that engineers utilize in this process: general purpose coding knowledge, domain-specific knowledge, and product-specific knowledge. We developed the Mousetrap code generation framework [17,16] which enabled the construction of compilers that rely on these same types of knowledge. In developing model compilers, we capture the knowledge leveraged by experienced engineers in a reusable form, store it in a knowledge base, and apply it to input specifications by the compiler to generate the target code.

We rely on transformation rules to codify programming knowledge. Transformation rules are recipes for taking a fragment of an input model and transforming it into a fragment of an output program. Each rule consists of three parts: a pattern that describes the fragment of the input program we want to operate on, a replacement that describes the final fragment of the output program we want to produce, and an applicability condition that tells us whether a given matched fragment of the input program can be legally transformed into the replacement fragment. Transformation rules are correctness preserving rewrite rules over parse trees. Pattern and replacement are written in the grammar of the programming language we are manipulating, but contain variables which stand for parts of the program we want to abstract away from. The applicability condition ensures that the rule is not applied in situations where the pattern matches a fragment of the input program but where we would introduce an error would we perform the replacement.

The heart of the Mousetrap system is a rewrite engine which traverses an input program, finds all the locales where a pattern in a set of transformation rules matches a fragment of the input program, and performs all those replacements that are permitted by the applicability conditions. The search for matches takes into account any equational theories that constructs of the programming language may be subject to, such as associativity, commutativity, idempotence, or a special list theory. The input program can be examined using various traversal strategies, from outside-in or from inside-out, in single steps, or until a fix-point is reached. In addition, the constructs used to express programming language grammar productions are typed, and program transformations take these types (as well as subtyping) into account. Rewriting is order-sorted.

Each of these transformation rules makes only a small change to the program. Consequentially, the program evolves in many steps, requiring thousands (or hundreds-of-thousands) of rewrites. Because these transformation rules are small and relatively simple, they are easy to show correct. But for the same reason the transformation rules have to be applied fully automatically. Interactive rule application is completely unfeasible.

We have divided the transformation from high-level designs to product code into a sequence of phases. Each phase essentially manipulates a different language, where each language gradually becomes closer to the target language in its semantics and underlying assumptions. The bulk of the transformations are within each phase or language layer; a simple set of transformations moves the program from one language layer to the next. At a rough-level of abstraction, the program proceeds through the following language layers: We begin with a canoncialization step where we replace similar constructs in the specification language with canonical forms that are easier to manipulate subsequently. Next we add domain-specific tasks. Next domain-specific specification constructs are realized. In the telecommunications domain, these are primarily extended finite state machines and the logical data layout defining a PDU. We then realize abstract data types, selecting an appropriate implementation based on domain or usage (for example, "set-as-bitvector" or "set-as-hashtable"). The program is then subject to extensive optimizations. Next we add product-specific implementation detail and map the program to the underlying computing or middleware platform. In this step we may provide automated memory management, process handling, light-weight multi-threading or simulation of concurrency, and so on. At this point, the program is transformed into the target language, usually C, and a final optimization step is applied.

In the following we list examples of transformations that are applied during the translation from designs to code. We apply an extensive set of standard techniques for realizing data structures and for optimizing data structures:

- Recognize clichés with particular efficient implementation
- Implement replicated processes as "call record" structures
- Combine identities with common sub-expression elimination
- Remove levels of indirection by lifting pointers
- Maintain information through finite differencing

- Compute change to data structures incrementally
- Propagate estimates of the size of data structures
- Allocate larger data structures in parcels of a size efficient for the target hardware
- Minimize heap allocation

Many possible optimizations are often not applied systematically by engineers when writing code by hand, but can be leveraged to great benefit by a code generator:

- In-lining of function and iterator calls
- In-lining of data structures
- Partial evaluation of function calls
- Constant propagation
- Context-dependent simplification
- Expression caching
- Common sub-expression elimination
- Special idioms for efficient implementation of primitives
- Source-level peephole optimizations
- Replacing shifts by masking and xor

Typical implementation choices that are applied by the Mousetrap system:

- Imposition of architectures, e.g., realizing processes as threads, as tasks, or eliminating them altogether
- Imposition of most efficient communication mechanism, such as interprocess communication, shared memory, remote procedure call, or method invocation on a distributed processing environment
- Imposition of non-standard data realization, such as inlining objects, exploding structures, or introducing pointers in order to minimize copying of data.

The resultant code size for infrastructure network elements compares favorably to hand-written code. In Fig. 8, examples "A1" and "A2" are network elements showing that that code size has been reduced by as much as 30% as compared with the hand-written application. Even for subscriber products, code size is approaching that of hand-written code. Application "A3" in Fig. 8 shows a subscriber device; its code size is only 9% above the estimate for hand-written code, and it is 42% smaller than the size of code obtained from the best commercial tool we tried.

Execution speed has met or exceeded performance targets for each delivered code generator. Figure 9 shows how the call execution time using the automatically generated code on two network elements (A1 and A2) closely tracks and at times improves over the call execution time of hand-written code for the same network element at various call loadings. A consequence of the better performance of the generated code for the middle call phases is a substantially reduced drop-call rate for the generated code.

The bottom line is that Mousetrap code generators have reached a level of maturity that allows them to be deployed for the development of performance-critical applications.

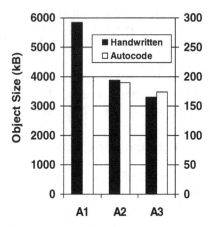

Fig. 8. Code size

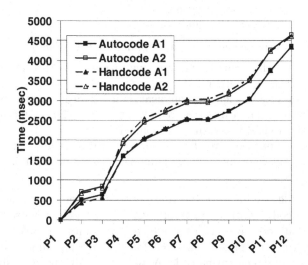

Fig. 9. Execution speed

7 Support Model

In order to support the widespread roll-out of model-driven engineering in our organization, we have formed a support team to assist Motorola businesses in the deployment of code generation.

The code generation support team maintains a large body of programming knowledge codified in the form of program transformation rules. This knowledge comprises general purpose programming knowledge, domain specific knowledge, and product specific knowledge, as described earlier. Once engineering has identified the domain constraints and the architectural constraints of a new product,

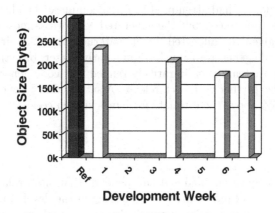

Development Week

Fig. 10. Iterative improvement of object size

the constraints are used to identify the subset of the programming knowledge relevant to this application. This relevant subset is extracted and packaged together with design and programming language parsers and printers as well as the rule application engine into a domain-specific compiler. This compiler is delivered to the application development team.

The domain-specific compilers transform the application designs into highly optimized product code. This code is optimized with respect to the domain constraints the development team had originally identified and will contain many other application-specific details. If the starting point is a subscriber device, for example, the code will be geared toward the needs and constraints of a subscriber device, as well as the peculiarities of the supported protocols and hardware. The generated code would not work, or would work very poorly, if used on an infrastructure product. If code for an infrastructure product were desired, a compiler specific to that domain would have been delivered.

If a completely new product or a product for a domain for which the programming knowledge has not yet been codified is to be developed, the code generation support team works with the application development engineers to identify and codify domain-specific and product-specific programming knowledge and then codifies this knowledge. Once the knowledge has been captured and is added to the Mousetrap rule base, the deployment process continues as described before.

The support team aims to deliver code generators that are optimized to the architectural and performance constraints of the chosen target platform and that take into account any other domain-specific information that is applicable. Identifying and codifying programming knowledge may require several iteration, until a solution is obtained that completely satisfies all constraints. A code generator is supported until the product that it is used in is retired. This close style of interaction is necessary, as often the requisite knowledge or constraints are not known ahead of time and are only discovered in light of delivered initial releases.

For example, Fig. 10 depicts consecutive releases of a code generator for a protocol stack on a subscriber device (the axis indicates consecutive development weeks). The developers had attempted to use a commercial code generator previously (shown as reference), but the generated code was almost twice as large as was feasible, given the allocated direct material costs. The first iteration of the Mousetrap code generator came in significantly better, but still far from the target. The support team then iteratively refined this code generator, bringing down the code size further with each release. A satisfactory level of performance was reached at 9% above the estimate for hand-written code.

8   Summary

In this paper, we have summarized the benefits that Motorola has obtained from the deployment of model-driven engineering in the development of reliable embedded systems, in particular, network elements for telecommunications systems. The benefits afforded by model-driven engineering result in both quality improvements and productivity improvements. In the development of telecommunication systems, a large portion of developed software, in our estimate at least three quarters of the total software, is amenable to leveraging model-driven engineering techniques.

We have also discussed each of the three elements we found most important for deployment of MDE. The first is a modeling language that provides the appropriate domain-specific abstractions and the ability to operationally execute the model. This element is critical for allowing the model to be a natural expression of the design without extra baggage and for enabling early testing. The second is a powerful domain-specific code generator. This element is one of the key enablers of MDE, allowing the model to be free of platform specifics and allowing the model to be maintained instead of the code. The third element is a deployment support team. As with any development paradigm, it is unrealistic to assume that engineers fresh out of college will have the necessary experience to be able to develop large-scale industrial systems. MDE adds the burden that it is sufficiently new and different to require a support team (process, language, modeling and abstraction, target platforms, etc.) to ensure success.

References

1. Baker, P., Loh, S., Weil, F.: Model-Driven Engineering in a Large Industrial Context—Motorola Case Study. In: MoDELS 2005. LNCS, vol. 3713, Springer, Heidelberg (2005)
2. Weigert, T., Reed, R.: Specifying Telecommunications Systems with UML. In: Lavagno, L., Martin, G., Selic, B. (eds.) UML for Real: Design of Embedded Real-Time Systems, Kluwer Academic Publisher, Amsterdam (2003)
3. Haugen, Ø., Møller-Pedersen, B., Weigert, T.: Structural Modeling with UML 2. In: Lavagno, L., Martin, G., Selic, B. (eds.) UML for Real: Design of Embedded Real-Time Systems, Kluwer Academic Publisher, Amsterdam (2003)
4. International Telecommunications Union, SDL Combined With UML, ITU-T Rec. Z.109 (2007)

5. International Telecommunications Union, Abstract Syntax Notation One (ASN.1) & ASN.1 Encoding Rules, ITU-T Rec. X.680–X.693 (2002)
6. Weigert, T., Dietz, P.: Automated Generation of Marshalling Code from High-Level Specifications. In: Reed, R., Reed, J. (eds.) SDL 2003. LNCS, vol. 2708, Springer, Heidelberg (2003)
7. European Telecommunications Standards Institute, Testing and Test Control Notation version 3, Part 1: TTCN-3 Core Language, ETSI ES 201 873-1 V2.2.1 (2003)
8. International Telecommunications Union, Specification and Description Language, ITU-T Rec. Z.100 (2000)
9. Dikel, D., Kane, D., Ornburn, S., Loftus, B., Wilson, J.: Applying Software Product-Line Architecture. IEEE Software 30, 49–55 (1997)
10. Baranov, S., Kotlyarov, V., Letichevsky, A., Weigert, T.: Leveraging UML to Deliver Correct Telecom Applications. In: Lavagno, L., Martin, G., Selic, B. (eds.) UML for Real: Design of Embedded Real-Time Systems, Kluwer Academic Publisher, Amsterdam (2003)
11. Boehm, B.: Software Engineering Economics. Prentice-Hall, Englewood Cliffs (1981)
12. Object Management Group, Unified Modeling Language (UML), Version 1 (1997)
13. Selic, B., Dhaussy, P., Ek, A., Haugen, Ø., Leblanc, P., Møller-Pedersen, B., Weigert, T.: SDL as UML: Why and What? In: France, R.B., Rumpe, B. (eds.) Proceedings of the 2nd International Conference on the Unified Modeling Language. LNCS, vol. 1723, pp. 446–456. Springer, Heidelberg (1999)
14. Weigert, T., Garlan, D., Knapman, J., Møller-Pedersen, B., Selic, B.: Modeling of Architectures with UML. In: Evans, A., Kent, S., Selic, B. (eds.) UML 2000. LNCS, vol. 1939, pp. 556–569. Springer, Heidelberg (2000)
15. Object Management Group, Unified Modeling Language (UML), Superstructure,Version 2.1.1 (2007)
16. Dietz, P., Marth, K., Berg, A.v.d., Weigert, T., Weil, F.: Practical Considerations in Automatic Code Generation. In: Tsai, J., Zhang, D. (eds.) Advances in Machine Learning Application in Software Engineering, Idea Group Publisher, Hershey (2006)
17. Boyle, J., Harmer, T., Weigert, T., Weil, F.: Knowledge-Based Derivation of Programs from Specifications. In: Bourbakis, N. (ed.) Artificial Intelligence And Automation, World Scientific Publishers, Singapore (1996)

TTCN-3 Quality Engineering: Using Learning Techniques to Evaluate Metric Sets

Edith Werner, Jens Grabowski, Helmut Neukirchen, Nils Röttger, Stephan Waack, and Benjamin Zeiss

Institute for Informatics, University of Göttingen
Lotzestr. 16–18, 37083 Göttingen, Germany
{ewerner,grabowski,neukirchen,nroettger,waack,zeiss}@cs.uni-goettingen.de

Abstract. Software metrics are an essential means to assess software quality. For the assessment of software quality, typically sets of complementing metrics are used since individual metrics cover only isolated quality aspects rather than a quality characteristic as a whole. The choice of the metrics within such metric sets, however, is non-trivial. Metrics may intuitively appear to be complementing, but they often are in fact non-orthogonal, i.e. the information they provide may overlap to some extent. In the past, such redundant metrics have been identified, for example, by statistical correlation methods. This paper presents, based on machine learning, a novel approach to minimise sets of metrics by identifying and removing metrics which have little effect on the overall quality assessment. To demonstrate the application of this approach, results from an experiment are provided. In this experiment, a set of metrics that is used to assess the analysability of test suites that are specified using the *Testing and Test Control Notation* (TTCN-3) is investigated.

1 Introduction

Quantitative methods like software metrics are a powerful means to assess and control software development [1]. In software development process maturity models, like *Capability Maturity Model Integration* (CMMI) [2] or *Software Process Improvement and Capability dEtermination'* (SPICE) [3], the usage of metrics is considered as an indicator of a high process maturity. For the quality assessment of test suites that are specified using the *Testing and Test Control Notation* (TTCN-3) [4,5], we have thus proposed a set of several TTCN-3 metrics [6]. When we presented and discussed these metrics at the Fifth International Workshop on System Analysis and Modelling (SAM'06), it was pointed out that the assessment of TTCN-3 specifications depends on the quality characteristic to be evaluated and that several metrics are needed to measure all aspects of a characteristic. Therefore, we developed subsequently a comprehensive test specification quality model [7] that takes various different quality characteristics into account to asses the quality of a test specification. Following the ISO/IEC 9126 standard [8], each quality characteristic is divided into further sub-characteristics

E. Gaudin, E. Najm, and R. Reed (Eds.): SDL 2007, LNCS 4745, pp. 54–68, 2007.

and each sub-characteristic is quantified using several metrics. By taking the measurements of the different metrics into account, a classification of the overall quality of a test specification can be made. But, as also pointed out at the discussion at SAM'06, this may lead to a cluttered set of metrics that is hard to interpret.

Hence, we developed a machine learning approach that can be used to optimise a set of metrics and that helps to judge whether a new metric should become part of the metrics set (i.e. measures a new quality aspect) or whether it is already subsumed by other metrics (i.e. the new metric leads to the same conclusion as other metrics already do). In this paper, we present our machine learning approach and show its practicability by applying it to a set of TTCN-3 metrics.

This paper is structured as follows: after this introduction, we provide foundations on software metrics and machine learning in Sect. 2. As our main contribution, we present our approach of using learning techniques to evaluate metric sets in Sect. 3. Then, in Sect. 4, we demonstrate the usage of this approach by applying it to a suite of TTCN-3 metrics. Finally, we conclude with a summary and outlook.

2 Foundations

In this section, foundations on software metrics and on pattern analysis using *Probably Approximately Correct* (PAC) learning are presented. In our case, the patterns to be learned will be the varying values of a metric set that contribute to a corresponding overall classification of the quality of a test specification.

2.1 Software Metrics

According to Fenton et al. [1], the term *software metrics* embraces all activities which involve software measurement. Software metrics are mostly used for management purposes and quality assurance in software development. They can be classified into measures for attributes of *processes*, *resources*, and *products*.

For each class, internal and external attributes can be distinguished. *External attributes* refer to how a process, resource, or product relates to its environment; *internal attributes* are properties of a process, resource, or product on its own, separate from any interactions with its environment. Internal product attributes are typically obtained by static analysis of the code to be assessed. External product attributes on the other hand are normally gained by accumulating quantitative data of interest during program execution.

Internal product metrics can be structured into *size* and *structural* metrics [1]. Size metrics measure properties of the number of usage of programming or specification language constructs, e.g. the metrics proposed by Halstead [9]. Structural metrics analyse the structure of a program or specification. The most popular examples are complexity metrics based on control flow or call graphs and coupling metrics.

Concerning metrics for measuring complexity of control structures, the most prominent complexity metric is the *cyclomatic complexity* from McCabe [10,11].

It is a *descriptive* metric, i.e. its value can be objectively derived from source code. By additionally using threshold values, this metric becomes also *prescriptive* [12], i.e. it helps to control software quality. For example, when threshold violations of the metric values are analysed, it can help to identify complex modules which shall be split into several simpler ones [11].

Metrics are often used in the context of a quality model. The ISO/IEC standard 9126 [8] defines such a quality model for internal quality, external quality, and quality-in-use of software products. It is possible to apply such quality models to test specifications as well [7]. The ISO/IEC quality model describes each distinct quality characteristic of a software product by further subcharacteristics that refine each characteristic. To quantify the quality with respect to each subcharacteristic, according metrics can be used. Based on these metrics and related thresholds, an overall classification of a given software product can be made. The actual scheme used for the overall classification may vary from project to project, e.g. one project may require a scenario in which all the calculated metric values need to be within the corresponding thresholds, whereas in other projects it may be sufficient if only a certain percentage of the involved metrics do not violate their thresholds.

To make sure that reasonable metrics are chosen, Basili et al. suggest the *Goal Question Metric* (GQM) approach [13]: First, the goals which shall be achieved (e.g. improve maintainability) must be defined. Then, for each goal, a set of meaningful questions that characterise a goal is derived. The answers to these questions determine whether a goal has been met or not. Finally, one or more metrics are defined to gather quantitative data which give answers to each question. The GQM approach, however, does not make any statement on the similarity of metrics and whether certain metrics are statistically replaceable by others.

There are numerous publications that try to tackle the orthogonality problem of software metrics, i.e. they try to identify those measures in a set of metrics that do not deliver any meaningful additional information. One early work of Henry et al. [14] demonstrated the high-degree relationship between the *cyclomatic complexity* and Halstead's complexity measures by means of Pearson correlation coefficients. A good overview on further related work is provided by Fenton et al. [1]: they list approaches to investigate the correlation of metrics using Spearmans' rank correlation coefficient and Kendall's robust correlation coefficient. To express the nature of the associations, *regression analysis* has been suggested. Furthermore, *principal component analysis* has been used to reduce the number of necessary metrics by removing those principal components that account for little of the variability. We are not aware of any approaches that use a learning approach as described in the remainder of this paper.

2.2   Extracting Pattern From Data

The so-called Keplers's third law states that the squares of the periods of planets are proportional to the cubes of their semimajor axes. The law corresponds to regularities present in the planetary data recorded by Tycho Brahe. Johannes Kepler's extraction of these regularities from Brahe's data can be regarded as an early example of pattern analysis.

There are various models to formalise such pattern analysis problems in diverse degrees of generality. A very prominent one is Valiant's learning model [15,16] that is outlined in the following.

We are given an *input space* $\mathfrak{X} \subset \mathbb{R}^n$. Usually we think of $\mathfrak{X}$ as being a set of encodings of instances or objects in the learner's world. Examples are rectangles in the Euclidean plane $\mathbb{R}^2$, two 2-dimensional arrays of binary pixels of a fixed width and height when it comes to recognising characters, or simply Boolean vectors of length n. The input space is the data source in this model. To this end, a random element $X \in \mathfrak{X}$ is given. It induces an arbitrary distribution P_X on $\mathfrak{X}$.

A *concept* over the input space $\mathfrak{X}$ is a $+1/-1$-valued function on $\mathfrak{X}$ or equivalently a subset of $\mathfrak{X}$. A *concept class* $\mathcal{C}$ is a collection of concepts. Examples are all rectangles in the Euclidean plane $\mathbb{R}^2$, pixel representations of a given alphabet, and all Boolean monomials of a fixed length k over the Boolean variables $x_1, x_2, \ldots, x_n$.

An algorithm A is a PAC learner of the concept class $\mathcal{C}$ by a hypothesis class $\mathcal{H}$, which usually comprises $\mathcal{C}$, if for every accuracy $\epsilon > 0$ and every confidence $\delta > 0$ there is minimal sample size $\mathrm{m}_A(\epsilon, \delta)$ such that for every target concept $g \in \mathcal{C}$, all $m \geq \mathrm{m}_A(\epsilon, \delta)$, and all distributions P_X the following property is satisfied. Let A be given access to a *learning sample*

$$U^{(m)} := ((X_1, g(X_1)), (X_2, g(X_2)), \ldots, (X_m, g(X_m))) \tag{1}$$

of length m, where $(X_1, X_2, \ldots, X_m)$ is a sample drawn independently from $\mathfrak{X}$ according to the distribution P_X. Then A outputs with probability at least $1 - \delta$ a hypothesis $H := A\left(U^{(m)}\right) \in \mathcal{H}$ satisfying $\mathrm{err}(H) \leq \epsilon$. This probability is taken over the random learning samples according to (1) and any internal randomisation, if the learning algorithm is a probabilistic one. The *error* $\mathrm{err}(h)$ of any hypothesis $h \in \mathcal{H}$ is defined by $P\left(h(X) \neq g(X)\right)$. The preceding condition is sometimes referred to as *consistency* of the learning algorithm A.

In order to devise a PAC learner, it is reasonable to output a hypothesis h that performs faultless on the learning sample (1). To ensure that this will work, especially to avoid what is called *overfitting*, it is, moreover, necessary to bound the *capacity* of the hypothesis class $\mathcal{H}$. Very popular capacity measures are the Vapnik-Cervonenkis dimension [17,18,19] and the Rademacher complexity [20]. For an overview see [21,22].

PAC learning can be canonically generalised to what might be called *pattern analysis* or *pattern extraction*. Starting point is the observation that the second components Y_i of the learning sample

$$U^{(m)} := ((X_1, Y_1), (X_2, Y_2), \ldots, (X_m, Y_m)) \tag{2}$$

need not always be totally depend on the first components X_i. Again we restrict ourselves to *classification problems*, that is to the cases, where the so-called *output variables* Y_i take values in the *output space* $\mathfrak{Y} = \{-1, +1\}$, The product

$\mathfrak{U} := \mathfrak{X} \times \mathfrak{Y}$ is denoted as *learning universe*. Using a random variable $U = (X, Y) \in \mathfrak{U}$, it is regarded as source of data. The first component X of U is called *input element*, the second component Y the *output variable*. Analogous to the cases of PAC learning, the distribution P_U with the random element U induced on the learning universe is not determined, but sometimes it has *guaranteed qualities*.

A pattern analysis algorithm A by a *pattern class* $\mathcal{P} \subset \mathrm{Map}(\mathfrak{U}, \{-1, +1\})$ takes a learning sample (2) as input. It computes a pattern $A(U^{(m)}) \in \mathcal{P}$ that "approximates" the *risk infimum* $\mathrm{risk}\,\mathcal{P} := \inf_{\pi \in \mathcal{P}} \mathrm{risk}\,\pi$ of the class $\mathcal{P}$ in the sense of consistency defined below. The risk of a pattern $\pi \in \mathcal{P}$, which is denoted by $\mathrm{risk}\,\pi$, in turn is defined to be the expected value $\mathrm{E}\,\pi(U)$ of $\pi(U)$. On overview on this setting is given in [22].

In this paper, we make only use of pattern classes consisting of patterns of the type $\ell_{0/1}(y, h(x))$, where h ranges over a hypothesis class $\mathcal{H} \subset \mathrm{Map}(\mathfrak{X}, \{-1, +1\})$, and $\ell_{0/1}$ is the so-called *0/1-loss function*: $\ell_{0/1}(y_1, y_2) = 1 - \delta(y_1, y_2)$, where δ is the Kronecker function.

An example for a guaranteed quality mentioned above is that Y equals $g(X)$, for some target concept g belonging to the concept class $\mathcal{C}$. If the pattern class is formed by means of a hypothesis class $\mathcal{H} \supseteq \mathcal{C}$, then $\mathrm{risk}\,\pi = \mathrm{err}\,h$ provided that $\pi(x, y) = \ell_{0/1}(y, h(x))$. That way PAC learning is a special case of pattern extraction. From now on we identify the pattern $\pi(x, y) = \ell_{0/1}(y, h(x))$ with the hypothesis $h(x)$, and consequently the pattern class $\mathcal{P}$ with the hypothesis class $\mathcal{H}$.

A pattern analysis algorithm A by $\mathcal{H}$ is called *consistent*, if for every accuracy $\epsilon > 0$ and every confidence $\delta > 0$ there is a minimal sample size $\mathrm{m}_A(\epsilon, \delta)$ such that for all $m \geq \mathrm{m}_A(\epsilon, \delta)$, and all distributions P_U the following condition is fulfilled. Taking the learning sample (2) as input, A outputs with probability at least $1 - \delta$ a hypothesis $H := A(U^{(m)}) \in \mathcal{H}$ satisfying

$$\mathrm{risk}\,H \leq \mathrm{risk}\,\mathcal{H} + \epsilon. \tag{3}$$

The problem with the risk of a hypothesis is that it cannot be calculated since the distribution P_U is not determined. Consequently, one cannot try to compute a hypothesis of minimal risk. The empirical risk minimisation induction principle *ERM* recommends a pattern analysis algorithm to choose a hypothesis h that minimises the *empirical* risk

$$\mathrm{risk}_{\mathrm{emp}}\left(h \,\big|\, U^{(m)}\right) := \frac{1}{m} \sum_{i=1}^{m} \ell_{0/1}\left(Y_i, h(X_i)\right) \tag{4}$$

on the learning sample (2). A pattern analysis algorithm A obeying ERM is consistent, if, for example, the Rademacher complexity $\mathrm{rc}_m(\mathcal{H})$ of $\mathcal{H}$ is an $o(1)$. In this cases the empirical risk of the output of A is a consistent estimator of the risk infimum in the sense of mathematical statistics.

In this paper ERM means that one has to minimise the number of misclassifications on the learning sample (2). Practically, one has to ensure that for sufficiently small accuracy and confidence – say $\epsilon = 0.005$ and $\delta = 10^{-6}$ – the learning sample length suffices to fulfil (3).

To get an idea of what the Rademacher complexity $rc_m(\mathcal{H})$ of a finite $\mathcal{H}$ with respect to samples of length m means, let us mention that $rc_m(\mathcal{H}) \leq \sqrt{2 \ln |\mathcal{H}|}/\sqrt{m}$ [23].

3   Using Learning Techniques to Evaluate Metric Sets

In this section we describe how to approximate a comprehensive software quality assessment scheme based on a set of n metrics by a restricted scheme supported by the "best" ν-subset $(0 < \nu < n)$ of these metrics in terms of learning techniques. To this end, we assign to a family of *parametrised* comprehensive schemes a concept class in the sense of PAC learning. For each ν-subset, the corresponding family of parametrised restricted schemes is, moreover, mirrored by a hypothesis class. We evaluate the performance of the approximation using the risk infimum of the best hypothesis class (see (3)).

In the following, we define the learning setup: The input space $\mathfrak{X}$ equals the Cartesian product of n intervals $[0, c_1], [0, c_2], \ldots, [0, c_n]$, that are the ranges of the n metrics. Thus each behavioural entity is represented by a vector of length n.

The concept class $\mathcal{C}$, which is equivalent to the parametrised comprehensive assessment schemes, consists of all concepts g such that for all $x \in \mathfrak{X}$

$$g(x) = +1 \quad \Longleftrightarrow \quad x_i > \tau_i \quad \text{for at most } k \text{ of the indices } \{1, 2, \ldots, n\},$$

and $g(x) = -1$ otherwise. Therein the *parameter* $(\tau_1, \tau_2, \ldots, \tau_n)$ is any element of $\mathfrak{X}$, and $k \in \{0, 1, \ldots, n-1\}$ is a constant. The concept g is equivalent to the following comprehensive software quality assessment scheme: A behavioural entity is positively evaluated, if and only if at most k of the n metrics violate their quality threshold given by $(\tau_1, \tau_2, \ldots, \tau_n)$.

We restricted ourselves to a "reasonable" concept $g_0 \in \mathcal{C}$ from the point of view of software quality assessment, rather than to learn the whole concept class in the sense of PAC learning. Our concept g_0 is determined by n threshold values $\gamma_1, \gamma_2, \ldots, \gamma_n$, one for each metric, based on our expertise in software testing. Then the learning samples were assumed to be drawn according to (1), with the target concept g being g_0 as guaranteed quality of the distribution P_U (see Section 2.2).

For each ν-subset $i_1 < i_2 < \ldots < i_\nu$ of $\{1, 2, \ldots, n\}$, we define the elements h of the hypothesis classes $\mathcal{H}(i_1, i_2, \ldots, i_\nu)$ determining a restricted scheme by

$$h(x) = +1 \quad \Longleftrightarrow \quad x_{i_j} > \tau_j \quad \text{for at most } \kappa \text{ elements } j \text{ of the set } \{1, 2, \ldots, \nu\},$$

where $\tau_j \in [0, c_{i_j}]$, for $j = 0, 1, \ldots, \nu - 1$, are the parameters of the hypothesis, and $1 \leq \kappa \leq \nu$ is a constant. Thus each ν-subset determines one restricted *model* of software assessment.

Clearly, learning a hypothesis of the above kind amounts to computing the ν *hypothesis thresholds* $\tau_1, \tau_2, \ldots, \tau_\nu$ from the training data. These thresholds need not be the same as the corresponding ones in the sequence $\gamma_1, \gamma_2, \ldots, \gamma_n$. This is due to the fact that we approximate n metrics by ν ones.

Without proof we notice that for a moderately large number n of metrics the pattern classes defined above are of relatively small capacity such that learning samples of reasonable size suffice to ensure (3) for acceptable accuracy and confidence.

What is a reasonable course of action in our learning setup to approximate a larger scheme by a smaller one and to evaluate the performance of the approximation? The one that follows is rather standard.

1. Represent all available behavioural entities as a vector of length n using the n metrics.
2. Classify them by the concept $g_0 \in \mathcal{C}$.
3. Randomly divide these data set into three parts: a training set (50%), a validation set (25%), and a test set (25%). This is because there are in fact two goals that we have in mind:

   Model selection: estimating the performance of the ν-subsets of our n-set of metrics to choose the best one.

   Model assessment: having chosen a final ν-subset of metrics, estimating the infimum risk.

4. In general, the training set is used to fit the models. In our case this means to compute for each ν-subset $\{i_1, i_2, \ldots, i_\nu\}$ of the index set $\{1, 2, \ldots, n\}$ a hypothesis $h(i_1, i_2, \ldots, i_\nu) \in \mathcal{H}(i_1, i_2, \ldots, i_\nu)$ in terms of its hypothesis thresholds that minimises the empirical risk (see (4)) on the training data.

5. Choose a best hypothesis $h\left(i_1^{(0)}, i_2^{(0)}, \ldots, i_\nu^{(0)}\right)$ on the validation set. This is done by computing the empirical risks of all hypotheses $h(i_1, i_2, \ldots, i_\nu)$ found in Step 4 on the validation data, the so-called *validation errors*.

6. Calculate the empirical risk of $h\left(i_1^{(0)}, i_2^{(0)}, \ldots, i_\nu^{(0)}\right)$ on the test set, the so-called *test error*, thus estimating the risk infimum risk $\mathcal{H}\left(i_1^{(0)}, i_2^{(0)}, \ldots, i_\nu^{(0)}\right)$ that in turn measures how well n metrics can be approximated by ν ones.

4 Application

To evaluate the practicability of our approach, we performed an experiment. In this experiment, we applied our approach to investigate whether it is possible to approximate a set of four metrics by a minimised set of one or two metrics only.

4.1 Metrics

In the following, the four metrics used in the experiment are introduced in more detail. The metrics are selected to capture different perceptions of complexity of behaviour within a TTCN-3 test suite with regards to the maintainability characteristic and its analysability subcharacteristic of the refined quality model for test specifications [7]. In TTCN-3, test behaviour is specified by test case, function, and altstep constructs. We start by describing a measure called *Number of Statements*.

Metric 1 (Number Of Statements NOS). The number of statement count NOS is mostly self explaining. Unlike the common lines of code (LOC) measure, counting the number of statements ignores information regarding the code itself such as the code's formatting or comments while retaining an intuitive measure of the code length.

Even though NOS delivers a measure for the code length per behavioural entity, it does not deliver any statement about code complexity. It is missing a sense of behavioural complexity. McCabe's *cyclomatic complexity* [10] attempts to deliver this, essentially by counting the number of branches of the control flow graph and thus penalising conditional behaviour.

Metric 2 (Cyclomatic Complexity $v(G)$). The cyclomatic complexity $v(G)$ of a control flow graph G can be defined[1] as:

$$v(G) = e - n + 2$$

In this formula, e denotes the number of edges and n is the number of nodes in G.

While the cyclomatic complexity $v(G)$ penalises conditional behaviour, it is missing another factor that comprises code complexity: deeply nested branches are not penalised any different than flat branches. For example, a conditional nested within another conditional is penalised the same as two subsequent conditionals even though nested conditionals obviously complicate things. Thus, we chose to add a simple nesting level metric to our set of metrics.

Metric 3 (Maximum Nesting Level MNL). The maximum nesting level MNL is obtained by inspecting all conditionals within a test behaviour and counting their nesting levels. For example, an if-statement within an if-statement would yield the nesting level 2. The maximum nesting level denotes the highest nesting level measured per behavioural entity.

Since structured test behaviour may invoke other callable behaviour (e.g. by calling other functions), the complexity of each code fragment also depends on the complexity resulting by calls to such other behavioural entities. For developers, deeply nested call structures can be bothersome as they have to look up and understand each called behaviour within the code piece in front of them when working on this code. The *Maximum Call Depth* provides such a measure.

Metric 4 (Maximum Call Depth MCD). The maximum call depth MCD is obtained by analysis of the call graph[2]. For each behaviour A, the corresponding graph of behaviours called by A is calculated recursively to include indirect

---

[1] Several ways of defining $v(G)$ can be found in literature. The above definition assumes that G has a single entry and a single exit point. In the presence of several exit points, this assumption can be maintained by adding edges from all exit points to a single exit point.

[2] In the call graph, a directed edge from node A to node B indicates that behaviour A calls behaviour B.

calls (i.e. the call relation is transitive); in this graph, the length of each path starting from A is measured and the resulting MCD value is the length of the longest distinct path. If the path contains a cycle due to a recursive call, the MCD value is ∞.

We calculate these four metrics for each behavioural entity (i.e. test case, function, altstep) of a TTCN-3 test suite and use the vector of calculated metric values to obtain an overall classification of the quality of a test behaviour with respect to the quality sub-characteristic *analysability*. To obtain such an overall classification, for each behaviour we compare the calculated metric values against corresponding thresholds. Each element of the vector may be classified as positive, i.e. does not violate its corresponding threshold value, or negative, i.e. does violate the corresponding threshold value. The overall classification of a behavioural entity is again a positive or negative verdict that depends on how many of the elements of the corresponding vector are classified as positive (indicating a good quality) or negative (indicating a bad quality) respectively.

4.2   Experimental Settings

To obtain a reasonable amount of data for applying and assessing our learning approach, we performed an experiment with several huge test suites that have been standardised by the *European Telecommunications Standards Institute* (ETSI). The first considered test suite is Version 3.2.1 of the test suite for the *Session Initiation Protocol* (SIP) [24], the second is a preliminary version of a test suite for the *Internet Protocol Version 6* (IPv6) [25]. Together, both test suites comprise 2276 behavioural entities and 88560 LOC.

The data used in this experiment was computed by our TRex TTCN-3 tool [26,27] using the metric thresholds given in Table 1. Based on our TTCN-3 experience, these basic thresholds were determined along the lines of the GQM approach mentioned in Sect. 2.1. TRex calculated a vector containing the values of the four metrics for every behavioural entity. Concerning the overall classification, we investigated two different scenarios:

Scenario 1. In the first scenario, every metric in the vector must be classified as positive to get a positive classification for this behavioural entity, i.e. a concept $g_0(x) = +1 \iff \forall i : x_i \leq \gamma_i$, where x_i are the metric values computed by TRex, γ_i are the corresponding metric thresholds as given in Table 1 and $i \in [1, 4]$. Using these thresholds, this scenario results in nearly 50% negative examples, i.e. behavioural entities that have a negative overall classification.

Scenario 2. In the second scenario, only three of the four metrics must be classified as positive to get an overall positive classification for the behavioural entity, i.e. a concept $g_0(x) = +1 \iff x_i > \gamma_i$, for at most one of the indices $i \in [1, 4]$. Using the same thresholds γ_i as in Scenario 1 (Table 1), this scenario leads to approximately 13% negative examples.

Table 1. Metric thresholds used for generating the data

Metric	γ
NOS	14
$v(G)$	4
MNL	3
MCD	10

Preprocessing

We implemented our learning approach and applied it to the data generated by TRex. For conducting the experiments, we randomly divided the data from the 2276 behavioural entities into three parts: The first part is used for learning and contains 50% of the behavioural entities. The second part contains 25% of the entities, this part is used for validation. Finally, the third part contains the remaining 25% and is used for testing. We have done such a partitioning for every experiment to have independent data sets.

The Different Experiments

We examine the best and the two best metrics that yield the closest approximation of the vector of four for every scenario, i.e. we try to find one metric and a combination of two metrics that predict the overall classification as good as possible.

For using just one metric, this means we have to find an occurring threshold. Therefore, we begin with the smallest possible threshold that divides all values of one metric in positive and negative examples. In each step we have the hypothesis thresholds τ_i and the positive (the metric value $\leq \tau_i$) and the negative (the metric value $> \tau_i$) examples in the hypothesis class $\mathcal{H}$. Then, we compare this with the overall classification, i.e. the concept class $\mathcal{C}$, and count the number of misclassifications. Performing the same steps for all possible thresholds we get the threshold that results in the smallest error. Afterwards, we proceed with the next metric and do the same. Finally we compare the metric/threshold combinations and choose the best. This means, we are looking for the smallest error in all metrics using a specific threshold.

For using two metrics, we try to find a combination of thresholds of two metrics that leads to the smallest error with respect to the overall classification. We do exactly the same as above, not searching a specific threshold but a threshold pair. So, we are searching in each of the possible metric combinations for the best threshold which leads to the smallest error.

4.3   Experimental Results

By investigating the two scenarios and for each scenario two different approximations (using either one or two metrics respectively), we obtain four different results.

Results for Learning the "Best" Metric in Scenario 1
For Scenario 1 (i.e. all four metrics must be classified as positive to yield a positive overall classification) and the assumption that the overall classification can be approximated by only one of the four metrics, the resulting data is provided in Table 2. If we select the biggest threshold it is clearly evident that all examples are classified as positive. Then the error is equal to the proportion of the negative examples. For a better overview we append this to the result table as *allNeg*. For any metrics, the resulting error is very big if it is the only metric used to predict the overall classification. For the best metric the risk infimum estimated on the testset is 19.61%. As usual we have estimated the risk only for the best metric. Hence, it is not advisable to replace the four metrics by only one metric. However, it is remarkable that the threshold chosen by the algorithms for the *MCD* metric is exactly the same as used for data generation. The other located thresholds are at least similar to those used for data generation.

Table 2. Learning the "best" metric in Scenario 1

Metric	Empirical risk	τ	Validation error	Test error
MCD	18.93	10	18.09	19.61
NOS	19.19	7	18.97	-
$v(G)$	29.80	2	34.22	-
MNL	33.57	2	37.41	-
allNeg	44.35	-	45.57	-

Results for Learning the "Best Two" Metrics in Scenario 1
When trying to approximate all four metrics using just two metrics, the results for Scenario 1 look like provided in Table 3. If the combination of the two metrics *NOS* and *MCD* is chosen, it is possible to reproduce the overall classification with a quite small risk infimum of 1.94%. The thresholds that have lead to this small error are exactly the same as chosen to generate the dataset. For all other combinations of metrics, the error is significantly larger and it is not advisable to use them instead.

Table 3. Learning the "best two" metrics in Scenario 1

Combination	Empirical risk	τ_1	τ_2	Validation error	Test error
NOS, MCD	2.11	14	10	1.76	1.94
$v(g)$, *MCD*	7.98	3	10	7.56	-
MNL, MCD	11.84	3	10	12.30	-
MNL, NOS	19.73	3	7	18.80	-
$v(g)$, *NOS*	19.82	3	7	18.98	-
$v(g)$, *MNL*	30.87	2	3	30.93	-
allNeg	44.74	-	-	43.94	-

Results for Learning the "Best" Metric in Scenario 2
In comparison with the first scenario, we here obtained a different ordering in the metrics, i.e. where MCD was the best metric in Scenario 1, it is now $v(g)$ (Table 4). The learned threshold for the first metric is exactly the same like the one chosen to generate the dataset. The estimated risk infimum for the best metric $v(G)$ is 5.57%. Similar to Scenario 1, a risk infimum of 5.57% is too high to use just one metric to compute the overall classification.

Table 4. Learning the "Best" Metric in Scenario 2

Metric	Empirical risk	τ	Validation error	Test error
$v(G)$	5.75	4	5.94	5.57
NOS	8.94	22	8.22	-
MNL	9.02	3	9.97	-
MCD	13.01	14	12.94	-
$allNeg$	13.01	-	12.76	-

Results for Learning the "Best Two" Metrics in Scenario 2
As in the previous experiment, the set of the best metrics as shown in Table 5 is a different one to Scenario 1. The estimated risk infimum for the combination $v(G)$, NOS that has the smallest validation error is 6.47%. Although the highest empirical risk in this experiment is 13.12% and therefore smaller than for the corresponding experiment in Scenario 1, the smallest empirical risk is much greater than for Scenario 1 and therefore less significant. Also, for NOS, the learned threshold $\tau_2 = 27$ differes very much from the threshold $\gamma = 14$ that was used to generate the data.

Table 5. Learning the "Best Two" Metrics in Scenario 2

Combination	Empirical risk	τ_1	τ_2	Validation error	Test error
$v(G)$, MNL	5.02	4	4	5.11	-
$v(G)$, NOS	5.46	4	27	4.93	6.47
$v(G)$, MCD	5.55	4	14	5.46	-
MNL, NOS	7.57	3	20	6.51	-
NOS, MCD	8.63	20	14	8.63	-
MNL, MCD	9.42	3	14	8.27	-
$allNeg$	13.12	-	-	12.85	-

5 Summary and Outlook

In the previous sections, we have presented a machine learning based method for the minimisation of metric sets. In this method, tuples of this metric set are first used to classify each measured entity of the software under investigation as either "good" or "bad". This classification is determined by threshold values for each metric in the set. The presented approach then attempts to approximate the same classification with a smaller set of metrics to reduce the number of necessary metrics in this set and to identify metrics with overlapping information.

We have tried this approach in two different classification scenarios on a set of four metrics substantiating the analysability quality characteristic of TTCN-3 test specifications. In the first scenario, the classification has been obtained by requiring that every metric value in the observed set must be smaller than its corresponding threshold value to be classified as "good". Given this setting, we have tried to approximate the entity classifications by using one single metric and by using a set of two metrics. According to the results, the risk of misjudging the classification of a behavioural entity by using just one single metric is quite high. By using a combination of two metrics, i.e. the NOS and MCD metrics, the approximated classification is very reasonable.

In the second scenario, only three of four metric values in the set have been required to be below their corresponding threshold values to be classified as "good". Again we have tried to approximate the classifications by using one single metric and a set of two metrics respectively. In both cases the risk of an incorrect assessment has been too high. The detailed reasons will be subject of further investigations.

In the experiments presented, we have applied our approach to metrics extracted from TTCN-3 test suites. We are currently working on quality assurance techniques for graphical languages such as the *Specification and Description Language* (SDL) and *Unified Modeling Language* (UML) which also includes metrics for models. We expect that our presented approach will also deliver reasonable results for metric sets designed to work on models. In addition, we want to evaluate metric sets used on Java implementations.

So far, we have only used a small set of metrics for the evaluation and therefore time and space complexity of our algorithm was not yet an issue. However, to make our technique applicable to larger sets of metrics as well, we plan to investigate the complexity of our method in more detail and optimise it accordingly.

AST *abstract syntax tree*
ANTLR *'ANother Tool for Language Recognition'*
CMMI *Capability Maturity Model Integration*
IDE *Integrated Development Environment*
EPL *Eclipse Public License*
ETSI *European Telecommunications Standards Institute*
GQM *Goal Question Metric*
IPv6 *Internet Protocol Version 6*
PAC *Probably Approximately Correct*
SDL *Specification and Description Language*
SIP *Session Initiation Protocol*
SPICE *Software Process Improvement and Capability dEtermination'*
SUT *System Under Test*
TTCN *Tree and Tabular Combined Notation*

TTCN-2 *Tree and Tabular Combined Notation*
TTCN-3 *Testing and Test Control Notation*
U2TP *UML 2.0 Testing Profile*
UML *Unified Modeling Language*

References

1. Fenton, N.E., Pfleeger, S.L.: Software Metrics. PWS Publishing, Boston (1997)
2. CMMI Product Team: CMMI for Development, Version 1.2. Technical Report CMU/SEI-2006-TR-008, Carnegie Mellon University, Software Engineering Institute (2006)
3. ISO/IEC: ISO/IEC Standard No. 15504: Information technology – Process Assessment; Parts 1–5. International Organization for Standardization (ISO) / International Electrotechnical Commission (IEC), Geneva, Switzerland (2003-2006)
4. ETSI: ETSI Standard (ES) 201 873-1 V3.2.1 (2007-02): The Testing and Test Control Notation version 3; Part 1: TTCN-3 Core Language. European Telecommunications Standards Institute (ETSI), Sophia-Antipolis, France, also published as ITU-T Recommendation Z.140 (February 2007)
5. Grabowski, J., Hogrefe, D., Réthy, G., Schieferdecker, I., Wiles, A., Willcock, C.: An introduction to the testing and test control notation (TTCN-3). Computer Networks 42(3), 375–403 (2003)
6. Zeiss, B., Neukirchen, H., Grabowski, J., Evans, D., Baker, P.: Refactoring and Metrics for TTCN-3 Test Suites. In: Gotzhein, R., Reed, R. (eds.) SAM 2006. LNCS, vol. 4320, pp. 148–165. Springer, Heidelberg (2006)
7. Zeiss, B., Vega, D., Schieferdecker, I., Neukirchen, H., Grabowski, J.: Applying the ISO 9126 Quality Model to Test Specifications – Exemplified for TTCN-3 Test Specifications. In: Bleek, W.G., Raasch, J., Züllighoven, H. (eds.) Software Engineering 2007, Bonn, Gesellschaft für Informatik. Lecture Notes in Informatics (LNI), vol. 105, pp. 231–242. Köllen Verlag (2007)
8. ISO/IEC: ISO/IEC Standard No. 9126: Software engineering – Product quality; Parts 1–4. International Organization for Standardization (ISO) / International Electrotechnical Commission (IEC), Geneva, Switzerland (2001-2004)
9. Halstead, M.: Elements of Software Science. Elsevier, New York (1977)
10. McCabe, T.J.: A Complexity Measure. IEEE Transactions on Software Engineering 2(4), 308–320 (1976)
11. Watson, A.H., McCabe, T.J.: Structured Testing: A Testing Methodology Using the Cyclomatic Complexity Metric. NIST Special Publication 500-235, National Institute of Standards and Technology, Computer Systems Laboratory, Gaithersburg, MD, United States of America (1996)
12. Fan, C.F., Yih, S.: Prescriptive metrics for software quality assurance. In: Proceedings of the First Asia-Pacific Software Engineering Conference, Tokyo, Japan, pp. 430–438. IEEE Computer Society Press, Los Alamitos (1994)
13. Basili, V.R., Weiss, D.M.: A Methodology for Collecting Valid Software Engineering Data. IEEE Transactions on Software Engineering 10(6), 728–738 (1984)
14. Henry, S., Kafura, D., Harris, K.: On the Relationships Among Three Software Metrics. In: Proceedings of the 1981 ACM Workshop/Symposium on Measurement and Evaluation of Software Quality, pp. 81–88. ACM Press, New York (1981)
15. Valiant, L.: A theory of learnability. Communications of the ACM 27(11), 1134–1142 (1984)

16. Valiant, L.: Deductive learning. Philosophical Transactions of the Royal Society London A 312, 441–446 (1984)
17. Vapnik, V., Chervonenkis, A.Y.: On the uniform convergence of relative frequencies of events and their probabilities. Theory of Probabilty and its Applications 16(2), 264–280 (1971)
18. Blumer, A., Ehrenfeucht, A., Haussler, D., Warmuth, M.K.: Learnability and the Vapnik-Chervonenkis dimension. Journal of the ACM 36(4), 929–969 (1989)
19. Vapnik, V.: The Nature of Statistical Lerning Theory. Springer, New York (1995)
20. Koltchinskii, V.I., Pachenko, D.: Rademacher processes and bounding the risk of learning function. High Dimensional Probability II, 443–459 (2000)
21. Kearns, M.J., Vazirani, U.V.: An Introduction to Computational Learning Theory. MIT Press, Cambridge (1994)
22. Shawe-Taylor, J., Cristianini, N.: Kernel Methods for Pattern Analysis. Cambridge University Press, Cambridge (2004)
23. Massart, P.: Some applications of concentration inequalities to statistics. Annales de la Faculté des Sciences de Toulouse, 245–303 vol. spécial dédié à Michel Talagrand (2000)
24. ETSI: Technical Specification (TS) 102 027-3 V3.2.1 (2005-07): SIP ATS & PIXIT; Part 3: Abstract Test Suite (ATS) and partial Protocol Implementation eXtra Information for Testing (PIXIT). European Telecommunications Standards Institute (ETSI), Sophia-Antipolis, France (July 2005)
25. ETSI: Technical Specification (TS) 102 516 V1.1 (2006-04): IPv6 Core Protocol; Conformance Abstract Test Suite (ATS) and partial Protocol Implementation eXtra Information for Testing (PIXIT). European Telecommunications Standards Institute (ETSI), Sophia-Antipolis, France (April 2006)
26. Baker, P., Evans, D., Grabowski, J., Neukirchen, H., Zeiss, B.: TRex – The Refactoring and Metrics Tool for TTCN-3 Test Specifications. In: Proceedings of TAIC PART 2006 (Testing: Academic & Industrial Conference – Practice And Research Techniques), Cumberland Lodge, Windsor Great Park, UK, 29th–31st August 2006, IEEE Computer Society Press, Los Alamitos (2006)
27. TRex Team: TRex Website (2007),
    http://www.trex.informatik.uni-goettingen.de

Using TTCN for Radio Conformance Test Systems

Javier Poncela-González, Juan Gómez-Salvador, Carlos Valero-Roldán,
and Unai Fernández-Plazaola

ETSI Telecomunicacion, Campus de Teatinos, s/n,
29071 Malaga, Spain
{javier,unai}@ic.uma.es

Abstract. While protocol conformance testing methodology is a well formalized field, radio testing methodology still relies on natural language specifications. This paper proposes an improvement on the quality of radio test specifications via the use of formal notation TTCN. This approach, and the fact that protocol and radio conformance testing share most of the underlying concepts, enables the use of a generic architecture for implementations of both types of testers, resulting in a reduction of the development efforts. This architecture has been validated with the implementation of radio test cases for the UMTS technology.

1 Introduction

Since its beginning, the effort in the field of conformance testing has been mainly centered in the area of protocol testing, where the testing methodology has attained a high level of formalization [1]. However, radio conformance testing has not evolved as much further. Radio test specifications are still provided only in natural language making them prone to ambiguous interpretations.

Traditionally, the fields of protocol and radio conformance testing have been considered as distant worlds, as the engineering groups related to each of them usually have non-overlapping backgrounds. While the protocol tests are focused on checking that sequence of messages exchanged between peer entities is performed in the correct order and the proper syntax, the aim of the radio tests is to certify the compliance of an implementation in aspects such as transmission and reception compatibility with other equipment. Nevertheless, most of the concepts are shared in both areas. For example, the set of documents internationally standardized for testing is nearly the same, as well as the documentation handled and provided by test laboratories.

In this paper we propose that TTCN is used to model radio test cases which would enhance the radio test specifications. Nowadays, these specifications are provided in natural language. Its quality could be improved by formalizing the test procedure with the use of TTCN, thus avoiding possible ambiguities and increasing its consistency [2]. With this approach it is possible to use the same architecture for radio and protocol test systems. One example of this architecture for protocol test systems, implemented using ITU description languages (SDL,

E. Gaudin, E. Najm, and R. Reed (Eds.): SDL 2007, LNCS 4745, pp. 69–85, 2007.

TTCN, ASN.1), can be found in [3]. A common architecture for both types of conformance tests can be obtained, which results in a reduction of the time and cost of the development, as some of the internal modules can be reutilized as well as the operator interface.

This paper is structured as follows. Section 2 gives an overview of the existing methodologies for protocol and radio conformance testing. Section 3 briefly comments the radio conformance test procedures. A proposal for a common test system architecture for protocol and radio test systems is proposed in Sect. 4. A detailed description of the main characteristics of this architecture for radio test systems is provided in Sect. 5. The architecture has been applied to the conformance testing of UMTS systems. A brief description of its radio test specification together with an example of application are presented in Sect. 6.

2   Conformance Testing Methodology

Nowadays, the conformance testing methodology is a well understood field. Firstly compiled in the late eighties by ITU [4], this methodology has been reviewed in order to achieve a higher formalization and, at the same time, to tackle distributed protocols testing. ETSI has been deeply involved in the advances of conformance testing, being one of the drivers of the TTCN language [5]. A tutorial, published by ETSI, on the standardized techniques for conformance testing can be found in [6].

Four types of tests can be applied to an implementation:

a) Basic interconnection: to check that main features are implemented and whether interconnection is possible.
b) Capability: to check observable external static capabilities.
c) Behaviour: check the dynamic conformance of the implementation.
d) Conformance resolution: in-depth checking of conformance.

Different configurations, shown in Fig. 1, are considered for the single layer testing process. The test designer will choose the most adequate configuration depending on the level and type of coordination between the UT and LT blocks and the accessibility of the upper IUT boundary. In ratio tests, the name Equipment Under Test (EUT) is used instead of Implementation Under Test (IUT); the term System Under Test (SUT) may be used in any context and encompasses the former two.

Test cases, each with a possible outcome of PASS, FAIL or INCONC, are grouped in Abstract Test Suites (ATSs). Though there could exist one Abstract Test Suite for each Abstract Test Method (ATM), an underlying principle is that only one ATS will be standardized for a given protocol layer.

Compiling a conformance testing standard is a laborious task, which, at the end, must provide one (or several) documents: a) The Test Suite Structure and Test Purposes (TSS&TP); b) One or more Abstract Test Suites (ATSs); c) The Test Management Protocol (TMP) if required. The TSS&TP is provided in natural language, while the ATSs are written in the TTCN formal notation.

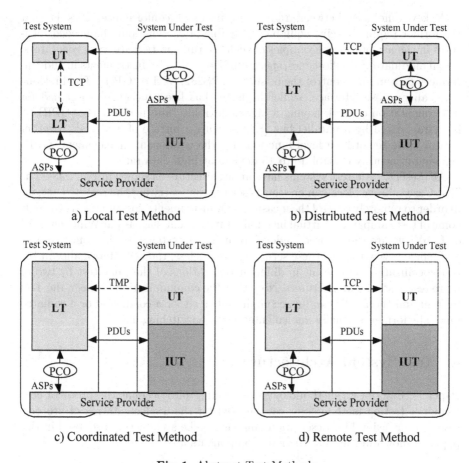

Fig. 1. Abstract Test Methods

When a manufacturer asks a test laboratory for a conformance certificate, several other documents are needed: a) Protocol Implementation Conformance Statement (PICS); b) Protocol Implementation eXtra Information for Testing (PIXIT); c) System Conformance Test Report (SCTR); d) Protocol Conformance Test Report (PCTR). The first two are needed in the test preparation stage; the last two are outputs produced by the test laboratory after the conformance assessment process has been performed.

3 Radio Conformance Testing

The development of conformance testing standards for the radio access of communication systems follows a path quite similar to the one employed for protocols. However, this process lacks the level of formalization achieved with protocols. Specifically, no Abstract Test Suite in formal language is produced, thus stopping the standardization process at the TSS&TP document.

A key difference between radio and protocol conformance tests is that the former require specific equipment capable of carrying out the needed measures in the air interface. Examples of such instrumentation are wave generators, signal modulators, oscilloscopes, spectrum analyzers, etc. Instruments include interfaces to remotely control them, such as RS232, VXI or GPIB. The first one is an all purpose interface, while the latter has been specifically designed for instrumentation control, having a higher flexibility and performance. GPIB [7] is characterized by a parallel bus (8 bits) with a bitrate of 8 MB/s[1], together with a basic set of high level functions for the equipment management. GPIB can simultaneously control up to 15 devices at high data rates.

At present, ratio test systems have an architecture as shown in Fig. 2 [8]. The Test Case Library block can be seen as scripts that carry out the required actions in order to remotely control the measurement instrumentation and report the outcome of test campaigns. Virtual instrumentation tools, such as LabWindows/CVI or LabView, are widely used to develop such test systems, as they offer an easy and efficient way to code these scripts. Nevertheless, the lack of formality in the test specification may result in different realizations of the same test by two or more test system manufacturers. Note that the communication between the Test System and the EUT[2] can be accomplished as either a conducted or a radiated link. The former is usually implemented using a switching unit.

4   Test System Architecture

Paper [3] describes a methodology that, taking into account the protocol conformance testing methodology, can be used for the implementation of protocol test systems using ITU description languages. The architecture proposed in this paper is shown in Fig. 3-a. Its main components are:

a) Graphical User Interface: controls the test campaign execution and reports and logs its outcome. It's written in Java to allow for portability to different operating systems.
b) Abstract Test Suite: divided in lower tester and upper tester parts, contains the compiled Test Cases.
c) Lower Subsystem: allows communication between the test system and the IUT. It comprises those layers above the physical layer that the test system must implement as indicated by the corresponding Abstract Test Method.

Looking at the architecture in more detail we can see that some of its parts can be either reused or automatically generated. The GUI can be designed so that it can serve in any protocol test system. Using TTCN C-code generators the Executable Test Suite (ETS) can be automatically generated from the standard TTCN modules. Supporting modules for the Executable Test Suite such as Test

---

[1] Originally 1 MB/s, increased to 8 MB/s in 2003.
[2] In ratio tests, the name Equipment Under Test (EUT) is used instead of Implementation Under Test (IUT).

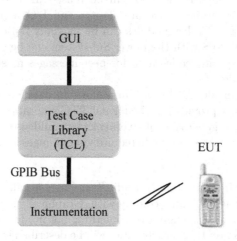

Fig. 2. Typical radio test system architecture

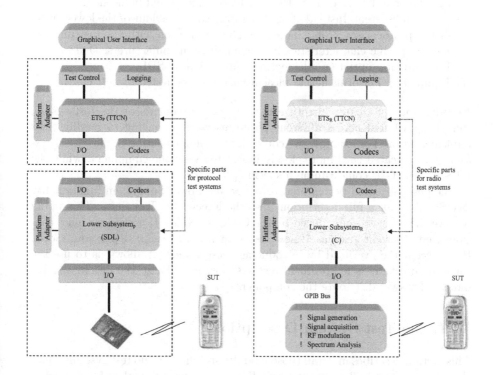

Fig. 3. (a) Protocol test system architecture (b) Radio test system architecture

Control, Platform Adapter and I/O can be reused in different test systems; this also happens with the Platform Adapter and I/O modules used by the Lower Subsystem. The Codec modules can be partially reused; the Codec used to communicate the ETS with the Lower Subsystem can be the same in all test systems. Only the specific codec used for peer messages must be generated for each technology under test.

This architecture could also be used in conformance radio testers (see Fig. 3-b) if such test cases were provided in the formal TTCN notation. In this way, code reusing and automatic generation of several blocks would also be achieved in radio test systems. Such an extension would require some changes in several of the blocks of the architecture:

a) Graphical User Interface (GUI): Radio Test Cases usually define a mask or a threshold that the IUT must comply with. Graphically showing the outcome is a useful tool for radio engineers, something not needed in protocol testing.
b) Abstract Test Suite: Its characteristics will be described in detail in Sect. 5.1.
c) Platform Adapter, Test Control, Logging and I/O: No changes would be needed.
d) Codec: As explained above, only the codec used by messages of the technology under test (e.g. UMTS, Bluetooth, WiMax) would be needed.
e) Lower Subsystem: Instead of implementing the behaviour of the lower layers of the protocol stack, it handles the communication with the instruments, hiding specific characteristics implemented by manufacturers. Due to this, it's more appropriate implementing it in C than in SDL.
f) Equipment: Performs actual measurements as requested by test cases.

An advantage of this architecture is that the components of the test system can be distributed across different platforms without having to modify their implementation. For example, we could think of implementing the lower subsystem in a dedicated card more closely integrated with the equipment, while the ETS and the GUI could run on a specific processor.

The designer could be tempted to merge the Lower Subsystem functionality (see Sect. 5.2 for a full description) into the Executable Test Suite. This would remove the overhead introduced by the Codec modules. However, we must consider that the radio tests are "slow" tests, at least, at the test procedure level. If we accept the overhead by introducing these codecs, it allows us to use the same architecture as for protocol test systems, modularize the design and (as indicated above) distribute the components.

5   Radio Test System Description

This section describes in detail those modules specific to radio test systems. Both the Abstract Test Suite and the Lower Subsystem own particular characteristics that distinguish them from those included in protocol test systems.

5.1   Abstract Test Suite

The main feature of the proposed architecture for radio test systems is the use of TTCN. This language would allow the standardization bodies to provide radio test suites in formal notation, thus leaving out any ambiguity that could arise in the natural language test specifications. At the same time, the validation effort would be reduced. This section describes the decisions taken and the main characteristics of this modelling.

In Sect. 2 the four ATMs defined by the conformance testing methodology have been presented. The main difference among these configurations is how the EUT is controlled during the test execution. There are two options to carry out this control: either automatically configuring the EUT for a test case, or manually. The first option completely automates the test procedure, but radio test specifications do not include a Test Controlling Protocol. Because of this, the second option has been chosen. Thus, the remote ATM (see Fig. 1-d) seems to be the most adequate configuration.

As in protocol tests, radio tests cases can be divided in three different sections that deal with the following duties:

a) Preamble: Sets the instrumentation and puts the EUT into the initial conditions demanded by the test case so that the test purpose can be verified.
b) Test body: Carries out the required actions on the EUT and the instrumentation in order to check the test purpose
c) Postamble: Although this stage does not explicitly appear in radio test specifications, it is required so that both EUT and instrumentation are put back into idle state.

The idle state must be defined so that every preamble starts under the same conditions as there is no fixed order for executing test cases. GPIB instrumentation allows two different states: local and remote. The local state, which does not allow the remote controlling, has been considered as idle.

The communication between the Abstract Test Suite and the instrumentation is made via messages. Each message will request one or several actions, depending on the specific instrumentation used, to be carried out by the Lower Subsystem. The communication must be designed taking into account GPIB bus behaviour and features. We require a confirmation for all messages sent to the instrumentation; it would be possible to only check the correct communication with the instruments at previously defined checkpoints, but we must consider the possibility of an error in the GPIB bus. As the instrumentation is provided by external devices, the probability of errors increases. The logical flow of the test case using the proposed set of messages is depicted in Fig. 4.

For every send event, a timeout is raised if its confirmation message, which can carry a positive or negative result, is not received in due time. If the confirmation is not received, it will mean that a communication error has occurred. The test execution can be stopped just after an error occurs, avoiding unnecessary waits for an INCONC verdict of the test case. This behaviour can be implemented in a parameterizable step in TTCN.

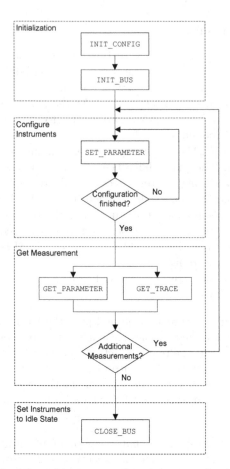

Fig. 4. Logical flow of test cases using the proposed set of messages

Although the type and number of needed messages may depend on the implementation, we have defined a set of messages that covers all required functionality. In the preamble stage, messages INIT_CONFIG and INIT_BUS have been defined. The first one tells the Lower Subsystem to read in the equipment configuration; afterwards, the instrumentation is initialized with the second message, setting them into GPIB remote state. At the same time, message CLOSE_BUS (used in postambles) will put the instrumentation into idle state.

Three messages have been used for configuring and retrieving data from the instrumentation.

- Message SET_PARAMETER configures and activates measurements.
- Message GET_PARAMETER obtains the instantaneous value of the active measurement. The request messages should include an instrument identifier and a command, which indicates the action to be performed by the instrumentation. The response counterparts should include an error code and, for the GET_PARAMETER message, the measured value.

– The third message is related to one of the functionalities typically needed in radio tests, the capture of a whole trace from an instrument. The points of the trace can be obtained either in one shot or by issuing a repetitive series of requests. This behaviour should be hidden from the ATS. Consequently, message GET_TRACE has been defined. The Lower Subsystem, which knows the interface with the instruments, will be responsible for implementing the appropriate actions to read in an entire trace.

Finally, one more message has been used for requesting actions from the operator. This message has been called ACTION_REQ and it can carry a text message. It is handled by the Test Control module.

Radio tests usually require an additional processing after having captured a trace by the instrumentation. This processing may require complex mathematical operations. Given that most of these (processing, for example, maximum/minimum search, filtering, bandwidth calculation, demodulation, bit synchronization, power integration) are common to radio test suites for different communication systems, we can think of them as a generic signal processing library that can be reused in different test systems, such as GSM, Bluetooth or UMTS. The functions in this library can be called from the TTCN code and linked at compilation time.

5.2 Lower Subsystem

The Lower Subsystem is the module responsible for the communication between the Abstract Test Suite and the Equipment Under Test. On one hand, it hides the physical communication characteristics; on the other hand, it takes into account possible interface differences as instrumentation can be built by different manufacturers. The implemented Lower Subsystem offers a generic API that can be used by any radio test case that is built using GPIB instrumentation.

One first issue is the type of interface offered by the instrumentation for its remote control. GPIB [7] has been chosen because of its flexibility and performance. The second issue to tackle is the set of remote commands that can be used. In Sect. 5.1 we have shown the messages used in the TTCN test modelling. The Lower Subsystem must map these messages into commands suitable for the specific instrumentation included in the test system. Several aspects must be considered:

a) The test system must be able to integrate instrumentation from different manufacturers.
b) Manufacturers usually only implement a subset of the GPIB standard.
c) Proprietary commands are often included to control capabilities that are specific for the instrument.
d) The same command may have different meanings for each device.

Configuration files can be used to solve these problems. Two types of configuration files have been used. The main configuration file (see Fig. 5) contains, for each instrument, an identifier, specific GPIB information (GPIB card address, GPIB address of the instrument and GPIB signalling mode) and a reference to an equipment configuration file.

```
# Configuration file for Test System
#id_equipo     GPIB_board     dir_GPIB     EOT_mode     file

Spec_An            0             20           2         specan.egp
Wave_Gen           0             29           2         wavgen.egp
```

Fig. 5. Main configuration file

```
# DEVICE: Spectrum Analyzer (specan.egp)

# Generic command     Specific device command

#      Non-query commands

Reset                  *RST
PeakPower              CALC1:MARK1:MAX
Span                   SENS1:FREQ:SPAN
Center                 SENS1:FREQ:CENT

Trigger                TRIG1:SEQ:SOUR
_FreeRun               IMM
_Line                  LINE
_RFPower               RFP

#      Query commands

PeakPower?             CALC1:MARK1:Y?
RefLevel?              DISP:WIND1:TRAC1:Y:SCAL:RLEV?
SweepTime?             SENS1:SWE:TIME?

Detector?              SENS1:DET1:FUNC?
_Average               AVER
_Sample                SAMP
_Rms                   RMS

ErrMsg?                SYST:ERR?
```

Fig. 6. Configuration file for spectrum analyzer FSIQ26 (Rohde&Schwartz)

The equipment configuration files (see Fig. 6) will provide the mapping between the command parameter of the primitives and the particular GPIB command for that instrument. This file contains, in one column, the command parameter of the primitives and, in a second column, its translation to the instrument's GPIB command. When the command requires a response from the instrument then character '?' is added at the end. Such commands are used to retrieve data from the instruments. The commands may carry options that must be also mapped. To distinguish them from the commands, they start with character '_' and appear right after the command itself.

With this mechanism new instruments can replace the existing ones by just defining their corresponding configuration files. Using these new files instead of the old ones will create a new test system with the same functionality as before, but with instrumentation from different manufacturers.

The Lower Subsystem has been written in C. Each message used in the Abstract Test Suite has, in the Lower Subsystem, a routine that implements its expected behaviour. These routines map the commands, hiding the actual implementation of the GPIB commands and can also perform low level error control. Table 1 lists these routines, their parameters and a brief description for each of them. The Instrument data type (see Figure 7) stores the configuration data for each instrumentation device. In case of error, all these routines return an error code and a description in parameter error. The Commands field of the structure holds the list of available commands for this instrument and the parameters that each command can carry.

```
typedef struct
{
    char  id_instr[L_ID_INSTR];
    int   gpib_board;
    short dir_gpib;
    int   eot_mode;
    char  arch_instr[L_ARCH];
    Commands *coms;
    void  *sig;
} Instrument;
```

Fig. 7 Instrument data type

When a message is received, the Lower Subsystem checks its type and then codifies the corresponding equipment commands, with the appropriate parameters as indicated in the message, looking at the translation table generated from the configuration files. The commands are executed sequentially and each result read from the bus and stored[3]. When all the commands associated with the message have been executed, a response is sent to the Executable Test Suite.

6   UMTS Radio Test System

UMTS is one of the mobile communication systems that are part of the 3G family [9]. This technology provides multiple, simultaneous and flexible connections with bitrates from 64 kbit/s up to 2 Mbit/s, worldwide roaming, security and negotiated QoS according to the user needs. It is expected that, with such speeds, services with high bandwidth demand such as multimedia services can be provided in a mobile environment.

The radio access technology is Direct Sequence CMDA (DS-CDMA), commonly referred to as WCDMA because bands are 5 MHz wide. The main characteristics of this technology are its robustness against interferences, its spectral efficiency, frequency reuse and flexible data rates. There are two working modes in WCDMA: Frequency Division Duplex (FDD), where one carrier is used for uplink and another carrier (separated 5 MHz) is used for downlink; and Time Division Duplex (TDD), where some slots in the carrier are used for uplink while other slots are used for downlink.

---

[3] Execution of commands is aborted if any of them is not successful. In this case, the error is read and reported back.

Table 1. Routines implemented in the Lower Subsystem

Function declaration	Description
int InitConfig (Instrument *instr, char *err)	Reads the configuration files. Must be called at the beginning of the test case.
int InitBus (Instrument *instr, char *err);	Sets the equipment into remote mode.
int SetParameter (Instrument *instr, char *id, char *com_gen, char *par_gen, char *err);	Executes the GPIB commands that do not require a response by the equipment.
int GetParameter (Instrument *instr, char *id, char *com_gen, char *par_gen, char *valor_dev_str, int l_valor_dev_str, char *err);	Executes the GPIB commands that require a response by the equipment.
int GetTrace (Instrument *instr,char *id, char *tx, char *ty, char *err)	Acquires the measurement trace.
int CloseBus (Instrument *instr, char *err);	Sets back the equipment into local mode; the front panel controls can be used again.

The radio test cases [10] are classified in four groups: transmitter characteristics (17), receiver characteristics (7), performance requirements (14) and requirements for support of Radio Resource Management (38). The list of transmitter test cases is shown in Table 2, which indicates the type of measurement that must be performed for each test case.

6.1 Example of Test Case Implementation

All test cases in the transmitter group have been implemented. As an example, we will describe the implementation of test case 5.9 (see Table 2), called Spectrum Emission Mask for the FDD variant. The purpose of this test case is to verify that the power of the User Equipment (UE) emission does not exceed the prescribed limits specified in the standard. The UE output power is measured at different offsets and compared with a reference emission mask.

The initial test conditions require that the UE is entered into loopback mode after a call has been setup (as described in [11], [12]). The test procedure must perform the following steps:

a) Set and send continuously Up power control commands to the UE until the UE output power is at maximum level.
b) Measure the power of the transmitted signal with a measurement filter as described in the standard. The centre frequency of the filter is stepped in contiguous steps and the measured power recorded for each step. The bandwidth of the filter is 30 kHz or 50 MHz, depending on the offset from the carrier centre frequency.
c) Calculate the ratio of the measured power compared to the reference power mask.

Table 2. List of transmitter test cases for UMTS

TS 34.121	Test Name	Measurement	TS 34.121	Test Name	Measurement
5.2	Maximum Output Power	Power level	5.6	Change of TFC	Power level
5.3	Frequency Error	Frequency	5.7	Power Setting in UL Compressed Mode	Power level
5.4	*Output Power Dynamics in the UL*	*<group>*	5.8	Occupied Bandwidth (OBW)	Spectrum
5.4.1	Open Loop Power Control in the UL	Power level	5.9	Spectrum Emission Mask	Spectrum
5.4.2	Inner Loop Power Control in the UL	Power level	5.10	Adjacent Channel Leakage Power Ratio (ACLR)	Spectrum
5.4.3	Minimum Output Power	Power level	5.11	Spurious Emissions	Spectrum
5.4.4	Out-of-Sync Handling of Output Power	Power level	5.12	Transmit Intermodulation	Spectrum
5.5	*Transmit ON/OFF Power*	*<group>*	*5.13*	*Transmit Modulation*	*<group>*
5.5.1	Transmit OFF Power	Power level	5.13.1	Error Vector Magnitude	EVM
5.5.2	Transmit ON/OFF Time Mask	Power level	5.13.2	Peak Code Domain Error	PCDE

Test Case Name		TC_TRM08_SpecEmissMask
Group		TRM/TC_TRM08/
Purpose		Verificar que la mascara espectral de emisión se cumple para distintas variaciones de la frecuencia portadora, tanto para altas como bajas frecuencias
Configuration		
Default		Check_T_global_trm08
Comments		
Selection Ref		TCS_TRM08
Description		Verificación de la mascara de emisión espectral para bajas y altas frecuencias.
Nr	**Label**	**Behaviour Description**
1		START T_global_trm08
2		+Inicializar_sistema
3		+Inic_an_esp_trm08_ftx_low
4		+Calc_SpecEmissMask_low
5		+EUT_ftx_high
6		+Inic_an_esp_trm08_ftx_high
7		+Calc_SpecEmissMask_high
8		+Check_res_trm08

Fig. 8. Code for test case Spectral Emission Mask

Test Step Name	Calc_SpecEmissMask_low	
Group	Calc_Steps/TC_TRM08/	
Objective		
Default	Check_T_global_trm08	
Comments		
Nr	**Label**	**Behaviour Description**	**Constraints Ref**
21		(TCV_frec_stop := TSO_RESTAR(TSC_fx_low,"2500000"))	
22		GPIB!SET_PARAMETER_REQ	Set_parameter_req(TSC_id, TSC_com_stop, TCV_frec_stop)
23		+Set_parameter_err_rsp	
24		START T_espera_1_s	
25		?TIMEOUT T_espera_1_s	
26		GPIB!GET_PARAMETER_REQ	Get_parameter_req(TSC_id, TSC_com_get_traza, TSC_par_traza)
27		+Get_parameter_err_rsp	
28		(TCV_arizq := TCV_par)	

Fig. 9. Code for test case Spectral Emission Mask

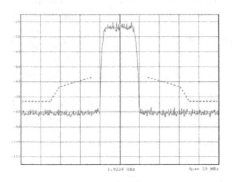

Fig. 10. Graphical result of the spectral emission mask test case

To carry out this test, we only need a spectrum analyzer; in particular we have used the FSIQ26 spectrum analyzer. The test cases were implemented in TTCN-2 because the common blocks (see Fig. 3) with protocol test systems were already built for this language version. However, the same architecture can be used with TTCN-3. In this case the common blocks around the Executable Test Suite would have to be adapted to the particular characteristics (structure, interfaces, data types, ...) of the C code generated by the TTCN compiler.

The test case has been implemented as follows (see Fig. 8 and Fig. 9):

1. The test system is initialized: the equipment configuration files are read (INIT_CONFIG) and the equipment is set into remote mode (INIT_BUS).
2. The spectrum analyzer is configured with the appropriate measurement filter parameters (bandwidth 30 kHz) via SET_PARAMETER messages.
3. The peak power is measured. The value is received in a GET_PARAMETER message.

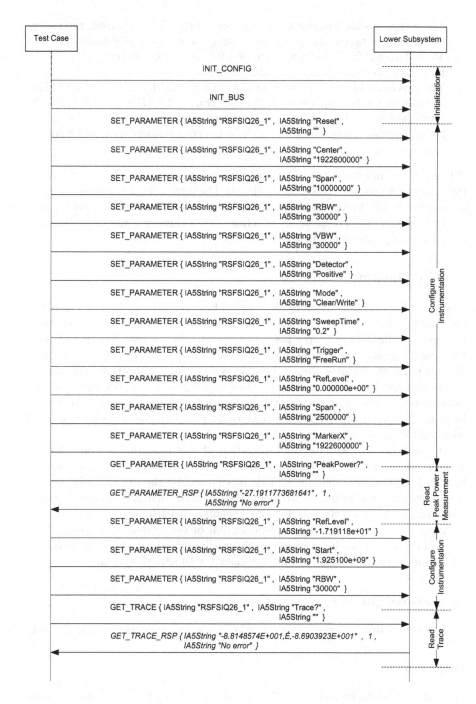

Fig. 11. Sequence of messages for test case Spectral Emission Mask until the first trace is obtained

4. Measurements for frequencies with offset up to +2.5 MHz from the carrier frequency are taken (steps of 5 kHz) using the GET_TRACE message.
5. Measurements for frequencies with offset down to -2.5 MHz from the carrier frequency are taken (steps of 5 kHz) as before.
6. The spectrum analyzer is configured for a bandwidth resolution of 50 kHz.
7. Measurements for frequencies with offset from -12.5 MHz up to +12.5 MHz from the carrier frequency are taken (steps of 25 kHz).
8. Measurements are compared with the reference emission mask and a verdict is generated.

When the test finishes a graphical report of the measured results is provided on the operator screen such as shown in Fig. 10. The dotted line represents the reference power levels. Figure 11 shows the sequence of messages exchanged between the test case and the Lower Subsystem from the beginning of the execution until the fourth step, where the first trace is read.

7   Conclusion

A methodology for radio conformance testing has been presented, which increases the quality of the radio test specifications as these are currently written in natural language. Using TTCN represents a step forward in the formalization of these test specifications. The validation process for test systems is simplified as some of their parts would have already been agreed by the qualification bodies.

The proposed architecture is derived as an extension from one that has provided good results in protocol conformance test systems. Several modules can be shared between both types of test systems, thus reducing the effort and cost required for the development.

This architecture enables the integration of instrumentation from different manufacturers as well as its straightforward substitution by other instrumentation with equivalent capabilities. This is achieved by the use of GPIB bus for the communication with the instrumentation and the definition of configuration files that particularize the interface implemented by each instrument.

As an example of use, the implementation of one transmitter test case for the UMTS system has been shown. Additionally, this architecture has also been used to implement the set of radio test cases for Bluetooth system.

Acknowledgments

This work has been partially funded by AT4 wireless and Spanish government.

References

1. Tretmans, J.: An Overview of OSI Conformance Testing, Formal Methods & Tools group. University of Twente, 2001. Translated and adapted from: Tretmans, J., van de Lagemaat, J., Conformance Testen. In: Handboek Telematica, vol. II, pages 4400, pp. 1–19. Samson (2001)

2. Kegley, K., Stavridou, V.: The Role of Formal Methods in Software Standards. In: Fourth IEEE International Symposium and Forum on Software Engineering Standards (1999)
3. Poncela, J., Sánchez, R., Tapia, P., Ferrer, R., Entrambasaguas, J.T.: Testbed Development for Communication Systems using Formal Languages. In: 2nd Workshop on SDL and MSC, Grenoble (June 26-28, 2000)
4. ITU-T X.290-X.296: OSI Conformance Testing Methodology and Framework for Protocol Recommendations for ITU-T Applications (1998)
5. ETSI ES 201 873: Methods for Testing and Specification (MTS): The Testing and Test Control Notation version 3, v 3.2.1 (2007)
6. ETR 021: Advanced Testing Methods (ATM): Tutorial on protocol conformance testing (1991)
7. IEEE Std. 488.1: IEEE Standard for Higher Performance Protocol for the Standard Digital Interface for Programmable Instrumentation (2003)
8. Baños, J.: Testing of Bluetooth Products in the Industrial Environment, IECON (2002)
9. 3rd Generation Partnership Project: http://www.3gpp.org/specs/specs.htm
10. 3GPP TS 34.121: 3rd Generation Partnership Project; Technical Specification Group Terminals; Terminal Conformance Specification: Radio transmission and reception (FDD)
11. 3GPP TS 34.108: 3rd Generation Partnership Project; Technical Specification Group Terminals; Common Test Environments for User Equipment (UE) Conformance Testing
12. 3GPP TS 34.108: Universal Mobile Telecommunications System (UMTS): Terminal logical test interface; Special conformance testing functions

Abbreviations

ATS	Abstract Test Suite
ATM	Abstract Test Method
ETS	Executable Test Suite
EUT	Equipment Under Test
FDD	Frequency Division Duplex
GPIB	General Purpose Interface Bus
GUI	Graphical User Interface
IUT	Implementation Under Test
SUT	System Under Test
TDD	Time Division Duplex
UE	User Equipment
UMTS	Universal Mobile Telecommunications System

Testing UML2.0 Models Using TTCN-3 and the UML2.0 Testing Profile

Paul Baker and Clive Jervis

Motorola Inc.
{paul.baker,clive.jervis}@motorola.com

Abstract. This paper describes a toolset for functional testing UML2.0 models by TTCN-3 test suites and its application within Motorola. The toolset incorporates support for part of the UML2.0 testing profile from which TTCN-3 can be generated. The toolset has been developed within Motorola for models developed using Telelogic Tau G2 and test suites using Telelogic Tester. The models are subsequently used for application code generation.

The basic integration of the Telelogic Tau and Tester, called *cosim*, has novel features, such as the ability to service operations declared as external to the model within TTCN-3, and to control model timer operations within TTCN-3. Translating UML2.0 data structures, such as classes, signal definitions, port definitions, and constants into TTCN-3 is done by a tool called UMB. The paper deals with complexities in mapping Tau UML2.0 types and structuring into TTCN-3.

To provide more rigorous test specification a tool supporting part of the UML2.0 Testing Profile has been developed which enables consistency of test specifications to be checked automatically and also the generation of executable TTCN-3 test suites for *cosim*.

The toolset is being used by several different product groups within Motorola, and the paper reports some experience and findings, including areas where TTCN-3 can be extended.

1   Introduction

Motorola has many projects using Telelogic's Tau G2 [10] for developing detailed UML2.0 [4] models that are subsequently used to generate application code using either Telelogic's [7], or Motorola's [3] code generators. In the past Motorola's strategy for functional testing SDL [6] models developed in Tau SDL Suite [9], was to use Telelogic's TTCN Suite [11] tool supporting TTCN-2 [13] that was integrated with the SDL Suite simulator in what Telelogic term cosimulation [8]. However, Telelogic does not currently provide similar functionality between their Tau G2 and Tester [12] tools for testing UML2.0 models with TTCN-3 [14] test scripts and so Motorola has developed its own integration, known as *cosim* which is reported in this paper along with supporting tools and some experience from its use.

E. Gaudin, E. Najm, and R. Reed (Eds.): SDL 2007, LNCS 4745, pp. 86–100, 2007.

In the remainder of this paper when we use UML and TTCN we refer to UML2.0, and TTCN-3, respectively. We also use Tau UML to reflect Telelogic's proprietary implementation of data beyond that defined in UML2.0.

In Sect. 2, we discuss some of the particular issues involved in testing functionality of models, and how we have devised solutions to these in *cosim*, such as external operations and timer handling. The *cosim* tool provides the basic integration between Tau Model Verifier and Tau Tester and is covered in Sect. 3. In Sect. 4, the UMB tool is reported, which translates static data declarations from a UML project into TTCN source code, such as signal and passive classes, as well as ports and constants. The section highlights some of the difficulties of mapping the Tau UML class/type and package system to TTCN.

Motorola has worked on support for the UML Testing Profile [1,5] using TTCN as an action language. In Sect. 5 we introduce the Motorola U2TP Tau addin that generates TTCN code for test architecture and the like from a UML Testing Profile representation and also generates TTCN test functions from behaviour represented in UML Sequence Diagrams. When used in conjunction with UMB, an entire test suite can be generated.

Section 6 comments on the TTCN language for UML model testing, and Sect. 7 gives some insight to the use of the test environment. Section 8 has concluding remarks.

2   UML Model Testing

The main benefit of developing detailed design models in a high level language such as SDL or UML is the ability to dynamically test the model prior to generating application code to discover functional defects earlier in the lifecycle [3]. Dynamically executing the model in isolation can be done interactively, much like using a traditional debugger, where a user sets breakpoints and can examine and alter values; however for repeatability and automation a test environment that uses test scripts requiring no human interaction is preferred. For SDL and UML models based on concurrent state machines the test language must be able to send and receive signals to/from the model and to handle concurrency/non-determinism, for which TTCN is very well suited.

Although model testing can be driven by a formal test script, one can still retain the advantages of model simulation, such as having both textual and graphical traces displayed in real-time, the ability to set break-points and examine values. Indeed, *cosim* uses these capabilities from Tau's UML Model Verifier and Tau Tester in generating execution logs and Sequence Diagrams.

Models used for application code generation present special challenges for testing; here we discuss two of these problems. In the first place there is the interface between the model and external interfaces, and secondly there is controlling model timers during testing. *cosim* has solutions to these two problems, which are covered in the following two subsections.

In the first case, *cosim* takes advantage of the TTCN language features for procedure based communication, and in the second case, we use signal based send/receive statements in TTCN, although there is a case to be made for having new statements specifically for external timers to be added to the language; this is further discussed in Sect. 6.

2.1 External Operations

Models developed for code generation inevitably have to interface to external entities, such as platform services (e.g database access, check-pointing, and error logging), and protocol stacks, etc. Whilst certain of these services, such as inter-process communication, may be handled by code used to integrate model generated code with its environment, leaving the developer to model communication using UML signals, other services have to be represented as external entities within the model – typically as class/type definitions and operation signatures.

To compile application code generated from a model, the user will need to supply code or libraries that implement such external entities. However, for model testing through model simulation it is usually impossible to include this external code – for example, the model development platform is different from the target platform, or the model generated code forms just one component of a complete executable so cannot be executed in isolation.

For model simulation the user usually has two options: either provide stub code for the external operations, or have the simulation tool (Tau Model Verifier here) dynamically prompt the user for return values during simulation.

The problem with stub code is that the stubs have to be written in the first place, and secondly different stubs may have to be written for different tests. For example, one test may be for normal model behaviour when an external operation returns successfully, and another test the error path behaviour when the same operation called with the same arguments returns an error code. In any event, stubs need to be configured along with the tests, not with the model.

The issue with prompting is that it requires user interaction, and the test values need to be documented and configured with the tests.

If optioned *cosim* automatically generates and compiles stub code during the build process for each Tau UML operation having the 'External' stereotype set. Then whenever an operation is invoked during test execution the stub encodes and transports all its 'in' and 'inout' arguments to Tau Tester along with the operation name. The *cosim* code on the Tau Tester side places such external calls into a *cosim* reserved port, which can then be picked up in a test script with the TTCN-3 `getcall` statement. The desired response can be made using the TTCN-3 `reply` statement, which causes *cosim* to encode and transport 'out', 'inout' and 'return' values back to the UML stub, again with the operation name; the stub in turn returns these values to the model simulation. The stub code blocks whilst the Tester side services the call. *cosim* uses a dedicated socket to transport procedure calls and responses between Tester and the Model Verifier.

Suppose we have the following external definition in UML of a Boolean operation called validate, that is intended to determine if a password is valid for a given user Id:

```
public <<External="true">> Boolean validate(Pass_t, UserID_t);
```

Now suppose that the following call is made to the operation during the model's execution:

```
validated = validate(password, userId);
```

The call will cause *cosim* to enqueue the call onto a TTCN port called proc_port that *cosim* uses for this purpose. The call encodes the operation name along with the values of password, and userId. The model's execution is now suspended[1] until a response is delivered by *cosim* from the TTCN execution. In TTCN, the call is detected by the getcall statement such as by the following statement (which here does not care what the parameter values are):

```
proc_port.getcall(validate: {?, ?} );
```

Once the call has been picked up in TTCN by a getcall statement, the test script can make any calculations it needs to before sending a response back via a reply statement, such as:

```
proc_port.reply(validate: {-, -} value true);
```

In this case the return value has been scripted to be true, and the '-' for the parameter values indicate that no value is specified, here because they are 'in' parameters.

The *cosim* code will encode and send back to the UML side any 'out' or 'inout' parameter values plus a return value if used for the operation, as in our example. These values are then returned to the blocked UML operation call which then unblocks allowing the Tau Model Verifier to proceed with the parameter/return values as sent by TTCN reply statement being returned to the run-time system.

'External' tagged artifacts in Tau UML may originate either through importing, say, C/C++ header files, or by the user applying the 'External' stereotype manually. The automatic generation of stubs works in either case, except that for imported C/C++ types/classes the user will have to supply the appropriate source code definition as per pure simulation builds.

2.2   Timers

Verifying models that contain timers via simulation presents some difficulties. The default mode of the Tau Model Verifier is to use 'simulated' time, however one can also chose real-time behaviour. In simulated time no timer will expire so long as there are internal or external signals waiting to be consumed. If there are none then the simulation will expire the timer that would fire first in real time – that is, the simulation will jump ahead in time to the point where the next timer will expire.

Using simulated time it is not possible to force a timer to expire in the Model Verifier whilst there are signals waiting to be consumed other than through

---

[1] Only the operation's body blocks, although this is moot as Tau's Model Verifier is single threaded.

manual intervention in the GUI; thus it is not possible to test automatically all possible scenarios. For real-time simulation there are different problems: some timers may be literally days long, so testing behaviour when they expire would be unrealistically slow, whilst on the other hand running *cosim* through the Tau GUIs on a real-time simulation means that a user's actions may effect behaviour. For example, if a user cannot initiate a test quick enough after starting the model simulation, a UML watchdog timer may expire before the TTCN has sent an appropriate signal (for simulated time, *cosim* takes care of this situation).

For theses reasons, *cosim* has an option in which model timers may be controlled from the test script. Here whenever a timer is set in the model, *cosim* sends a signal to Tester on a reserved port that can be picked up in a test script by a regular `receive` statement. The signal has as parameters the name of the timer, its duration, and a unique number to distinguish multiple timers of the same name. Only if a corresponding expire timer signal is sent back from TTCN will the timer expire in the UML model.

3   The *Cosim* Integration

The heart of the test suite is a tool called *cosim* that integrates the Tau G2 Model Verifier with Tau Tester. It consists chiefly of one set of code that integrates with the Tau G2 generated code API and one set that integrates with the Tester API (Telelogic's implementation of the TTCN TRI and TCI interfaces [15,16]). The user generates executables for the UML model and TTCN test suite using Telelogic's own code generators through the normal tools' menu systems using build scripts provided by *cosim*.

Since *cosim* uses Telelogic's own C code generators, all UML and TTCN language features that are supported by Telelogic are *de facto* supported by *cosim*, there are no additional constraints. However there are UML elements that are not supported by Telelogic C code generation, such as user defined UML templates, an hence these cannot be accommodated by *cosim* either.

In the case of Tau UML, the user points the build artifact to the *cosim* kernel, and for Tester the user uses a *cosim* make configuration file. *cosim* can be run either via the tools' GUIs (the Model Verifier on UML side), or directly from the command line/shell so that batch execution can be scripted. In either case, textual and sequence diagrams of both the model and test suite executions can be recorded.

Communication between the two tools is via three sockets using a dedicated encoding/decoding scheme: two sockets are for asynchronous messages exchange (one in each direction between the two tools), and one for servicing synchronous external operation calls made by UML model.

Tau tester provides several modes of execution of TTCN test suites, which are all supported by *cosim*. For example individual tests can be executed interactively through its test management GUI, or a test plan file can be specified that executes a number of tests in sequence.

Signals that are sent out of a UML port are directed by *cosim* to a port of the same name in TTCN and vice versa. That is the system port names of TTCN tests must match the names of the ports of the active class being tested in UML. Furthermore the type names in TTCN must match the corresponding signal name in UML. Notice that the direction of signals on a UML port will be the opposite of the same signals in the corresponding TTCN port. Thus if signal appears in the required interface of a port of the UML active class under test, then it must be declared in the 'in' direction of the corresponding TTCN port type. The converse is true for signals appearing on a realized interface. The UMB tool will construct appropriate TTCN port type definitions from a UML model as described in Sect. 4.

UML external operations that are to be serviced by TTCN do not require any port declarations in a UML model, but the corresponding signatures must be listed in a TTCN port type as 'inout's that is instantiated with the name proc_port, as *cosim* injects procedure calls to this port.

Similarly if *cosim* is handling (non-parameterized) UML timers, types called StartExtTimer and FireExtTimer must be declared and defined on a port called P_ExtTimers. When the UML model sets a timer it may be detected in a TTCN test case by a **receive** statement for signal StartExtTimer on port P_ExtTimers. To force the Model Verifier to expire the timer, the test script will send signal FireExtTimer over this port. The signals are defined bellow, in which the timerHandle will be a unique number defined dynamically by *cosim* to distinguish all timers, but particularly relavent for multiple timers of the same name, timerName is the timer identifier as a character string and timerVal is its duration as an integer:

```
type record StartExtTimer
{
    integer timerHandle,
    integer timerVal,
    charstring timerName
};

type record FireExtTimer
{
    integer timerHandle
};
```

The timer handling required modifications to be made to a Tau kernel header file so that *cosim* code replaced the normal timer queue handling provided for simulated time. Currently the timer handling feature of *cosim* works only for non-parameterised timers.

cosim produces detailed log files on both Model Verifier and Tester sides that can be used to debug problems. For example, if there is a decode error of a signal or operation parameter due to a type mismatch between the UML representation and the TTCN representation, the logs will detail both the original encoding and the point and reason where the decoding failed.

4   The UMB Tool

The UMB tool has two primary functions: translating all class and data definitions within a UML model into TTCN-3 equivalents, and providing a GUI for defining TTCN templates. Here we concentrate on the translation capabilities of UMB as this encompasses the issues of mapping UML entities into TTCN, which is not always straightforward.

The UML entities translated by UMB and the corresponding TTCN representation are given in Table 1.

Table 1. UMB translations of UML entities

UML Entity	TTCN Entity
class	record type
signal	record type
port	port type
syntypes, enumerations, etc	type
external operations	signatures
const	constant
package	module/group

Class definitions in UML are translated to record types in TTCN, as are signal definitions. If an attribute/parameter is not declared as a 'part' in UML and is an aggregate type, then the TTCN types will correspond to a pointer representation as described below. However, most signal parameters are passed by value, i.e. declared as 'part'.

Port definitions from UML result in a port type declaration in TTCN, however the signal directions are reversed, so that when a signal is sent out from a UML model, it may be received by a port of the same name in TTCN, and vice-versa.

UML constants are translated by UMB to TTCN, however since the defining expression may not be directly translatable to TTCN, only simple arithmetic expressions are translated, or constants whose defining expression is a literal value, or another constant.

4.1   Class/Type Translations

Since UML and TTCN are different languages, it is to be expected that the type systems do not match – indeed even for base types, there is no guarantee that, say, a Tau UML Integer has the same range as a TTCN integer (by default it doesn't – Tau UML Integers are 32 bit and Tester's 64). Thus some Tau UML types have to be modeled in TTCN requiring both UMB and *cosim* to be

Table 2.

Tau UML Type	Base TTCN Representation
Integer	integer
Boolean	boolean
Real	float
Char	char
Charstring	charsting
Octetstring	octetstring
Bit	bit
Bitstring	bitstring
class	record
enum	enumerated
choice	union
syntype (with constraint)	type (with constraint)
Array< , >, String<>	record of (integer, type)
Powerset<>	set of
Ref, CPtr<>	union of null_type and record of

consistent. For example, there are no pointer types in TTCN, but Tau UML has a template for pointers (as support for imported C types and operations) and can pass parameters by reference.

To provide a degree of implementation independence, all Tau UML atomic types are translated by prefixing the name with 'UML_', the definitions of which are provided in a *cosim* supplied TTCN module called **predefined**. Thus it is possible to change the range of **UML_Integer**, defined as a subrange of TTCN **integer** type, without having to alter the *cosim* encoders. For example, a Tau UML Real is translated to 'UML_Real' whose definition is:

```
type float UML_Real (-1.7976931348623157E308 .. 1.7976931348623157E308);
```

Table 2 lists many of the UMB/*cosim* mappings of Tau UML types to the core TTCN types; in each case this will be via a type definition possibly with subrange constraint. Tau UML arrays are translated as TTCN lists, using **record of**. Each element of the list is a pair consisting of an index and a value. If the UML array has a fixed size a corresponding length constraint is used in the TTCN translation. The reason using **record of** and pairs is to accommodate arrays of unbounded size and to simplify the *cosim* encoders, since arrays may be implemented as linked lists by the Tau code generator.

Of particular complexity is the translation of the **CPtr** template, used explicitly in Tau UML representation of C pointer types and implicitly in pass-by-reference signal/operation parameters. Since TTCN has no equivalent, the types using this have to be modelled as the union of two types. The first type being a singleton provided in the *cosim* **predefined** package as **null_type**, and the second as a **record of** the dereferenced type. A null pointer is represented by the singleton value of the **null_type**. A non-null value is represented by the **record** of type, which will contain a list of dereferenced values – one value supplied in the case of a plain derefererencing, and a list if the pointer represents an array of values. The latter may occur if a UML external operation originates from an imported a C/C++ header file that uses pointers for this purpose.

UMB also translates operations in a UML model that are tagged with the 'External' stereotype into TTCN signatures. These signatures can be used in test scripts to service external operation calls made by the model, using the `getcall` and `reply` statements. For non-static class operations, the signature has an extra leading 'inout' parameter passed as a pointer representation of the class itself, so that the class state information is available to the test script.

4.2   Package/Module Structure

UMB preserves UML package structure in the translation by using TTCN modules and groups. However, unlike UML packages, TTCN modules cannot be nested. UMB translates top level packages to modules, and nested packages to groups. Nesting one deep become groups within modules, and further nesting become groups within groups, etc..

UMB also creates the appropriate TTCN import statements in modules that correspond to UML import or access dependencies. Further, as TTCN import statements are not wholly transitive, UMB creates the extra import statements to match UML scoping. Nonetheless, scoping that matches UML scoping exactly cannot be reproduced within TTCN, which may result in name clashes. For example, nested UML packages may reuse the same identifier unambiguously, but groups in TTCN do not provide separate scope from enclosing modules or groups.

File and directory structure is also replicated by UMB, so that a Tau UML source '.u2' file becomes a TTCN source file of the same name but having extension '.ttcn'. UMB prompts the user for a home directory into which the generated TTCN files and directories will be created.

Using UMB on a complex model can produce many TTCN source files, some projects have exceeded 50 files. To populate a TTCN project with these *cosim* includes a Tau Tester addin that adds any files found on disk into the project, and warns if there are project files not present on disk. The addin also ensures that project's make configuration files are current with the *cosim* distribution being used.

4.3   Template Generation

UMB provides a GUI in which TTCN templates can be generated. The tool provides a nested view of the type structure of the template that may be expanded and collapsed as desired. For each field, the user can specify an actual value, pattern, expression, template parameter, or template reference. The GUI is useful because it presents to the user the complete type structure, rather than having the user remember it. Fig. 1 has a screen shot of the UMB's template GUI.

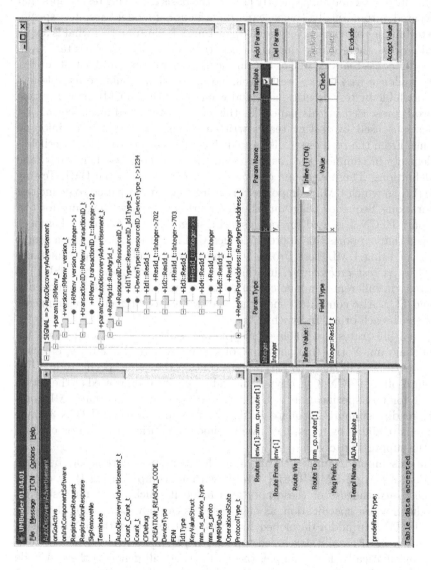

Fig. 1. UMB Template GUI

5   UML Testing Profile

Within Motorola some testing teams develop informal test specifications in the form of natural language and ad-hoc diagrams, which tend towards further manual work during inspections and test execution. Such test specifications are then manually inspected and subsequently used as the basis of writing test scripts that are executed automatically. Hence, exploring the use of model-based test specification techniques provided a very good opportunity for automating what is a very manual process, thereby introducing the ability to automatically check test specifications for consistency as well as automatically generate executable test scripts.

The challenge was to explore rigorous notations that would be useable and understandable by test practitioners, and would fit with the UML model testing framework presented in this paper. To this end, we reviewed a number of test specifications used by testing teams written in natural language or informal diagrams. From the review, we discovered that different approaches nonetheless had elements in common such as: test configuration, test case behaviour, and data definitions. These elements can be readily expressed in the UML Testing Profile [1,5] in which UML Composite Structure Diagrams are used to define test configurations, Sequence Diagrams and Interaction Overview Diagrams for test behaviour; TTCN-3 is used for value specification[2]. A Tau G2 addin has been developed that supports this approach, called U2TP. Figure 2 illustrates a simple example of using UML Test Profile to define a test configuration, sometimes referred to as *test architecture*, in which a single system under test (SUT) is connected via different communication ports to two different test components, TC1 and TC2. Also connectors show that the two test components communicate directly with each other for synchronisation.

Figure 3 illustrates a possible corresponding test case definition using a Sequence Diagram. Notice that the name of signals refer to the data type passed between entities, and that the parentheses contain the value specification.

In our toolkit, TTCN-3 data types and value specification is used as the action language for test specification in UML. One reason for this is that UML tools do not readily support adequate UML instance specification. TTCN-3 value notation is readable by users, has a well-defined semantics, and can be checked using the supporting tools.

From this simple example it is apparent that test specifications can be made more rigorous using UML Testing Profile without compromising their clarity. In some cases, the use of these notations made it much easier for testers to comprehend a test specification, as many aspects can now be visualized.

The U2TP Tau addin developed by Motorola to support the UML Testing Profile uses an internally developed tool called *ptk* [2] to generate TTCN test scripts automatically. For example, the U2TP tool will generate the test code for setting up the test configuration (see Fig. 4), as well as the code for test behaviour including TTCN test case functions, defaults, verdict handling, etc.

---

[2] Note that UML2.0 does not prescribe an action language. We use TTCN-3 as it supports value specification (similar to instance specification within UML 2.0).

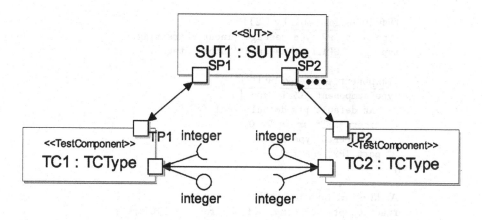

Fig. 2. Simple Test Configuration Using the UML Testing Profile

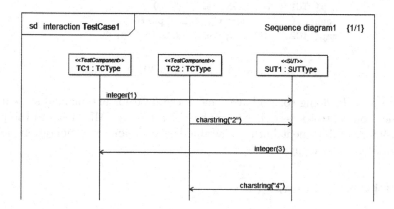

Fig. 3. Simple Test Case Specification Using the UML Testing Profile

From the UML port definitions U2TP will generate corresponding port types that convey the same signals as in the UML test specification, for example, the SUTType instance in Fig. 2 has ports SP1 and SP2 (n.b. the realized/required signals are not shown in the diagram), and in Fig. 4 the corresponding TTCN port type declarations, SP1_Type and SP2_Type generated by U2TP are shown. From each instance in the composite structure diagram of Fig. 2, U2TP will generate a corresponding TTCN component type, again as shown in Fig. 4, in which its ports are declared based on the generated port types. Thus, generated TTCN component TC2_TCType represents the UML part TC2, and the component declares port TP2 to be of port type TP2_Type. Finally, the way the components are connected in the composite structure diagram contained in Fig. 2 generates a corresponding function called ptk_testcomp_config in TTCN that does the same (note that in TTCN configurations are dynamic) as can be seen in Fig. 4.

In addition to generating test code the U2TP tool will also generate a Microsoft Word document containing the UML test specification with appropriate

Definitions generated by U2TP:
```
type port SP2_Type message {inout charstring}
type port SP1_Type message {inout integer}
```

Components generated by U2TP
```
type component TC2_TCType {
    var default ptk_defaultresult;
    timer MaxTimer := 20.0;
    port port0_Type port0;
    port TP2_Type TP2
}
```

Architecture built by U2TP
```
function ptk_testcomp_config() runs on MTCType {
    TC1 := TC1_PTCType.create;
    TC2 := TC2_PTCType.create;
    map( TC1 : TP1 , system : SP1 );
    connect( TC1 : port1 , TC2 : port0 );
    map( TC2 : TP2 , system : SP2 )
}
```

Fig. 4. TTCN-3 Code generated by UTP tool

annotations. In doing so, we have remove the need for one manual step in the test development process. That is, by having a formal UML model in the place of an informal document both executable test code and documentation can be produced automatically.

6 TTCN-3 Language

On the whole, TTCN-3 is a big improvement for model testing over TTCN-2 in terms of language features and in usability, due having the core language in plain text. It is not surprising that the type system is different from Tau UML, but it is rich enough to be able to model the former's types. In particular the procedure based communication for servicing UML external operations has proved more than sufficient – having operation declarations in the form of signatures, and the getcall and reply statements[3] for servicing calls.

One deficiency in comparison to UML is the lack of nested modules, which either leads to having more import statements than would otherwise be necessary, or to having non-scoped groups - the approach taken by UMB. In any case, because the scope rules are more restrictive in TTCN, it is not always possible to map a UML model to TTCN without having name clashes.

The fact that *cosim* has been able to control UML timers within TTCN, proves that TTCN-3 would benefit from having native statements for this purpose. In line with getcall, there could be gettimer, etc.; the default semantics of which should be non-blocking.

---

[3] Although not used by *cosim*, there are the matching call and getreply statements.

Tau UML has the CPtr<> template type to deal with external C/C++ code. It would be useful if TTCN had something similar rather than leaving it to the user to invent solution as done by UMB/*cosim*.

7   Experience

Multiple projects within Motorla are or have used the model test environment, and each project may have several models. There are examples of tests exchanging some 1,000 messages between the model and a single test script, and hundreds of tests scripts for a single model. Most users use simulated time for model test, whereas servicing external operations vs. writing their own stubs is a more even split.

Testing does reveal some systematic modeling errors, such as passing signal parameters by reference rather than by value using 'part', however standard programming errors are more likely to occur, such as incorrect loop index or array bounds, and cut/paste errors when duplicating similar functionality has be incorrectly modified in the copied version.

Teams also report the benefit of developing model tests and then reusing them to test application code running on the target machine where this is possible. In this case, the application code is generated by the Motorola Mousetrap code generator [3] that includes the encoders/decoders for marshalling signals. Corresponding encoders are also produced by Mousetrap for incorporation with the Tester run-time API. Here the reported benefit is the ease of debugging tests (as well as models) through the Tau Tester and Model Verifier GUIs used in model test prior to and rather than from executables running directly during application testing.

8   Conclusion

The main test environment described here has been developed over three years, and has been successfully used by diverse teams in different sectors within Motorola, although the U2TP addin is more recently developed. The test environment is supported and developed by the Motorola's Software Design Automation group for use by all Motorola, and is the only test tool used by Tau UML models developed for code generation.

Groups are keen to extend the test environment capability for application testing, because building and executing models/tests in *cosim* has been kept as user-friendly as possible. However, although there is a Motorola standard encoder/decoder solution via Mousetrap, application communication is project dependent.

The more recent addition of support for part of the UML Testing Profile is under evaluation as users are keen to extend their use of UML beyond modeling systems and applications.

We have suggested areas where TTCN-3 could be extended, such as handling external timers and support for types that use pointers in the system under test. However, users find TTCN-3 an improvement over TTCN-2, particularly because of the textual syntax of the core language.

References

1. P. Baker, Z.R. Dai, J. Grabowski, Ø. Haugen, I. Schieferdecker, C. Williams.: Model-Driven Testing Using the UML Testing Profile. Springer, Berlin (2007)
2. Baker, P., Bristow, P., Jervis, C., King, D., Mitchell, W.: Automatic Generation of Conformance Tests from Message Sequence Charts. In: Sherratt, E. (ed.) SAM 2002. LNCS, vol. 2599, Springer, Heidelberg (2003)
3. Dietz, P., Marth, K., Berg, A.v.d., Weigert, T., Weil, F.: Practical Considerations in Automatic Code Generation. In: Tsai, J., Zhang, D. (eds.) Advances in Machine Learning Application in Software Engineering, pages. 92. Idea Group Publisher, Hershey (2006)
4. Object Management Group (OMG): UML Superstructure Specification, Version 2.0, formal/05-07-04 (August 2005)
5. Object Management Group (OMG): UML 2.0 Testing Profile, Final Adopted Specification. ptc/04-10-14 (April 2004)
6. Specification and Description Language (SDL-2000). International Telecommunications Union – Telecommunications Standards Sector (ITU-T) Recommendation Z.100, Geneva (2001)
7. Telelogic Code Generation:
   http://www.telelogic.com/products/tau/g2/
   design-high-quality-software.cfm
8. Telelogic cosimulation:
   http://www.telelogic.com/products/tau/ttcn/
   co-simulate-and-test-your-system-design.cfm
9. Telelogic SDL Suite:
   http://www.telelogic.com/products/tau/sdl/overview.cfm
10. Telelogic Tau G2: http://www.telelogic.com/products/tau/g2/overview.cfm
11. Telelogic TTCN Suite:
    http://www.telelogic.com/products/tau/ttcn/
    overview.cfm
12. Telelogic Tester:
    http://www.telelogic.com/products/tau/tester/overview.cfm
13. Conformance Testing Methodology and Framework – Part 3: The Tree and Tabular Combined Notation (TTCN), ITU Recommendation X.292 (1997)
14. The Testing and Test Control Notation version 3; Part 1: TTCN-3 Core Language, ETSI ES 201 873-1 V3.1.1 (2005-06)
15. The Testing and Test Control Notation version 3; Part 5: TTCN-3 Runtime Interface (TRI), ETSI ES 201 873-5 V3.1.1 (2005-06)
16. The Testing and Test Control Notation version 3; Part 6: TTCN-3 Control Interface (TCI), ETSI ES 201 873-6 V3.1.1 (2005-06)

Specifying Input Port Bounds in SDL

Reinhard Gotzhein, Rüdiger Grammes, and Thomas Kuhn

Networked Systems Group
University of Kaiserslautern, Germany
{gotzhein,grammes,kuhn}@informatik.uni-kl.de

Abstract. According to the SDL semantics, input ports "may retain any number of input signals", and therefore may grow without upper bound. While this is a convenient property on design level, it may lead to illegal behaviour on concrete hardware platforms when a queue overflow occurs, especially in the context of distributed embedded systems with severe storage constraints. In this paper, we present a straightforward extension of SDL in order to specify input port bounds formally. In our solution, bounds are associated with signals and input ports. We define both the concrete and abstract grammar and the formal dynamic semantics of the proposed SDL extension. We have implemented the extension in Cmicro, and illustrate our solution by examples from the Assisted Bicycle Trainer, a wireless sensor network.

1 Introduction

Model-driven development (MDD) [1] is a software engineering approach that places the abstract, formal system model in the center of the development activity. The idea is that models guide and direct all development activities, including system design, performance assessments, and automatic code generation from design models. Specification techniques, such as ITU-T's Specification and Description Language – SDL [2], are used to specify models [3]. Transformations of SDL models are supported by reuse techniques, for instance, design patterns and design components, and by commercial SDL compilers [4].

Among the target domains of MDD are embedded systems in general, and networked control systems (NCS) [5] in particular. Typically, these systems have scarce resources in terms of storage, communication bandwidth, and energy, which requires particular care of the system developer already in the design phase. To cope with scarce resources, SDL language subsets that lead to "predictable" resource usage have been proposed [6]. For instance, the size of an agent set can be limited, or dynamic agent creation can be avoided entirely. SDT Cmicro [4] is an SDL-to-C compiler supporting an SDL language subset tailored to embedded systems.

Dynamic agent sets are but one source of unbounded resource consumption. Another source are input ports of SDL agents, which – according to the SDL semantics [2,7] – "may retain any number of input signals", and therefore may grow without upper bound. While this is a useful property on design level, it

E. Gaudin, E. Najm, and R. Reed (Eds.): SDL 2007, LNCS 4745, pp. 101–116, 2007.
© Springer-Verlag Berlin Heidelberg 2007

may lead to illegal behaviour on system platforms with insufficient storage to queue incoming signals in all possible system executions. Some SDL runtime systems try to cope with this problem by entering an error state in case of queue overflow. From this state, the SDL system is restarted, which means that all signals retained in input queues are discarded. Restart is, of course, not a solution if the overload situation occurs frequently, and certainly not an appropriate choice in real-time systems.

In practical cases, it is often possible to assure an upper input port bound, for instance, by applying flow control mechanisms, by limiting the number of instances of a signal, or by analysing the reachability graph of the specified system. However, failures in distributed embedded systems could lead to event storms that overload the SDL system temporarily. To cope with such situations, incoming signals could be discarded in a well-defined manner, or could replace queued signals if the input port queue is already filled. Although these measures are different in nature, they all have the capability of solving the problem of input port overflow in implementations derived from SDL models. However, a behaviour ensuring an upper bound of an input port cannot be explicitly specified in SDL – other than in the case of the size of agent sets.

So far, there is little work related to the formal specification of queue bounds. Although it is not possible to formally specify upper input port bounds in SDL, current code generation methodologies rely on the developer for setting sufficient upper bounds for signal queues [8]. Especially for microcontrollers, model checking is suggested as a methodology to determine accurate queue sizes. However, model checking is only feasible if all properties of a model are known to the model checker. In case of an SDL specification, this includes all relevant properties of the environment. Open SDL systems need to be turned into closed SDL systems before they can be processed by a model checker. In [9], an approach for generating a model for the SDL environment that is usable in a model checker is presented. Unfortunately, it is sometimes impossible to specify the worst case behaviour of the SDL environment without considering an infinite state space, which will cause a model checker to fail. In this case, the only solution is to determine the maximum queue size by testing, which cannot guarantee a correctly dimensioned signal queue and therefore cannot guarantee the absence of potential queue overflows.

In this paper, we propose an extension of SDL for the specification of input port bounds. More specifically, upper bounds for the number of signals of the same type can be formally specified for each input port. If the bound is reached and another signal arrives, the oldest signal of the same type is deleted from the input port, and the new signal is appended. This solution is especially suitable in the context of networked control systems (NCS), where typically only the most recent sensor values are of interest.

The paper is organised as follows. In Sect. 2, we present an extension to SDL to specify input port bounds. To maintain compatibility with existing SDL tools, we also define an extension through annotations. To illustrate the usage, we show excerpts from the SDL specification of the Assisted Bicycle Trainer: a mobile sensor network for group training of cyclists. In Sect. 3, we incorporate the extension to SDL into the dynamic formal semantics, which turns out to be straightforward. Based on an alternative input port bound definition by annotations, we have modified the SDL-to-C compiler Cmicro [4] (Sect. 4), and have performed simulations to show the benefits in a microcontroller setting (Sect. 5). In Sect. 6, we discuss pros and cons of specifying input port bounds, followed by conclusions in Sect. 7.

2   An SDL Extension for Input Port Bounds

Input port bounds can be specified in different ways, for example:

- *Explicit input port bound specification*: A bound is specified for all input ports of an agent set.
- *Implicit input port bound specification*: A bound is specified for each element of the set of signals in all channels or gates leading to an agent set[1]. The bound for the input ports is derived as the sum of the bounds for signals consumed by the agents' state machines.

In both cases, the bound is applied to the input port of each instance of the agent set. If the number of instances in the agent set is itself bounded, then the number of signal instances (of a given signal type) that can be queued is bounded too, assuring predictable resource consumption.

The *explicit* input port bound specification has the advantage that the number of queued signals of different types can vary within the specified bound. In the *implicit* case, bounds can be specified on a per-signal-type basis. Thus, for each signal type, there is a guaranteed number of slots in the input port, which cannot be filled by signals of other types. This solution is especially suitable for networked control systems, where the most recent value of each sensor is to be kept in the input port. This property cannot be guaranteed by the explicit input port bound specification. Therefore, we adopt the implicit input port bound specification, which covers all interesting cases that have occurred in our projects so far.

For implicit input port bound specification, we introduce two complementary syntactical SDL language extensions:

- *Global bound specification*: Bounds are specified together with signal definitions, with the default being "unbounded" if no bound is given.
- *Local bound specification*: Bounds are specified for individual elements of the set of signals in all channels or gates leading to the agent set, with the default being "global bound" if no local bound is defined.

The specification of global bounds is very concise, since there is only one definition per signal. On the other hand, the specification of local bounds gives

---

[1] We omit the treatment of implicit input signals, exceptions, and timer signals. For timer signals without parameters, for instance, the upper signal instance bound is always 1.

more flexibility, as different bounds can be associated with agent sets that receive signal instances of the same type – a frequent case in our projects. Also, if the signal definition is imported from a package – another frequent case –, it is preferable to specify local bounds in order to keep the package unchanged. Note that both styles can be combined such that the global bound defines the default value, which can be overruled by a local bound.

Local bound specification. To specify local bounds, we extend the concrete and abstract syntax of SDL. In the concrete syntax, we add an optional attribute <signal bound> to the signal list associated with channels and gates, put into square brackets. In the abstract syntax, the extension is represented by an attribute *Signal-local-bound-**set*** of *Agent-definition*, containing all signal types for which a bound has been specified, together with the specified *nat*-value.

Concrete Grammar

| <signal list item> | ::= | <signal identifier>
 [<signal bound>] |
| <signal bound> | ::= | <left square bracket>
 <Natural simple expression>
 <right square bracket> |

Abstract Grammar

Agent-definition	::	*Agent-name* *Number-of-instances* *Signal-local-bound-**set*** *Agent-type-identifier*
Signal-local-bound	::	*Signal-name* *Signal-bound*
Signal-bound	=	*Nat*

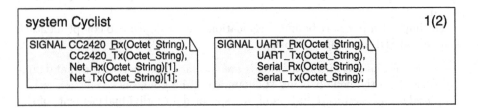

Fig. 1. SDL specification of Assisted Bicycle Trainer on system level (excerpt)

Global bound specification. To specify global bounds, we extend the concrete syntax by adding an optional attribute <signal bound> to <signal definition item>. In the abstract syntax, this is transformed to the local bound specification, i.e., all signal bounds are directly associated with agent definitions.

Concrete Grammar

<signal definition item>   ::=   <signal name>
                                      [<formal context parameters>]
                                      ...
                                      [<sort list>]
                                      [<signal bound>]

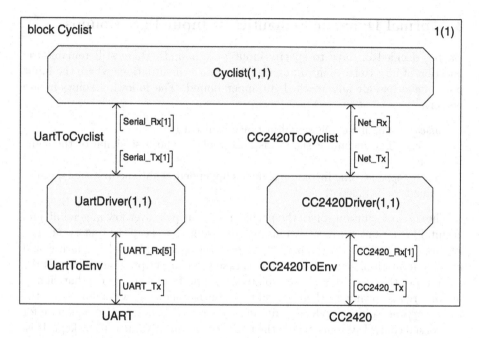

Fig. 2. SDL specification of Assisted Bicycle Trainer on process level (excerpt)

Figure 1 shows how global bounds are specified on SDL system level. Here, a global bound of 1 is associated with the definitions of the SDL signals Net_Rx and Net_Tx. For all other signals, the default "unbounded" holds. Local bounds are specified on process level and associated with elements of signal lists (see Fig. 2). For instance, a local bound of 5 is specified for incoming signals of type UART_Rx. The reasoning behind this choice is that up to 5 sensors are connected via serial lines. Periodically, these sensors deliver status values (e.g., current speed, heart rate, pedal force) to the cyclist system, where they are accumulated in the SDL process UartDriver before being forwarded in one signal of type Serial_Rx to the SDL process Cyclist. If for some reason - for instance, reduced duty cycles[2] due to energy shortage - these signals cannot be processed

---

[2] In NCSs, a duty cycle is the ratio between active and total period.

before the next set of sensor values is received, the new sensor values are used instead. Periodically, the SDL process Cyclist broadcasts aggregated sensor values via ZigBee (communication processor CC2420) to all other cyclist nodes. Local and global bounds are specified to limit the number of queued signals outbound (Net_Tx) and inbound (CC2420_Rx and Net_Rx) to 1. From the global and local signal bounds, it can be derived that the input port bounds of Cyclist, UartDriver, and CC2420driver are 2, 6, and 2, respectively. Note that in case of substructures, only local bounds for signals consumed by the state machines of the given agent set are to be specified (well-formedness condition).

3   Formal Dynamic Semantics of Input Port Bounds

Having decided on how to specify input port bounds, there still remains the question of how to treat incoming signal instances in situations where the input port queue has already reached its upper bound. The following solutions are perceivable:

- *discard*: The incoming signal instance is discarded.
- *replace*: The incoming signal instance replaces the first signal of the same type.
- *delete/append*: The incoming signal is appended, while the first signal of the same type is deleted.

The *discard* solution solves the problem of input port overflow in general, and is suitable in event storm situations, where it suffices to keep the first event. The *replace* solution is an interesting candidate, if the specified bound is 1, as it would avoid starvation of signals - new signals take the place of previous signals of the same type. However, this would violate the property of input ports that signals are ordered according to their arrival time. In the following, we elaborate on the *delete/append* solution, which maintains that property and is also adequate for networked control systems, where the most recent sensor value is to be kept. It is, however, also possible to support several solutions, and to let the system designer specify which one to apply.

3.1   Delete/Append Semantics of Input Port Bounds

Defining semantics for input port bounds, we modify the signal flow model of the formal dynamic semantics of SDL [7], defined using Abstract State Machines (for an introduction to ASMs, see [10]). We define new derived functions, predicates and rule macros for reading bounds from the abstract syntax, and for inserting signals into bounded queues. Of the signal flow model, only rule macro DELIVERSIGNALS ([7], Section 2.3.2.1) is modified[3]. Note that while the formal dynamic semantics defines the semantics of SDL-2000, all definitions in this section apply to SDL-96 as well.

---

[3] Note that transition selection and, in particular, the semantics of the *save* construct are not affected.

The derived function *bound* forms the interface to the abstract syntax. It returns the input port bound for input port g and signal type s. If no bound is specified for signal s in the agent that owns g, the value zero is returned.

$bound(g$: GATE, s: SIGNAL) : NAT $=_{\text{def}}$
   let $slb = take(\{b \in g.myagent.agentAS1.s\text{-}Signal\text{-}local\text{-}bound\text{-}\textbf{set}$:
                           $b.\textbf{s-}Signal\text{-}name = s.\textbf{s-}Signal\text{-}name\})$
      if $slb \neq undefined$ **then** $slb.\textbf{s-}Signal\text{-}bound$ **else** 0 **endif**
   endlet

We define two derived predicates to determine if a signal can be inserted into the input queue (the *schedule* of a gate) without violating the specified bound. *Insertable*(s,g) holds if the number of signals of type s in the input queue of g is smaller than the bound, or if no bound is defined. *Insertable*(s) holds if signals of type s can be inserted into some input port of the current agent set without violating a bound.

$Insertable\,(s$: SIGNAL, g: GATE): BOOLEAN $=_{\text{def}}$
   $bound(g,\ s) = 0 \vee |\{\ si \in g.schedule\ |\ si.signalType = s\}| < bound(g,\ s)$

$Insertable\,(s$: SIGNAL): BOOLEAN $=_{\text{def}}$
   $\exists\ sa$: $sa \in$ SDLAGENT $\wedge\ sa.owner = Self \wedge\ Insertable\,(s,\ sa.inport)$

If a signal of type s is inserted into a queue that already holds the maximum number of signals of this type, the oldest signal in the queue of the same type is deleted. Function *deleteByType*$(s,siSeq)$ returns a queue without the first - and therefore oldest - signal of type s in queue *siSeq*.

$deleteByType(s$: SIGNAL, $siSeq$: SIGNALINST$*$): SIGNALINST$* =_{\text{def}}$
   if $siSeq = empty$ **then** $empty$
   elseif $siSeq.head.signalType = s$ **then** $siSeq.tail$
   else $< siSeq.head >\,^{\cap}\,deleteByType(s,\ siSeq.tail)$
   endif

INSERTINPORT is a rule macro for the insertion of signals into the input queue of agents. If signal si can be inserted without violating the bound of the input queue, the macro is equivalent to INSERT ([7], Section 2.1.1.2) on unbounded queues (line 3). Otherwise, the signal is inserted into a queue from which the oldest signal of the same type was deleted (line 5).

Rule macro DELIVERSIGNALS delivers signals from gates of agent sets to the input queues of contained agents. Underlined are the modifications made to DELIVERSIGNALS to support bounded queues, using the functions and predicates defined above. Calls to rule macro INSERT are replaced by INSERTINPORT, respecting the bound defined for the input queue for the corresponding agent and signal type.

```
1  INSERTINPORT(si: SIGNALINST, t: Time, g: GATE)≡
2      if Insertable( si.signalType, g) then
3          g.schedule := insert( si, t, g.schedule)
4      else
5          g.schedule := insert( si, t, deleteByType(si.signalType, g.schedule))
6      endif
7      si.arrival := t
```

DELIVERSIGNALS covers two cases. In the first case (lines 6-8), the signal is addressed explicitly by PID, and the target is deterministic. In the second case (lines 10-12), the signal can be delivered to any agent in the agent set.

Signals should only be deleted if absolutely necessary. In the second case, choosing an arbitrary agent can lead to a signal being deleted, although another agent of the agent set has fewer signals of the corresponding type in its input port than specified by the bound. Therefore, we choose an agent where the number of signals of type s in input port g is smaller than the bound (i.e., INSERTABLE(s,g) is true), *if* such an agent exists in the current agent set (i.e., INSERTABLE(s) is true), and an arbitrary agent from the agent set otherwise.

```
1  DELIVERSIGNALS ≡
2    choose g: g ∈  Self . ingates  ∧   g . queue ≠ empty
3      let  si  =  g . queue . head  in
4        DELETE(si, g)
5        if  si . toArg ∈  PID  ∧   si . toArg ≠  undefined  then
6          choose sa: sa ∈  SDLAGENT ∧ sa . owner = Self ∧   sa . self  = si . toArg
7            INSERTINPORT( si ,  si . arrival ,  sa . inport)
8          endchoose
9        else
10         choose sa: sa ∈  SDLAGENT ∧   sa . owner = Self ∧
                  Insertable( si . signalType)  →  Insertable( si . signalType, sa . inport)
11           INSERTINPORT( si ,  si . arrival ,  sa . inport)
12         endchoose
13       endif
14     endlet
15   endchoose
```

3.2   Signal Starvation and Replace Semantics

The delete/append solution formalized above can lead to signal starvation. Consider a scenario with two signal types a and b, with signals of these types arriving alternately. Further, let the bounds for a and b be set to 1. If signals of type a are always consumed before the next signal of that type arrives, no deletions will occur with regard to a. If, however, signals of type b are never consumed before the next signal of that type arrives, then according to the delete/append semantics, the old signal is deleted and the new signal appended *after* the previous signal of type a. This effect would lead to starvation of signals of type b.

Signal starvation can be avoided by replacing signals instead of deleting and appending them. In other words, the incoming signal is not appended to the queue in cases where the bound has been reached, but overwrites the oldest signal in the queue. There are two problems with this solution. First, the SDL semantics states that signals in the input port queue are ordered by arrival time. This property would be violated by replacing the oldest signal. Second, if the signal bound is greater than 1, overwriting of the oldest signal would result in an overtaking of signals of the same type. Overwriting the newest signal would solve that problem, but certainly is not a good idea either. For these reasons, we have not chosen the replace semantics in our solution.

4   Implementation of Input Port Bounds

To implement the proposed extension for specifying input port bounds, several SDL tools are to be modified. In particular, changes of the SDL editor, the SDL analyzer, and the SDL compiler are necessary. As far as commercial tool environments are concerned, these changes can only be implemented by the tool provider, because the source code is usually not publicly available. To avoid this difficulty, we propose an alternative signal bound definition by annotations, which is compatible with existing SDL editors. Furthermore, we provide an implementation of signal bounds in Cmicro, an SDL-to-C compiler that is part of the Telelogic TAU SDL Suite.

4.1   Defining Signal Bounds by Annotations

Instead of using the SDL extension introduced in Sect. 2, signal bounds can be expressed by annotations. This has several advantages. First, annotations are compatible with existing SDL editors, and are processed into SDL-PR with comments. Second, annotations defining signal bounds can be introduced in different places of an SDL specification, for instance, on system level, thus avoiding the modification of imported packages. To define signal bounds by annotations, we use the following syntax:

$\#BOUND(agentIdentifier, signalType, signalBound)$

By using agent identifiers instead of agent names, annotations can be placed on different structural levels. In general, the structural context of the annotation applies, improving readability. In Fig. 3, the signal bounds specified in Fig. 1 and Fig. 2 are expressed through annotations of this kind. Note that the formal comment is attached to the block Cyclist, therefore, it suffices to use process names to uniquely identify input ports. In order to express global bounds, we can associate annotations with signal definitions – an option we omit here.

4.2   Implementing Signal Bounds in Cmicro

In this section, we elaborate on implementing signal bounds in Cmicro, an SDL-to-C compiler of the Telelogic TAU SDL Suite targeted to embedded systems. Since these systems suffer severe storage constraints, it is particularly important to support signal bounds. Our solution consists of three steps. First, all annotations defining signal bounds are extracted into a definition file. Second, our SDL Environment Framework (SEnF) is extended to support signal bounds. Third, the Cmicro runtime library is modified.

Definition file. The SDL-PR file is parsed twice, once by the SDL-to-C compiler, and once by our preprocessor that extracts all annotations expressing signal bounds. The output of the preprocessor is a definition file that is used by the SDL Environment Framework (SEnF). For the example in Fig. 3, the following definition file is produced:

```
1  BOUND(CC2420Driver, CC2420_Rx, 1)
2  BOUND(CC2420Driver, Net_Tx, 1)
3  BOUND(UartDriver, UART_Rx, 5)
4  BOUND(UartDriver, Serial_Tx, 1)
5  BOUND(Cyclist, Serial_Rx, 1)
6  BOUND(Cyclist, Net_Rx, 1)
```

Extensions of the SDL Environment Framework. We have extended our
SDL runtime environment "SEnF"' with a function *signalBoundExceeded* that
checks whether a signal bound has been exceeded. This function is generated at
compile time, and is specific to the generated SDL system. With respect to the
limited memory of embedded systems, we have decided to create an implementation that is stored in ROM, which usually is substantially larger than RAM on
these devices. Therefore, we transform the definition file, which was generated
by the preprocessor, into the function *signalBoundExceeded*:

```
1  // Check if a signal bound was exceeded
2  // - This requires a changed mk_queue.h
3  int signalBoundExceeded(
4      xPID receiverPid,
5      xmk_T_SIGNAL signalId,
6      int signalsInQueue)
7  {
8      // Checking signal bounds
9      #include <signalbounds.def>
10
11     // Signal bound not exceeded
12     return 0;
13 }
```

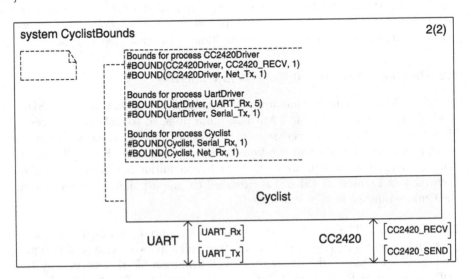

Fig. 3. SDL specification with annotations (excerpt)

The C-preprocessor is used to generate a tailored function *signalBoundExceeded* for every signal type for which a bound has been specified. The generated definition file is included, with the BOUND macros in the definition file being transformed into statements checking the signal bounds. The implementation of the BOUND macro depends on the SDL compiler used. The definition for the Cmicro SDL-to-C compiler is as follows:

```
1  #define BOUND(agentIdentifier, signalID, signalBound) \
2      if ( \
3          ( receiverPid == GLOBALPID(XPTID_ ## agentIdentifier)) && \
4          ( signalId == signalID) && \
5          ( signalsInQueue >= signalBound) \
6      ) return 1;
```

Cmicro runtime library. The Cmicro runtime library requires a modification of the function implementing the INSERTINPORT rule macro. By default, the Cmicro library keeps all SDL signals in a global linked list. When inserting a new signal into the input port of a process, this list is inspected.

```
1  for( rover = XMK_QUEUE_ADR; *rover != ( T_E_SIGNAL xmk_RAM_ptr) NULL;
       rover = &(( *rover )->next ) );
```

We have modified this behaviour to check signal bounds for the inserted signal while traversing the list. All signals of the same type as the inserted signal waiting at the same gate are counted. A reference to the oldest signal is stored for deletion in case the signal bound was exceeded. The special case where the signal that has activated the current transition is still in the queue must be considered, otherwise the same signal could be deallocated twice.

```
1  // Count queued signals of same type as inserted signal
2  int queuedSignalsOfType = 0;
3
4  // Inspect the signal queue
5  rover = XMK_QUEUE_ADR;
6
7  while (*rover != ( T_E_SIGNAL xmk_RAM_ptr) 0) {
8      if ((rover->rec==p_Message->rec)&&(rover->signal==p_Message->signal))
          {
9          if (( oldestSignal == 0) && ( oldestSignal != XMK_CURRENTSIGNAL))
10             oldestSignal = *rover;
11         queuedSignalsOfType++;
```

The generated *signalBoundExceeded* function is used to check if the signal bound for the inserted signal was exceeded. In that case, the oldest signal is removed from the queue to stay within the specified bounds.

```
12             if ( signalBoundExceeded(p_Message->rec, p_Message->signal,
                   queuedSignalsOfType) != 0) {
13                 // Signal bound exceeded
14                 if ( oldestSignal == 0) {
```

```
15        // - Technically, the signal that caused the queue to
             overflow is
16        //   not in the queue anymore
17        // - The SDL queue must be of maximal size of at least the
             sum of
18        //   all signal bounds + 1
19        // - Leave the signal alone and let rover point to the next
             signal
20        //   The signal will be removed by the runtime environment
             after
21        //   the current transition has ended. Freeing now is
             dangerous.
22        rover = &(( *rover )->next );
23    } else {
24        // Delete current signal
25        T_E_SIGNAL xmk_RAM_ptr curSignalBackup =
             XMK_CURRENTSIGNAL;
26        XMK_CURRENTSIGNAL = oldestSignal;
27        xmk_RemoveCurrentSignal();
28        XMK_CURRENTSIGNAL = curSignalBackup;
29    }
30
31    // One signal less in queue
32    queuedSignalsOfType--;
```

After traversing the queue, the signal is appended at the end of the queue. This behaviour of Cmicro has not been modified.

5 Simulation Experiments

With the Telelogic Cmicro SDL-to-C compiler extended by signal bounds as described in Sect. 4, we have performed simulation studies of the Assisted Bicycle Trainer (ABT). In the simulation, we are using the signal bounds specified in Sect. 2 and Sect. 4, yielding a global queue bound of 10^4. The ABT is a wireless sensor network, with up to 5 sensors connected via UART. In the simulation, we assume that these sensors start operation by transmitting one sensor value per second. All sensor values received in the interval of one second are then consumed by UartDriver (see Fig. 2), accumulated, and forwarded to Cyclist. To ensure proper operation, a timer set to 1 second is used to trigger UartDriver. After receiving and processing the accumulated sensor data, Cyclist broadcasts these data via CC2420Driver.

The simulation starts with a nominal number of 5 sensor values per second. After 3 seconds of simulation time, the total number of sensor values per second is increased by one every second, up to 15. Since UartDriver starts consuming values only after the timer has expired, and the signal bound for UART_Rx is 5, this means that old signals are deleted from the queue as soon as the signal bound has

---

[4] Recall that Cmicro uses one global input port queue.

been reached, and new signals are appended. In Fig. 4, the resulting behaviour is shown. The solid curve represents the number of received sensor values per second, starting with 5. The dotted curve marks the number of deleted sensor values per second, which is the number of received values minus 5. Finally, the dashed line shows the number of accumulated sensor data broadcasts per second, which is 1. Obviously, the system behaves as expected, even in periods where too many sensor values are produced.

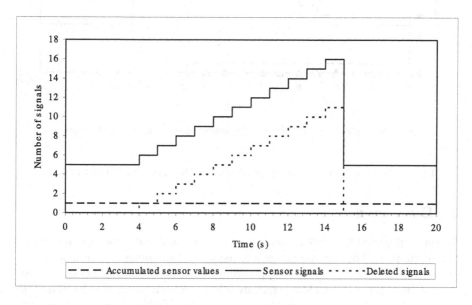

Fig. 4. Assisted Bicycle Trainer: Simulation with specified signal bounds

In Fig. 5, the same scenario has been simulated using the original Telelogic Cmicro compiler, i.e. without implementing signal bounds. We have set the global queue size to 14, which results from the intended global queue bound of 10 plus 1 timer signal plus 3 internal Cmicro slots. In the simulation, sensor data are accepted until the actual queue size exceeds 14. Note that queue slots that are reserved for other signal types in the implementation supporting signal bounds are also used for sensor data, therefore, more than 5 sensor values may be stored. This works fine as long as all incoming signals can be appended to the queue. As soon as the queue is filled, Cmicro starts discarding incoming signals[5], regardless of their type. In the simulated system, this has the effect that the timer signal that is supposed to trigger UartDriver to receive and accumulate sensor data is discarded as well. As a consequence, no further sensor data are removed from the queue, therefore, no sensor data are accumulated and forwarded to Cyclist, which leads to a complete system failure.

---

[5] Alternatively, Cmicro may be configured to raise an exception in case of queue overflow.

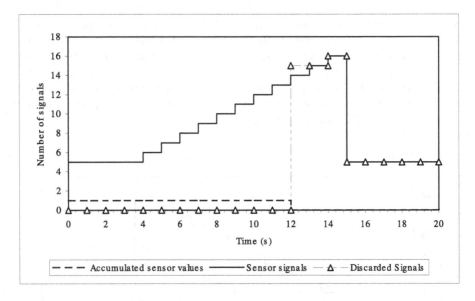

Fig. 5. Assisted Bicycle Trainer: Simulation without specified signal bounds

6   Discussion

All types of embedded systems may suffer from unpredictable memory consumption at runtime. This can happen due to asynchronous communication, resulting in queue overflows. It can also happen due to synchronous interaction, e.g., recursive procedure calls, yielding stack overflows. In both cases, non-deterministic or illegal system behaviour can be the consequence. In this paper, we have presented one strategy to handle queue overflows by specifying queue bounds in a problem-specific way at design time, and by defining the system behaviour in case of signal arrivals when the input port is filled. Other strategies handle queue overflows and stack overflows at runtime:

– *Queue overflows*: One technique used in existing runtime environments is exception handling. Exceptions are raised when an undesired system state is entered. Depending on the runtime environment, either the specified system or the runtime environment is forced to handle the exception. Existing runtime environments follow two strategies for handling exceptions due to queue overflows. Either the system is halted immediately, or the signal that caused the overflow is dropped. Both strategies will leave the system in an unpredictable and unknown state, resulting in non-deterministic system behaviour. Predictable behaviour can only be restored by resetting the system into a known state. Further, we observe that exception handling due to queue overflow is undesirable in general. The internals of queue handling are specific to the runtime environment. Therefore, resolution strategies for queue overflow are not specified, and may therefore depend on the platform. Specifying application specific strategies like deferring signals in the case of full queues is also not efficient, since then, low-priority data signals can block high-priority control signals for an unpredictable amount of time.

– *Stack overflows*: Stack overflows are handled by the runtime environment or by the operating system. Usually, it is not possible to return to a stable system state once a stack overflow has occurred. Therefore, the only possibility of handling stack overflow is to reset the system to a well-defined state, resulting in data loss and a delay due to the reset procedure.

While it is possible to combine the strategies above with our solution to queue bounds, they cannot be used to avoid system misbehaviour due to unpredictable memory consumption, which is a more general problem. The informal runtime semantics of UML2 is similar to the formal semantics of SDL. Some UML2 tools, e.g. Telelogic TAU G2 [11], even translate UML models into SDL systems. This shows that the applicability of the work presented in this paper is not limited to the domain of SDL systems.

7 Conclusions and Future Work

The SDL semantics states that input ports "may retain any number of input signals". However, executing specifications on a concrete hardware platform, this property cannot be guaranteed, leading to illegal behaviour in cases of insufficient memory.

In this paper, we have proposed an extension of SDL to support the specification of input port bounds. We have presented both an extension of the concrete and abstract syntax of SDL, and an extension based on annotations compatible with the concrete syntax of SDL-96 and existing SDL editors. We have defined the semantics of input port bounds formally, by adapting the dynamic semantics of SDL-2000. The required changes consisted of 20 additional lines of ASM rules, and the modification of only 3 lines. Based on annotations, we have implemented input port bounds into the Telelogic Cmicro SDL-to-C compiler, and have presented simulation studies based on this implementation.

We believe that the extension proposed in this work is of interest for future standardized versions of SDL. As such, it should be discussed in the standardization committee of ITU-T. Also, tool providers with customers in the embedded systems domain using SDL as design language could have a strong interest. In our future work, we intend to adapt our own SDL-to-C++ compiler ConTraST [12] to support input port bounds. Furthermore, we will use the extension in our projects in the ubiquitous computing domain.

References

1. Book, M., Beydeda, S., Gruhn, V.(eds.): Model-driven Software Development. Springer, Heidelberg (2005)
2. ITU-T: Specification and Description Language(SDL). ITU-T Recommendation Z.100. International Telecommunications Union (August 2002)

3. Gotzhein, R.: Model-driven by SDL - Improving the Quality of Networked Systems Development (Invited Paper). In (NOTERE 2007). 7th International Conference on New Technologies of Distributed Systems, Marrakesh, Morocco, June 4-8, 2007, pp. 4–8 (2007)
4. Telelogic AB: (Telelogic Tau Generation 1), www.telelogic.com/products/tau/index.cfm
5. Walsh, G.C., Ye, H., Bushnell, L.: Stability Analysis of Networked Control Systems. IEEE Transactions of Control Systems Technology 10, 438–445 (2002)
6. Grammes, R.: Formal Operations for SDL Language Profiles. In: Gotzhein, R., Reed, R. (eds.) SAM 2006. LNCS, vol. 4320, pp. 49–63. Springer, Heidelberg (2006)
7. ITU-T: SDL formal definition: Dynamic semantics. ITU-T Recommendation Z.100 Annex F3 International Telecommunications Union (November 2000)
8. Wasowski, A.: On Efficient Program Synthesis from Statecharts. ACM SIGPLAN Notices 38, 163–170 (2003)
9. Sidorova, N., Steffen, M.: Embedding chaos. In: Cousot, P. (ed.) SAS 2001. LNCS, vol. 2126, pp. 319–334. Springer, Heidelberg (2001)
10. ITU-T: SDL formal definition: General overview. ITU-T Recommendation Z.100 Annex F3 International Telecommunications Union (November 2000)
11. Telelogic AB: (Telelogic Tau Generation 2), www.telelogic.com/products/tau/g2/index.cfm
12. Fliege, I., Grammes, R., Weber, C.: ConTraST - A Configurable SDL Transpiler And Runtime Environment. In: Gotzhein, R., Reed, R. (eds.) SAM 2006. LNCS, vol. 4320, pp. 222–234. Springer, Heidelberg (2006)

Translatable Finite State Time Machine

Krzysztof Sacha

Warsaw University of Technology, Nowowiejska 15/19, 00–665 Warszawa, Poland
k.sacha@ia.pw.edu.pl

Abstract. The paper describes syntax, behavior and formal semantics
of a new class of timed automata, which are tailored for modeling the
behavior of real-time systems. A formal method for automatic generation
of programs is developed around this model. The method starts from
modeling the desired behavior of the system under design by means of
a UML-based state machine with the ability to measure time, and ends
up with a complete program written in one of the IEC 1131 languages.
The translation process is done automatically, and the semantics of the
resulting program is isomorphic to the semantics of the model.

1 Introduction

Control applications are usually reactive in that they must respond to a series
of events according to a strictly defined stimulus-response pattern. Finite state
machines (FSM) are one of the best known models that have been recognized
as useful to specify such requirements. The advantages of a classical FSM model
are conceptual simplicity and mathematical precision. The model is executable
and analyzable, and has the potential for automatic code generation. What is
missing in a classical finite state machine is the ability to model time.

Several time extensions to FSM have been developed and described in the literature. The most widely accepted models of timed automata [1,2] and timed I/O
automata [3] are used mainly for modeling and verification of time-dependent
behavior of state systems. Still another models of time triggered automata [4]
and PLC-automata [5,6] are used for code generation. Neither of these models
accounts for hierarchical structuring of states that is defined in the UML [7].

The goal of this paper is to present an original model of a finite state time
machine that extends the classical Moore automaton in the dimension of time.
The work is aimed at the development of programs for polling-type controllers,
i.e. programmable logic controllers (PLC) and their software-based counterparts,
known as soft-PLC. An early version of the model, described in [8], allowed for
only one running timer at a state (similar restriction holds for a PLC-automaton
[5,6]). What is new in this paper, is a support for several timers running at
each state, and a more formal treatment of the hierarchy of states and history
indicator defined in UML.

PLC controllers are used in industry for solving time- and safety-critical problems, like traffic or process control. A PLC controller is a device that has several

E. Gaudin, E. Najm, and R. Reed (Eds.): SDL 2007, LNCS 4745, pp. 117–132, 2007.
© Springer-Verlag Berlin Heidelberg 2007

inputs and outputs where sensors and actuators can be plugged in. The controller executes in a cyclic manner, and every cycle consists of the following three phases: Polling the inputs, executing the program and updating the outputs. Cyclic pattern of execution and the duration of each cycle introduce an explicit granularity of time, which is measured and guaranteed by the operating system. Output signals of the controller are discrete and change only at the edge of two consecutive cycles of execution.

Programming of a PLC deals with the computing phase of the execution cycle only. The core part of the computation relates to calculations of Boolean conditions that define the next state of the controller and the values of two-state output signals. The programming languages, standardized in [9], include: Instruction List (IL), Structured Text (ST), Ladder Diagram (LD) and Function Block Diagram (FBD).

A finite state time machine defines the algorithm for computing the output signals of a controller with respect to input signals and time. Once the algorithm has been defined, it can be verified and validated, and then converted into a target program code automatically. Because the translation of the model is formally proven, no further verification of the target program is necessary. It is worth noting that FSM-based models are recommended by IEC for modeling the behavior of safety related systems [10].

The paper is organized as follows. Sect. 2 provides the reader with a short overview of the subset of UML-based statecharts that are used in the paper. Sect. 3 gives a formal definition of finite state time machine that defines the semantics of the statechart model. The process of converting a finite state time machine into a program is described in Sect. 4. The description is illustrated using a case study of a plant controller. Final remarks and plans for future work are given in Conclusions.

2   UML Statecharts

PLC controllers are used in many real applications as part of a bigger system that consists of several components coupled and working together. The required behavior of such a system, and of all of its components, can be described by a set of UML-based models [11]. The conceptual tool that is offered by UML to model this part of processing, which is done by a PLC, is statechart – a model that describes the states an object can have and how events (input signals) affect those states over time.

Basically, statechart is a graph that shows how an object reacts to events that originate in the outside world. It consists of states that capture distinct modes of the object behavior and transitions between states that are caused by events and accompanied with actions. The modeling concept is simple and consistent with the theory of finite state machines. Relating this model to a PLC one can note that events correspond to the occurrences of input signals and actions correspond to changes of the output signals. States and transitions between states are defined by a controller program.

Modeling real systems that can have hundreds of states requires means for managing the complexity. Therefore UML adds further elements to this simple model:

- Hierarchy of states.
- Entry and exit actions of a state that are executed on entering and exiting the state.
- Internal transitions that are handled without causing a change in state.
- Deferred events that are memorized for handling in another state.
- Guards, i.e. Boolean conditions that enable or disable transitions.
- Time events that correspond to the expirations of predefined periods of time.

UML does not define any formal operational semantics for this model. Therefore multiple approaches have been developed and described in the literature, based on specification languages [12,13], graph transformations [14] or by converting the model to hierarchical automata and providing a semantics by a Kripke structure [15]. All those formalisms deal with a restricted subset of UML statecharts, extensively use advanced mathematical formalisms and are very hard to understand for software and control engineers.

The approach presented in this paper is much simpler and remains as close to the model of a finite state machine as possible. The effects of the extensions defined in UML on the semantics of a finite state machine are discussed in the rest of this section.

Hierarchy of states. One way to capture the behavior of a complex system is to describe its behavior using many levels of abstraction. UML offers hierarchical statecharts, in which a state can have many sub-states nested to an arbitrary level. Transitions between states can originate in and can lead to a state at an arbitrary level of nesting. A simple example of a hierarchical statechart is shown in Fig. 1.

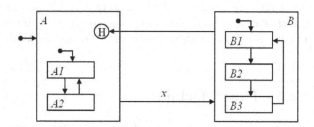

Fig. 1. A hierarchical statechart

Hierarchy of states alone does not add any new semantics to the model, in that a hierarchical diagram can always be converted into a "flat" one. In fact, an automaton is always in one of the leaf states of the hierarchy. A transition that originates in a super-state can be considered an abbreviated notation for a bunch of transitions that originate in each of its internal sub-states. The meaning of a transition that leads to a super-state is also clear, because such a transition leads to the initial sub-state of this super-state. For example, transition x from state A to B in Fig. 1 stands for a pair of transitions: One from state $A1$ to $B1$ (the initial state of B) and the other one from state $A2$ to $B1$.

The problem lies in the history indicator (circled H in Fig. 1). A transition that leads to such an indicator must enter the last sub-state on exit of a super-state. This way the history indicator introduces a hidden memory, which stores the last sub-state on exit of this super-state, which contains the history indicator. This can be expressed in the "flat" model by multiplication of states. An algorithm for flattening the hierarchy of states is described in Sect. 4.

Entry and exit actions. Entry and exit actions of a state can easily be reassigned to transitions that input or output the state. No new semantics to the model is added.

Internal transitions. An internal transition is a transition that performs an action without changing the state. This is equivalent to the concept of Mealy automaton, whose output depends on the current state and the current input, as opposed to Moore automaton, whose output depends on the current state only. Both types of automata have been proved equivalent.

Deferred events. A deferred event is an event, which does not trigger any action or transition immediately, but is stored in order to make a transition in one of the future states. Such a feature violates the rule that the only memory of an automaton is state. A state before observing a deferred event and the state after this event has occurred are different states that can be modeled separately.

Guards. Guard conditions deal with the attributes of an object in object-oriented modeling, and do not apply to modeling of PLCs.

Time events. A substantial extension to the model of a finite state machine is the introduction of time. A time event originates inside the automaton, and breaks the rule that the reaction of the automaton to an external event depends on the current state only. An additional memory of timers that measure the flow of time is needed. This feature will be treated in detail in the next section.

3   Finite State Time Machine

Finite state machine is a recognized tool for defining the algorithms of processing the enumerative sets of events. The automaton-like graphical models are formal, as well as understandable to engineers and computer programmers. What is missing in a classical finite state machine is the ability to model time. In this section we define a new model of a finite state time machine that adds time to the classical Moore automaton.

Definition. A *finite state time machine* is a tuple $A = (S, \Sigma, \Gamma, \tau, \delta, s_0, \varepsilon, \Omega, \omega)$, where

S is a finite set of *states*,

Σ is a finite set of *input symbols*,

Ω is a finite set of *output symbols*,

Γ is a finite set of variables called *timer symbols*,

$\tau : \Gamma \to 2^S \times R^+$ is an injective function, called *timer function*
   (with projections denoted $\tau_S : \Gamma \to 2^S$ and $\tau_R : \Gamma \to R^+$, respectively),

$\delta : S \times \Sigma \times 2^\Gamma \to S$ is a partial function, called *transition function*, such
   that: $[(s, a, \Theta) \in Dom(\delta)] \Leftrightarrow (\forall t \in \Theta)[s \in \tau_S(t)]$

$s_0 \in S$ is the initial state,

$\varepsilon \in R^+$ is the granularity of time,

$\omega : S \to \Omega$ is an output function.

Notation: R^+ is the set of positive real numbers, $Dom(\delta)$ is the domain of function δ. Cardinality of a set X will be denoted $card(X)$, and an empty set will be denoted ϕ.

It can be noted from the above definition that a finite state time machine is finite, and looks much like a Moore automaton with three additional elements: Γ, τ, ε. The rationale that stands behind the timer symbols can be explained as follows. The only memory of a Moore automaton is state. Adding time to such an automaton adds an additional kind of memory that stores durations of time intervals. This additional kind of memory is explicitly shown as a set of timer symbols. A finite state time machine responds to input symbols and timer symbols that appear when a time interval expires. Each timer symbol will be converted in the implementation process into a timer device that measures time.

3.1   Execution of a Finite State Time Machine

Moore automaton models a device that cooperates with its environment. The execution of an automaton starts in state s_0. The environment generates a sequence of input symbols $a_0, a_1, \ldots, a_k, \ldots$ and the automaton moves through a sequence of states $s_0, s_1, \ldots, s_k, \ldots$ such that $s_{k+1} = \delta(s_k, a_k)$ for $k = 0, 1, \ldots$. Each state s_k of the automaton corresponds to an output symbol $q_k = \omega(s_k)$. This way the automaton responds to a sequence of input symbols $a_0, a_1, \ldots, a_k, \ldots$ with a sequence of output symbols $q_0, q_1, \ldots, q_k, \ldots$.

A finite state time machine adds to the model the dimension of time. Each timer symbol $t \in \Gamma$ is a variable, which takes values from the set R^+. The current valuation of a variable t is interpreted as the duration of a period of time.

Timer symbols in Γ can be set in an arbitrary order defined by a function:

$t : \{1 \ldots n\} \to \Gamma$ where $n = card(\Gamma)$

Particular timers from Γ are now denoted $t^1 \ldots t^n$.

The current value $\tilde{t}$ of timer symbols can be described as a vector of values:

$\tilde{t} : \{1 \ldots n\} \to R^+$ where $n = card(\Gamma)$

The current values of particular timers are denoted $\tilde{t}^1 \ldots \tilde{t}^n$.

The execution of a finite state time machine starts in state s_0, with the values of all timers equal to 0. For a given state s_k and a valuation of timers $\tilde{t}_k$, $k = $

$0, 1, \ldots$, there exists a set Θ of expired timers, defined as:

$$\Theta(s_k, \tilde{t}_k) = \{t^i \in \Gamma : s_k \in \tau_S(t^i) \text{ and } \tilde{t}_k^i \geq \tau_R(t^i)\}$$

The machine executes in state s_k with the valuation of timers $\tilde{t}_k$, $k = 0, 1, \ldots$, by taking an input symbol a_k and moving to the next state s_{k+1} defined by the transition function:

$$s_{k+1} = \delta(s_k, a_k, \Theta(s_k, \tilde{t}_k))$$

When the machine enters a state s_{k+1}, $k = 0, 1, \ldots$, time advances and the values of timers change reflecting the elapsed time interval ε:

$$\tilde{t}_{k+1}^i = \begin{cases} \tilde{t}_k^i + \varepsilon & \text{if } s_{k+1} \in \tau_S(t^i) \text{ and } s_k \in \tau_S(t^i) \\ 0 & \text{otherwise} \end{cases}$$

When the valuation of timers $\tilde{t}$ changes, the set Θ of expired timers may change as well. This way a finite state time machine can respond to the flow of time, even if $s_{k+1} = s_k$ and $a_{k+1} = a_k$. Please note that the last argument of δ is a set of all timers expired in a given state and time, hence, no conflict exists if several timers expire at the same time instant.

Each state s_k of the automaton corresponds to an output symbol $q_k = \omega(s_k)$. By that means the automaton responds to an input sequence $a_1, \ldots, a_k, \ldots$ with an output sequence $q_1, \ldots, q_k, \ldots$. The output symbol $q_0 = \omega(s_0)$ depends on the definition of function ω only, and has no direct relation to any input symbol of the machine.

Finite state time machine models a time-driven device, which advances time with a fixed increment of ε time units. After each such increment the values of timers and the machine state are updated as described by the transition function. The device responds to a timed sequence of input symbols $a_1, \ldots, a_j, \ldots$ that occur at time $\vartheta_1, \ldots, \vartheta_j, \ldots$ [2]. The flow of time within the input sequence is not synchronized to ε-increments of the machine. This means that a finite state time machine may or may not capture a symbol a_j of a timed input sequence, if $\vartheta_{j+1} - \vartheta_j < \varepsilon$.

3.2 Examples

Example 1. Consider a train-detecting sensor [5] that signals 'a' if a train is approaching, 'b' if not, and '$Error$' if a failure of the device has been detected. The sensor can stutter for a time Δt after a train has passed the sensor. The control system is expected to filter the stuttering and to react on the '$Error$' signal immediately.

The behavior of the required system can be described precisely using an automaton that could measure time (Fig. 2). The automaton starts in state N and reads the input. If the train approaches, the input reads 'a' and the automaton moves to state A. Now the input can stutter, but the automaton does not react to signal 'b', until it has continued to be in state A at least through the period Δt. Afterwards, if 'b' still holds, the automaton returns back to state N and continues as before. If the input reads '$Error$', the automaton moves to state X.

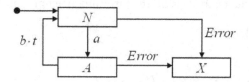

Fig. 2. Filtering device with detection of errors

The notation in Fig. 2 shows that a transition can be enabled by a combination of an input symbol and a timer symbol.

Formal definition of the filtering device can be written as follows:

$S = \{N, A, X\}$
$\Sigma = \{a, b, \text{Error}\}$
$\Omega = \{\text{no approach, approach, don't know}\}$
$\Gamma = \{t\}$
$\tau: \quad \tau(t) = (\{A\}, \Delta t)$
$\delta: \quad \delta(N, a, \phi) = A \qquad\qquad \delta(N, b, \phi) = N \qquad\qquad \delta(N, \text{Error}, \phi) = X$
$\qquad\quad \delta(A, a, \phi) = A \qquad\qquad \delta(A, b, \phi) = A \qquad\qquad \delta(A, \text{Error}, \phi) = X$
$\qquad\quad \delta(A, a, \{t\}) = A \qquad\quad \delta(A, b, \{t\}) = N \qquad\quad \delta(A, \text{Error}, \{t\}) = X$
$\qquad\quad \delta(X, a, \phi) = X \qquad\qquad \delta(X, b, \phi) = X \qquad\qquad \delta(A, \text{Error}, \phi) = X$
$s_0 = N$
$\omega: \quad \omega(N) = \text{no approach} \qquad \omega(A) = \text{approach} \qquad \omega(X) = \text{don't know}$

The granularity of time ε defines the responsiveness of the system. The response on the output to a change of the input signal cannot be guaranteed earlier than after time ε. The length of the acceptable delay has not been defined in [5].

Example 2. Consider a timed automaton [2], which measures time using two clocks: t^1, t^2 (Fig. 3). Clock t^1 is reset and starts measuring time when the automaton moves from $s0$ to $s1$ reading input a. A check $(\tilde{t}^1 < 1)$ in state $s2$ allows for a transition from $s2$ to $s3$ only within 1 time unit after processing a. A similar mechanism of starting clock t^2 while reading b and checking its value while reading d ensures that the delay between b and the transition from $s3$ to $s0$ is always greater than 2.

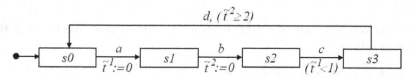

Fig. 3. Timed automaton

A definition of the equivalent finite state time machine can be the following:

$S = \{s0, s1, s2, s3\}$
$\Sigma = \{a, b, c, d\}$
$\Gamma = \{t^1, t^2\}$
$\tau: \quad \tau(t^1) = (\{s1, s2\}, 1) \quad \tau(t^2) = (\{s2, s3\}, 2)$
$\delta: \quad \delta(s0, a, \phi) = s1 \qquad \delta(s0, \xi, \phi) = s0 \qquad$ for all $\xi \in \{b, c, d\}$
$\qquad \delta(s1, b, \Theta) = s2 \qquad \delta(s1, \xi, \Theta) = s1 \qquad$ for all $\Theta \subseteq \{t^1\}, \xi \in \{a, c, d\}$
$\qquad \delta(s2, c, \phi) = s3 \qquad \delta(s2, c, \{t^2\}) = s3$
$\qquad \delta(s2, c, \{t^1\}) = s2 \qquad \delta(s2, c, \{t^1, t^2\}) = s2$
$\qquad\qquad\qquad\qquad\qquad \delta(s2, \xi, \Theta) = s2 \qquad$ for all $\Theta \subseteq \{t^1, t^2\}, \xi \in \{a, b, d\}$
$\qquad \delta(s3, d, \phi) = s3 \qquad \delta(s3, d, \{t^2\}) = s0$
$\qquad\qquad\qquad\qquad\qquad \delta(s3, \xi, \Theta) = s3 \qquad$ for all $\Theta \subseteq \{t^2\}, \xi \in \{a, c, d\}$

$s_0 = S0$
$\varepsilon = 1$

Output elements Ω, ω do not exist in timed automata and can be defined arbitrarily.

4   Program Generation

PLC controller is a device that cooperates with its environment through a set of input and output signals. The controller executes in a loop, which begins with polling the inputs and ends up with setting the output signals. What can be observed from the outside of the controller is a sequence of output signals, yielded in response to a sequence of the input signals. Cyclic execution of a controller can be described in a pseudo-code, which creates a reference model for PLC execution:

```
state = initial_state();
loop_forever {
    input = poll_the_input();
    timers = set_timers(state,active_timers());
    state = next_state(state,timers,input);
    output = count_output(state);
    set_the_output(output);
}
```

The operating system of a PLC controls the flow of time and executes the following actions:

- sets the initial state (*initial_state*),
- executes the loop (*loop_forever*),
- sets the output (*set_the_output*) and polls the input (*poll_the_input*) just between the two consecutive loop cycles,
- controls time flow and sets the expired timers (*set_timers*).

What the programmer must do is to write a code for:

- selecting the active timers (*active_timers*),
- calculating the next state of the controller (*next_state*),
- calculating the output (*count_output*).

4.1   Defining a Finite State Time Machine for an UML Statechart

The required behavior of a PLC program is defined by means of a hierarchical statechart (Sect. 2). The hierarchy of states can be described as a pair $H = (Sc, h)$ where:

Sc is a finite set of *states* of the statechart,
$h : Sc \rightarrow 2^{Sc}$ is a partial function, such that:
$\quad (\exists sc^0 \in Sc)(\forall sc \in Sc)[sc^0 \notin h(sc)]$ – there exists a root of the hierarchy,
$\quad (\forall sc \neq sc^0)(\exists sc' \in Sc)[sc \in h(sc')]$ – each but root state has a super-state,
$\quad (\forall sc, sc' \in Sc)[h(sc) \cap h(sc') = \phi]$ – the sets of sub-states are disjoint,

It can be proved that a hierarchy of states H is a directed tree graph. Function h assigns a set of sub-states to each super-state. The root state sc^0 of the tree encircles the entire hierarchy and usually is not shown in the graphical diagram of a statechart. The set of leaves of the tree can be defined as:

$$L = \{sc \in Sc : h(sc) = \phi\}$$

A compound state s of the hierarchy is a partial function, defined for each $sc \notin L$:

$$s : Sc \rightarrow Sc \qquad \text{such that: } (\forall sc \notin L)[s(sc) \in h(sc)]$$

It can be proved that for each compound state $s \in Sc$ there exists only one path $P^s = sc^0 \dots sc^n$ from the root state to a leaf state such that $sc^i \in h(sc^{i-1})$ for $i = 1 \dots n$. Path P^s will be called an active path in s, and the leaf state at the end of P^s will be called an active state, denoted $sc(s)$.

The hierarchy of states is coded into the states of bits (flip-flops) inside the PLC controller. The coding algorithm traverses the hierarchy in a top-down manner and assigns a separate group of bits to code the sub-states of each super-state. The result is a vector of bits, capable of storing all possible values of function s. A valuation of bits within this vector represents a compound state s of the hierarchy. Each such valuation is also a state s of the equivalent "flat" finite state time machine. This way the set S of states of the finite state time machine consists of all compound states of the hierarchy.

For example, only one bit is needed at the highest level of the hierarchy in Fig. 1 to distinguish the states A and B, one additional bit to code the sub-states $A1$ and $A2$ that are nested within the state A and another two bits to code the sub-states $B1$, $B2$ and $B3$ within the state B. Such a 4-bit coding covers all the possible states within the hierarchical state diagram. At the same time each particular combination of the four bits defines an individual state of a "flat" finite state time machine.

The other elements of a finite state time machine $A = (S, \Sigma, \Gamma, \tau, \delta, s_0, \varepsilon, \Omega, \omega)$ are defined in the following way:

- the set of input symbols Σ corresponds to the set of events that are assigned to transitions within the UML state diagram,
- the set of timers Γ corresponds to the set of time events within the statechart and the timer function τ is derived from the definitions of those time events,
- transition function δ captures all the transitions defined within the UML statechart in such a way that:
  1. Each transition of a statechart from a state $sc \in Sc$ adds to the domain of function δ one element for each leaf state sc^i that is nested at an arbitrary level within this state sc; each such element is a triple (s, a, Θ), in which $s \in S$ has the active state $sc(s) = sc^i$.
  2. The value of function δ for such an element is a new state $s' \in S$ such that the active state in path $P^{s'}$ is the initial state $s_0(sc')$ of the target, if the target is a state $sc' \in Sc$, or is a sub-state $s(sc')$ of the target, if the target is a history indicator within a state sc'.
- the state s_0 is the coded initial state of the UML statechart,
- the set of output symbols Ω and the output function are derived from actions that are defined within the UML statechart.

Granularity of time ε is the only element that must explicitly be added to the model, as UML state diagram is not of discrete type. However, as pointed out in Sect. 3.1, granularity of time defines a constraint for the timing within the timed input sequence, which is generated by the environment.

4.2   Mapping of a Finite State Time Machine into a PLC Program

The semantics of a PLC program, i.e. the meaning within its application domain, is a mapping, which converts a sequence of input signals into a sequence of output signals. If we establish a mapping between the input signals of a PLC and the input symbols of a finite state time machine, and another mapping between the output signals of a PLC and the output symbols of a machine, we can think about a finite state time machine as of a model of a PLC program.

The behavior of a PLC program is defined formally within the reference model by the semantics of its programming language, which may be one of the IEC 1131 languages [9], e.g. ladder diagram or structured text. The behavior of a finite state time machine has also been defined formally in Sect. 3.1 . By that means a method for translating a high level abstract model of finite state time machine $(S, \Sigma, \Gamma, \tau, \delta, s_0, \varepsilon, \Omega, \omega)$ into a PLC program can formally be defined. The method consists of the following steps:

1. Mapping of sets $S, \Gamma, \Sigma, \Omega$ into states, timers, input signals and output signals of a PLC.
2. Defining function *active_timers* consistently with function τ.
3. Defining function *next_state* consistently with function δ.
4. Defining function *count_output* consistently with function ω.
5. Code generation.

The mappings of sets $S, \Gamma, \Sigma, \Omega$ into states, timers, input signals and output signals of a PLC can be arbitrary one-to-one mappings.

5 Case Study

A bottling line (Fig. 4) consists of a bottle supply with a gate, a conveyor system, a scale platform and a bottle-filling pipe with a valve. Bottles to be filled are drawn one by one from the supply of bottles and moved to the scale platform by the conveyor. As soon as the bottle is at required position, a contact sensor attached to the platform is depressed and the bottle-filling valve is opened. The scale platform measures the weight of the bottle with its contents. When the bottle is full, the bottle-filling valve is shut off, and an operator manually removes the bottle from the line. Removing the bottle releases the contact sensor, and the entire cycle repeats automatically.

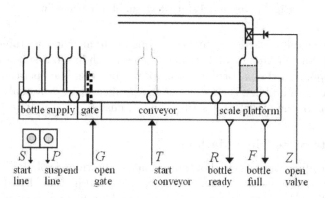

Fig. 4. Bottling line

The current line status is described by a set of two-state signals issued by the plant sensors and switches:

S start the line: A manual signal that enables the repetitive line operation;
P suspend the line: A manual signal that suspends temporarily the bottling process;
R bottle ready: A signal from the electrical contact of the platform sensor;
F bottle full: A signal issued by the scale.

The controller reads the current line status and yields the three control signals:

G open the gate of the bottle supply (a pulse signal of the length Δt_1);
T start the conveyor;
Z open the bottle-filling valve.

There are three different modes of control of the bottling line: *Working* (regular line operation), *Blocked* (when something went wrong) and *Suspended* (a

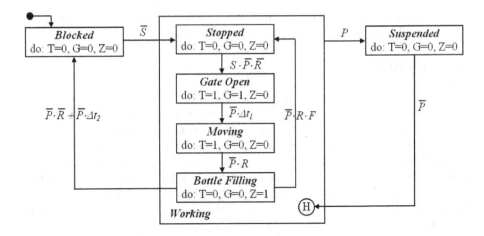

Fig. 5. Optimized state diagram of a bottling-line

maintenance mode). Particular modes of control are modeled as states of a statechart (Fig. 5). *Working* mode is a super-state, which has four sub-states nested that correspond to the particular phases of the bottling line operation.

The process of building the requirements specification, safety analysis and the optimization of the model, is described and discussed in detail in [8,16].

5.1   Finite State Time Machine

A selected coding for states and output signals is shown in Table 1. There are six states at the lowest level of nesting shown explicitly in Fig. 5 and listed in Table 1. However, the history indicator adds an additional implicit memory of the former sub-states of the state *Working* that are to be re-entered from *Suspended*. Hence, there are in fact four sub-states nested in the state *Suspended* that correspond to sub-states of the state *Working*.

Table 1. The coding of states (flip-flops: $M1, M2, M3, M4$, output signals T, G, Z)

$M1$	$M2$	$M3$	$M4$	Bottling line state	T	G	Z
0	0			*Blocked*	0	0	0
1	0	0	0	*Stopped*	0	0	0
1	0	0	1	*Gate Open*	1	1	0
1	0	1	1	*Moving*	1	0	0
1	0	1	0	*Bottle Filling*	0	0	1
1	1	*	*	*Suspended*	0	0	0

Finally, there are nine states, sixteen input symbols, three output symbols and two timers in the finite state time machine, which defines the semantics of the state diagram in Fig. 5. These sets together with the timer function and the transition function are defined below:

$S = \{Blocked,\ Stopped,\ GateOpen,\ Moving,\ BottleFilling, Suspended\text{-}Stopped,$
$\quad Suspended\text{-}Open,\ Suspended\text{-}Moving,\ Suspended\text{-}Filling\}$
$\Sigma = \{S \cdot P \cdot R \cdot F, S \cdot P \cdot R \cdot \overline{F}, S \cdot P \cdot \overline{R} \cdot F, S \cdot P \cdot \overline{R} \cdot \overline{F}, \dots, \overline{S} \cdot \overline{P} \cdot \overline{R} \cdot \overline{F}\}$
$\Gamma = \{t^1, t^2\}$
$\tau:\ \tau(t^1) = (\{GateOpen\}, \Delta t_1)$
$\quad\ \tau(t^2) = (\{BottleFilling\}, \Delta t_2)$
$\delta:\ \delta(Blocked, \overline{S}, \phi) = Stopped$
$\quad\ \delta(Stopped, P, \phi) = Suspended\text{-}Stopped$
$\quad\ \delta(Stopped, S \cdot \overline{P} \cdot \overline{R}, \phi) = GateOpen$
$\quad\ \delta(GateOpen, P, \phi) = Suspended\text{-}Open$
$\quad\ \delta(GateOpen, P, \{t^1\}) = Suspended\text{-}Open$
$\quad\ \delta(GateOpen, \overline{P}, \{t^1\}) = Moving$
$\quad\ \delta(Moving, P, \phi) = Suspended\text{-}Moving$
$\quad\ \delta(Moving, \overline{P} \cdot R, \phi) = BottleFilling$
$\quad\ \delta((BottleFilling, P, \phi) = Suspended\text{-}Filling$
$\quad\ \delta(BottleFilling, P, \{t^2\}) = Suspended\text{-}Filling$
$\quad\ \delta(BottleFilling, \overline{P} \cdot R \cdot F, \phi) = Stopped$
$\quad\ \delta(BottleFilling, \overline{P} \cdot \overline{R}, \phi) = Blocked$
$\quad\ \delta(BottleFilling, \overline{P}, \{t^2\}) = Blocked$
$\quad\ \delta(Suspended\text{-}Stopped, \overline{P}, \phi) = Stopped$
$\quad\ \delta(Suspended\text{-}Open, \overline{P}, \phi) = GateOpen$
$\quad\ \delta(Suspended\text{-}Moving, \overline{P}, \phi) = Moving$
$\quad\ \delta(Suspended\text{-}Filling, \overline{P}, \phi) = BottleFilling$

In all other cases $\delta(s, a) = s$ and $\delta(s, a, \Theta) = s$. These transitions are not shown in Fig. 5. The usual Boolean notation for the subsets of input symbols is used in the above definition of the function δ, e.g.: $S \cdot \overline{P} \cdot \overline{R}$ represents the set $\{S \cdot \overline{P} \cdot \overline{R} \cdot F, S \cdot \overline{P} \cdot \overline{R} \cdot \overline{F}\}$.

5.2 Program Generation

Each timer symbol of a finite state time machine is implemented within a PLC controller by a separate timer block of a ladder diagram. A Boolean condition that sets a timer depends on the coding of this state, which is assigned to the timer by the timer function τ. For example, the conditions to set timers t^1 and t^2 are the following:

(a1) Set $t1 = M1 \cdot \overline{M2} \cdot \overline{M3} \cdot M4$
(a2) Set $t2 = M1 \cdot \overline{M2} \cdot M3 \cdot \overline{M4}$

The transition function of a finite state time machine defines conditions to set or reset flip-flops. It is implemented by a sequence of Boolean expressions that depend on the coding of states, input signals, timers, and the definition of function δ. A complete sequence of Boolean expressions that implement the transition function is as follows:

(b1) Set $M11 = \overline{S} \cdot \overline{M1} \cdot \overline{M2}$

(b2) Set $M12 = P \cdot M1 \cdot \overline{M2}$

(b3) Set $M13 = \overline{P} \cdot t1 \cdot M1 \cdot \overline{M2} \cdot \overline{M3} \cdot M4$

(b4) Set $M14 = S \cdot \overline{P} \cdot \overline{R} \cdot M1 \cdot \overline{M2} \cdot \overline{M3} \cdot \overline{M4}$

(b5) Res $M11 = (\overline{P} \cdot \overline{R} + \overline{P} \cdot t2) \cdot M1 \cdot \overline{M2} \cdot M3 \cdot \overline{M4}$

(b6) Res $M12 = \overline{P} \cdot M1 \cdot M2$

(b7) Res $M13 = \overline{P} \cdot R \cdot F \cdot M1 \cdot \overline{M2} \cdot M3 \cdot \overline{M4} + \overline{S} \cdot \overline{M1} \cdot \overline{M2}$

(b8) Res $M14 = \overline{P} \cdot R \cdot M1 \cdot \overline{M2} \cdot M3 \cdot M4 + \overline{S} \cdot \overline{M1} \cdot \overline{M2}$

....

(c1) $M1 = M11$

(c2) $M2 = M12$

(c3) $M3 = M13$

(c4) $M4 = M14$

The expressions to set timers are placed in the sequence before the expressions that implement the transition function. This way the values of timers are updated as soon as possible after entering a new state. Moreover, they are stable during the entire program execution cycle.

Output function defines conditions to set or reset the output signals in relation to the current state of the finite state time machine. A sequence of Boolean expressions that implement the output function can be defined as follows:

(d1) $G = M1 \cdot \overline{M2} \cdot \overline{M3} \cdot M4$

(d2) $Z = M1 \cdot \overline{M2} \cdot M3 \cdot \overline{M4}$

(d3) $T = M1 \cdot \overline{M2} \cdot \overline{M3} \cdot M4 + M1 \cdot \overline{M2} \cdot M3 \cdot M4 = M1 \cdot \overline{M2} \cdot M4$

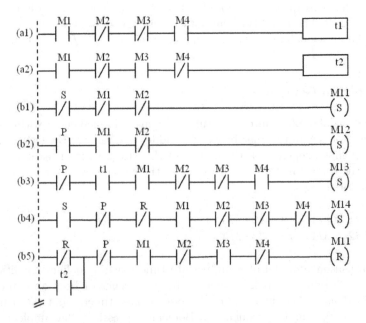

Fig. 6. A part of the program for a bottling line controller

The sequence (a1) ... (d3) of Boolean expressions, generated by an automatic tool from a statechart, or a set of statecharts, defines in all detail a program for a PLC. Such a program can be expressed in the language of a ladder diagram or an instruction list [9,17].

Each expression is converted into a single line of the ladder. Disjunction of terms is represented by parallel branches within the line, while conjunction of symbols is represented by serial connection of elements within a given branch. Negation of an argument is implemented by a normally closed contact. Each timer symbol is implemented by a separate timer provided by the language. A part of the program for a bottling-plant controller is shown in Fig. 6.

Finite state time machine can also be implemented using a procedural language, e.g. C. A description of such a conversion is outside the scope of this paper.

6   Conclusions

This paper describes an original extension to Moore automata, which is aimed at the modeling of time. The extended model is translatable, and can be used as a basis for automatic code generation. The paper describes a formal definition of a finite state time machine and a method for building the implementation. The application of the model and the method is illustrated by a case study of a bottling line controller. The advantages of the method are: Formality, simplicity, ability of automatic code generation and the potential for formal analysis.

A disadvantage is complexity that results from exponential growth of the sets of input symbols and states. However, the concept of input symbol helps in making the specification unambiguous, and the concepts of hierarchical state diagram and history indicator make part of the state space invisible to the modeler. The full size of the state space appears only at the level of a finite state time machine. Appropriate representation can make automatic verification of systems of 10^{20} states feasible [18].

The method described in this paper has been devised mainly for didactic purposes and has been extensively used within the control systems lab in order to implement programs for PLC controllers. The experience is such that the method helps the students in bridging the gap between their math knowledge and C programming skills at one side, and the reality of industrial control at the other. The first version of a tool for automatic program generation (ladder diagram for PLC) is currently being tested.

The plans for future work are aimed at extending the model towards concurrent operations that are allowed in the UML-based statecharts. Moreover, we are working on methods of model verification, preferably using UPPAAL model checker [19].

The size of code generated in procedural languages and the accuracy of time in generated code are open problems that are still waiting for research.

References

1. Alur, R., Dill, D.L.: A theory of timed automata. Theoretical Computer Science 126, 183–235 (1994)
2. Alur, R., Dill, D.L.: Automata-theoretic verification of real-time systems. In: Formal Methods for Real-Time Computing, Trends in Software Series, pp. 55–82. John Wiley & Sons, Chichester (1996)
3. Kaynar, D.K., Lynch, N.A., Segala, R., Vaandrager, F.W.: The Theory of Timed I/O Auto-mata. Synthesis Lecture on Computer Science, Morgan & Claypool Publishers (2006)
4. Krcal, P., Mokrushin, L., Thiagarajan, P.S., Yi, W.: Timed vs. Time Triggered Automata. In: Gardner, P., Yoshida, N. (eds.) CONCUR 2004. LNCS, vol. 3170, pp. 340–354. Springer, Heidelberg (2004)
5. Dierks, H.: PLC-Automata: A New Class of Implementable Real-Time Automata. In: Rus, T., Bertran, M. (eds.) AMAST-ARTS 1997, ARTS 1997, and AMAST-WS 1997. LNCS, vol. 1231, pp. 111–125. Springer, Heidelberg (1997)
6. Tapken, J., Dierks, H.: MOBY/PLC – Graphical Development of PLCAutomata. In: Ravn, A.P., Rischel, H. (eds.) FTRTFT 1998. LNCS, vol. 1486, pp. 311–314. Springer, Heidelberg (1998)
7. Unified Modeling Language (UML), version 2.1.1, http://www.omg.org/technology/documents/formal/uml.htm
8. Sacha, K.: Automatic Code Generation for PLC Controllers. In: Winther, R., Gran, B.A., Dahll, G. (eds.) SAFECOMP 2005. LNCS, vol. 3688, pp. 303–316. Springer, Heidelberg (2005)
9. IEC 1131-3, Programmable controllers – part 3: Programming languages, IEC (1993)
10. IEC 61508, Functional Safety: Safety-Related Systems, IEC 1998/2000
11. Douglass, B.P.: Real-Time UML. Addison-Wesley, Reading, Massachusetts (1998)
12. Aredo, D.B.: Semantics of UML Statecharts in PVS, Research report No. 299, Department of Informatics, University of Oslo (2000)
13. Börger, E., Cavarra, A., Riccobene, E.: Modeling the dynamics of UML state machines. In: Gurevich, Y., Kutter, P., Odersky, M., Thiele, L. (eds.) ASM 2000. LNCS, vol. 1912, pp. 223–241. Springer, Heidelberg (2000)
14. Kuske, S.: A Formal Semantics of UML State Machines Based on Structured Graph Transformation. In: Gogolla, M., Kobryn, C. (eds.) UML 2001 – The Unified Modeling Language. Modeling Languages, Concepts, and Tools. LNCS, vol. 2185, pp. 241–255. Springer, Heidelberg (2001)
15. Pintér, G., Majzik, I.: Program Code Generation Based on Uml Statechart Models. Periodica Polytechnica Ser. El. Eng. 47(3–4), 187–204 (2003)
16. Sacha, K.: A Simple Method for PLC Programming. In: Colnaric, M., Adamski, M., Węgrzyn, M. (eds.) Real-Time Programming 2003, pp. 27–31. Elsevier, Oxford (2003)
17. Siemens, SIMATIC S7-200 Programmable Controller, System manual, Siemens (1998)
18. Burch, J.R., Clarke, E.M., McMillan, K.L., Dill, D.L., Hwang, L.J.: Symbolic model checking: 10^{20} states and beyond. Information and Computation 98(2), 142–170 (1992)
19. Lamport, L.: Real-Time Model Checking is Really Simple. In: Borrione, D., Paul, W. (eds.) CHARME 2005. LNCS, vol. 3725, pp. 162–175. Springer, Heidelberg (2005)

Enhanced Use Case Map Traversal Semantics

Jason Kealey and Daniel Amyot

SITE, University of Ottawa, Canada
jkealey@shade.ca, damyot@site.uottawa.ca

Abstract. The Use Case Map (UCM) notation enables the use of graph-ical scenarios to model grey-box views of a system's operational require-ments and behaviour, in context. The scenario traversal mechanism is the most popular UCM analysis technique but its current tool support in UCMNav is limited and hard to use, and the high coupling of its fea-tures makes it difficult to maintain and evolve. This paper presents major enhancements to the recent jUCMNav Eclipse plugin consisting of a new scenario traversal semantics accompanied by enhanced trace transfor-mations to Message Sequence Charts. In addition, this paper identifies a set of semantic variation points which lay the groundwork for notational clarifications and user-defined semantic profiles.

1 Introduction

The *Use Case Map* (UCM) notation [5] is a part of the proposal for ITU-T's User Requirements Notation (URN) [1,10]. UCMs visually model operational sce-narios cutting through a system's component structure, providing a high-level, grey-box view of system behaviour in context. Because of their visual nature and apparent simplicity, UCMs are quickly understood by many stakeholders. Fur-thermore, UCMs are useful in various development phases such as requirements modelling and analysis, test case generation, performance modeling, and business process modelling, and this in numerous application domains[1].

Among the techniques used to analyze and transform UCM models, the *sce-nario traversal mechanism* is likely the most popular and best supported one. This mechanism essentially provides an operational semantics for UCMs based on an execution environment. By providing an initial context, called *scenario def-inition*, the traversal mechanism determines which scenario paths of the UCM model will be followed, until no progress is possible. There are many typical applications of such traversal semantics, including:

- **Model understanding and scenario visualization:** Complex UCM models involve many paths and diagrams that invoke one another. The traversal can highlight which scenario paths are followed in a given context (e.g., see Figs. 1 and 2). In addition, the traversed paths can be visualized in a linear form, e.g. by transforming them to Message Sequence Charts

---

[1] The UCM Virtual Library, http://www.UseCaseMaps.org/pub/, contains a collec-tion of over 140 papers and theses illustrating these topics.

E. Gaudin, E. Najm, and R. Reed (Eds.): SDL 2007, LNCS 4745, pp. 133–149, 2007.

(MSC) [9], hence avoiding the need to flip back and forth through many diagrams.

- **Model analysis:** Scenario definitions act like test cases for the UCM model itself and enable the detection of unexpected behaviour (deadlocks, races, interactions, etc.) as well as the regression testing of evolving models.
- **Test goal generation:** Once validated, the scenarios extracted via the traversal mechanism can serve as a basis for design/implementation-level test goals, e.g., in MSC, UCM sequence diagrams, or TTCN-3 format.
- **MDA-like transformations:** The traversal mechanism can use platform-dependent information sources on top of UCM models and scenario definitions in order to generate partial design models (e.g., in MSC or UML).

UCMNav is a UCM modelling, analysis, and transformation tool developed over the past decade. Though it includes a scenario traversal mechanism [2,3] and transformation procedures to various target languages (including MSCs [13]), it suffers from major limitations and usability, extensibility, and maintainability issues. jUCMNav, its Eclipse-based successor, is a complete re-implementation of the modelling tool which now supports URN in its entirety, i.e. UCM combined with the Goal-oriented Requirements Language (GRL) [16].

This paper introduces major analysis enhancements to jUCMNav by providing an extensible scenario traversal mechanism accompanied by trace transformations to MSCs. The new scenario traversal engine supports a more complex data model in addition to being designed for extensibility. Furthermore, this paper identifies a set of semantic variation points for which the behaviour is unclear in UCMs as well as potential alignment with common workflow patterns, laying the groundwork for notational clarifications and user-defined semantic profiles.

Section 2 introduces an example UCM model featuring an active scenario, setting the stage for the introduction of the new scenario traversal semantics in Section 3. Section 4 describes the new scenario traversal listener infrastructure which is used by the three-step MSC generation algorithm. Section 5 discusses related work and summarizes UCM semantic variation points; clearing up semantic issues is a necessary step towards future enhancements to the notation and jUCMNav. Section 6 finally presents conclusions and future work.

2   An Example Use Case Map Model with Scenarios

An example is used here to illustrate parts of the UCM notation and typical usage. It also emphasizes some of the complexities of the traversal mechanism and limitations of the current UCM notation. The interested reader can access more comprehensive tutorial material online[2]. Although the scenario traversal mechanism is only explained in Section 3, note that both figures in this section highlight a particular scenario in a different color (i.e., the active scenario).

---

[2] See http://www.UseCaseMaps.org and http://jucmnav.softwareengineering.ca/twiki/bin/view/ProjetSEG/JUCMNavTutorials

Our sample UCM model describes an online e-commerce front-end to a warehouse selling physical products. The company's business processes do not allow it to show real-time product availability on its website; because this process is manual, an unfortunate web customer can order a product that is not available in the warehouse. Should this occur, the web store will inform the user that his order includes back-ordered products. Consequently, the user will either decide to wait for the product to become available, cancel the back-ordered items, or cancel the order completely.

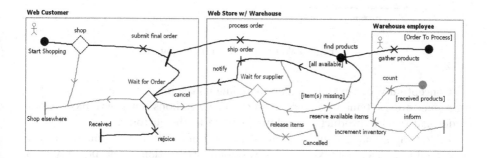

Fig. 1. Example Use Case Map with an active scenario

Fig. 1 describes the top level process which can be read from the *start points* (filled circles) following the paths until *end points* (bars) are reached. Along the way, various path elements are encountered such as *responsibilities* (shown as X's), *Or-forks* (mutually exclusive alternatives), *Or-joins* (path merging), and *stubs* (diamonds). *Condition labels* on alternatives and pre/post-conditions are shown between square brackets (the logical conditions themselves are formalized using a data model). Stubs contain sub-maps (called *plugins*) and can either be static or dynamic (dotted outline). The former contains only one plugin whereas the latter offers different possibilities and the one that is used is selected by the traversal engine depending on the stub's selection policy.

Fig. 2 describes the Wait for Order plugin map and illustrates a few other UCM constructs. The *And-fork* introduces the concept of concurrency in Use Case Maps and its counterpart (not used here), the And-join is used for synchronizing paths. Fork and joins can be used independently and do not need to be well nested. Looping paths are also allowed. Another way to model synchronization in UCMs, which we use here, is to make use of the *waiting place* (filled circle on path) or the *timer* (clock icon). Although both path nodes block until a connected path arrives, the timeout has the added capability of following a *timeout path* (zigzag symbol) if the connected path never arrives. Section 5 will provide insights on how the UCM notation could be enhanced with additional workflow patterns to improve the readability and precision of this plugin map.

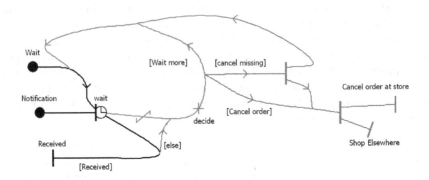

Fig. 2. Wait for Order plugin map

Conceptually, our example scenario highlights the primary use case where the customer orders items which are in stock. The warehouse employee receives the order, gathers the products and ships them off to the customer.

In [2,3,13], scenario definitions are composed of a list of start points that are triggered in a given context (a set of variable initializations), and possibly with post-conditions required to be fulfilled at the end of the execution. Responsibilities are allowed to change the values of the variables. Once executed, the traversal results are visualized as a coloured path over the original UCM.

The UCMNav implementation of this mechanism suffers from many limitations. The only data type allowed is Boolean. Conditions and assignments are described using a very simple action language with a non-standard syntax. The same start points cannot be triggered multiple times. Scenario definitions are not reusable, leading to scalability and management issues. The traversal is combined with a trace linearization algorithm (for MSC generation) that is prone to errors; hence it is difficult to debug and maintain. The traversal is rigid, without semantic variation points and without tolerance for errors (it often blocks if something unexpected happens or is not initialized properly). Only one scenario can be run at a time. Finally, UCMNav has a dependency on external tools for MSC generation (e.g., UCMExporter [3]) and visualization (e.g., Telelogic Tau), hence hindering usability. The following sections will address these issues and discuss the new solution implemented in jUCMNav.

3 New Traversal Semantics

3.1 Data Model and Operators

This section describes the data model and operators now available in jUCMNav. jUCMNav supports Boolean variables, integer variables, and variables of user-defined enumeration types whereas UCMNav only supported Boolean variables. All variables are global in scope, which is more appropriate for requirements (targeted by URN) than implementation. jUCMNav supports more operators to work with these data types and although they remain very simple, the set supported by jUCMNav greatly improves expressiveness for conditions:

- **Integers** {..., -2, -1, 0, 1, 2, ...}: Support for comparison (equals, not equals, greater than, less than, greater or equal to, less or equal to) and arithmetic operators (additive inverse, addition, subtraction, multiplication);
- **Booleans** {true, false}: Support for comparison (equals, not equals) and logical (not, and, or, xor, implies) operators;
- **User-defined enumerations** { {INITIAL, ACTIVE}, ... }: Support for definition and for comparison (equals, not equals) operators.

The concrete grammar is omitted here for simplicity but it should be noted that it does support the SDL syntax for these data types and operators[3]. The action language used to modify variables in responsibilities supports assignments and if-else statements on top of the operators listed above. The pseudocode parser was automatically generated from a grammar in Backus-Naur Form (BNF) using JavaCC/JJTree [11]. Integers were not added with the intension of supporting complex mathematical computations; their main use in UCMs is to better support loop constructs which were previously represented using complicated sets of Boolean variables. As for enumerations, they are well adapted to Or-forks or stub selection conditions that have multiple possible branches.

3.2   Metamodel Enhancements

The URN metamodel (implemented in jUCMNav [16]) was enhanced to support scenario definitions. The relevant portion is presented as a class diagram in Fig. 3. A UCM model can contain a set of scenario groups which, in turn, contain scenario definitions. A particular scenario definition is represented as:

- An ordered list of scenario start points, where duplications are allowed;
- A set of variable initializations;
- A set of scenario post-conditions (logical conditions expressed using the language described in the previous section);
- A set of scenario preconditions;
- An ordered list of scenario end points that must be reached during execution;
- An ordered list of included scenarios (for reusability and management).

Only the first three of these elements were supported in UCMNav. Our contribution to this model is the support of additional elements that make UCM scenarios closer to test cases. The UCM modeller can now define where the traversal should end, to facilitate model verification. Furthermore, scenario inclusion now allows a modeller to reuse existing scenario definitions and incrementally build the test suite. In particular, default variable initializations can be defined in one central location and overridden if necessary in including scenarios. This is also useful when new variables are added to an evolving UCM model.

---

[3] See http://jucmnav.softwareengineering.ca/twiki/bin/view/ProjetSEG/HelpOnLine

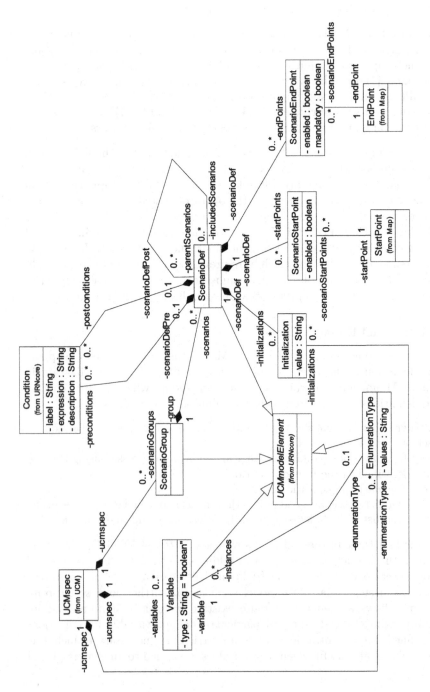

Fig. 3. UCM scenarios metamodel

All preconditions, post-conditions, start points, and end points are also included but cannot be overridden in the parent scenario: the union of these elements is always executed before the parent scenario's elements.

3.3   Architecture and Algorithm Overview

This section presents the scenario traversal engine's high-level architecture and algorithms. jUCMNav provides a default semantic interpretation of the various constructs according to common understanding and the draft standard, but as will be presented in Section 5, there are many issues that are up for clarification.

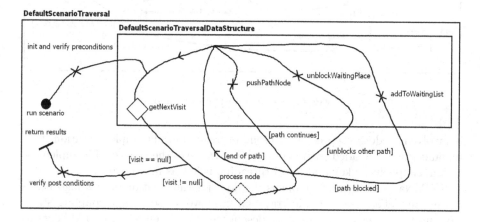

Fig. 4. Default Scenario Traversal

The default scenario traversal algorithm is architecturally separated in two: DefaultScenarioTraversal and DefaultScenarioTraversalDataStructure, as shown in the UCM of Fig. 4. The former defines the flow of control in the traversal algorithm and how each UCM path node should be processed, according to the default semantics of each path node. The latter encapsulates data structures such as the stack of path nodes that have to be processed and the waiting list (a queue of path nodes that cannot be processed at this time). By using a stack and a blocked node list, one defines a depth-first traversal algorithm. A breadth-first implementation could be trivially added by simply changing the stack to a queue inside the DefaultScenarioTraversalDataStructure.

The core of the traversal engine is represented here as the process node dynamic stub. Each path node is treated differently according to its type, related node connections, and related conditions. Section 5 will detail the ones that are particularly challenging. The traversal engine's second most important responsibility is to decide on the path node that should be executed next, which is defined in the getNextVisit stub and refined by the plugin map shown in Fig. 5.

The default scenario traversal data structure uses a node stack and a waiting list internally: this depth first behaviour respects the general traversal behaviour presented in [2] that was implemented in UCMNav. Because concurrency

DefaultScenarioTraversalDataStructure

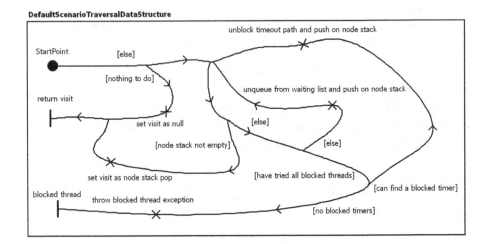

Fig. 5. Get Next Visit plugin map

is involved, it does keep track of pseudo-threads but the implementation itself remains single-threaded. As maintainability is one of the goals of this implementation, simplicity is key and multi-threading is left as future work.

jUCMNav's infrastructure opens the door for the creation of new algorithms by any modeller: our scenario traversal framework uses a low coupling strategy and the *chain of responsibility* design pattern [7], enabling tool builders to override the default traversal algorithm via a plugin to jUCMNav.

3.4   Validation Methodology

To validate the correctness of the implementation, jUCMNav's set of unit tests was augmented significantly. For the parser aspects only, over one hundred tests were created, to verify the correctness of the BNF grammar given to the parser generator. Furthermore, another fifty tests that make use of the new scenario features were created to cover the base traversal cases. The automated tests focus on the low-level aspects of the scenario generation, for the most part. As for checking the high-level behaviour, the MSC export plugin presented in Section 4 was used for that purpose. Although primarily implemented as a way to visualize scenario execution using a widespread notation, the exported files provide a manual mechanism to double-check scenario traversals.

4   New Scenario Export Mechanism

4.1   Scenario Metamodel and Existing Tool Support

The generation of MSCs from jUCMNav execution traces has been planned since its inception. In parallel to jUCMNav's creation, initiated two years ago, a team of undergraduate students created an Eclipse-based MSC Viewer that reads the scenario files generated by the old UCMNav and converted by a filter called UCMExporter [3]. This is no longer necessary with jUCMNav, which uses the MSC Viewer metamodel to describe the result of traversals.

jUCMNav exports the XML serialization of the metamodel depicted in Figs. 6 and 7 using the Eclipse Modeling Framework (EMF) [6]. The metamodel is heavily inspired by the XML DTD used by UCMExporter [3]. It contains concepts for groups of scenarios, component definitions and instances, and events, conditions, and messages ordered in sequences or in parallel (no choice as alternatives are resolved by the traversal semantics). The different types of events correspond to UCM path nodes traversed during execution.

jUCMNav creates a model instance using the information collected during a scenario traversal and serializes the result to a file. Working on this instance, another tool could generate an MSC (for use in Telelogic Tau, for example), UML sequence diagrams or TTCN-3 test skeletons.

4.2   Architecture and Algorithm Highlights

The transformation of UCM scenario execution traces to MSCs is implemented as a jUCMNav export plugin (available via Eclipse's standard Export menu). The export mechanism creates a .jucmscenarios file, which can be loaded by the MSC viewer. The MSC generator itself is implemented as a simple listener to the scenario traversal algorithm. This approach decouples the traversal from the export mechanism which in turn increases the maintainability of the application as a whole; a vast improvement over the older tools.

Simply put, the export plugin executes selected UCM scenario definitions with the MSC generator listening to the various notifications and iteratively building the scenarios. Generating an instance of the ScenarioSpec metamodel from the scenario traversal is actually a three-step process, which cleverly reuses jUCMNav's internal structure and scenario traversal mechanism: 1) generate a flat UCM while traversing; 2) make it well-formed; 3) export XML scenario.

First, the traversal listener generates a new URN model that represents a *flat* view of the scenario execution (a partial order without any Or-forks, Or-joins, or stubs). jUCMNav's auto-layout feature can be used to render the UCM diagram. This greatly improves debugging capabilities and this transformation has become a feature in its own right.

Algorithmically, the flatting process maps incoming notifications to the creation of a particular element in the target map. By reusing the same internal commands used by the UCM editor when a user builds a diagram, the new targetdiagram is thus syntactically valid. Each executed scenario is represented in its own map and the original scenario definitions are cloned and can be re-executed verbatim on the generated URN model. An example of such a flat scenario, generated from our example model, can be seen in Fig. 8 (left).

Second, the generated URN model is checked for well-nestedness according to the definition in [2]. If it is not well-nested (e.g., left part of Fig. 8), the model is transformed and additional concurrency constraints are imposed to

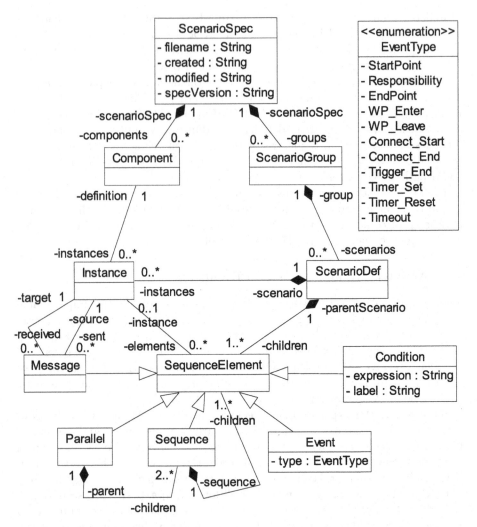

Fig. 6. Exported UCM scenario metamodel (1/2)

ensure that it can be expressed in a linear form (such as an MSC or UML sequence diagram). One well-nested version of this scenario can be seen in Fig. 8 (right). Here, the direction arrows carrying plugin traversal events (as metadata) are constrained to be executed after *process order* to make the result well-nested.

Third, the ScenarioSpec instance is built by traversing the well-nested URN model. The main complexity here is the synthesis of synchronization messages necessary to ensure causality across multiple instances. The inferred messages are based on the techniques presented in [3]. Additional simplifications were possible in our implementation due to a less restrictive architecture (UCM-Exporter was implemented as XML transformations) and because jUCMNav's

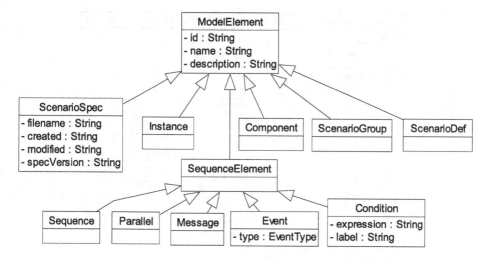

Fig. 7. Exported UCM scenario metamodel (2/2) - Model elements

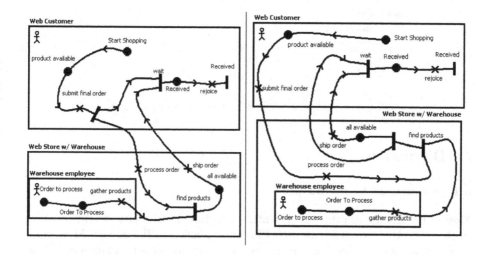

Fig. 8. Flattened scenario and its well-nested version

query framework was reused. This output can then be visualized in the MSC Viewer that is packaged with jUCMNav, as seen in Fig. 9.

In this transformation, UCM components are converted to MSC instances, UCM start/end points to self messages, UCM responsibilities to MSC actions, UCM timers to MSC timer set/reset/timeout events, and UCM conditions to MSC conditions. Explicit UCM concurrency (And-forks) is shown using MSC *par* inline statements. The inter-instance messages are synthesized to preserve the UCM causality, and names are created automatically according to the context.

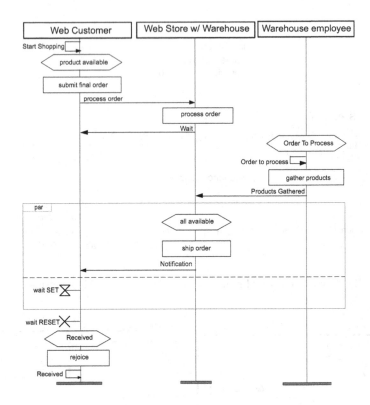

Fig. 9. Message Sequence Chart exported from Fig. 8

5   Discussion

5.1   Return on Contributions

Most of UCMNav's limitations presented in Section 2 and related to the previous work in [2,3,13] have been addressed in our extension to jUCMNav. More complex and usable data types are available, together with an action language whose concrete syntax is compatible with SDL. Scenario definitions now supportpost-conditions, expected end points, and start points that can be triggered multiple times. Scenarios can be included in other scenarios, hence improving management and scalability. Visual scenario highlight is supported; traversed paths and elements are shown in a different colour and offer a hit count indicating the number of times they were traversed. Multiple scenarios can be executed, enabling coverage analysis of a set of test scenarios. The traversal, linearization, and MSC generation are entirely decoupled, and intermediate UCM representations (with scenarios) can be exported, enabling other types of analysis and transformations. The traversal can be guided by user preferences (e.g., for the required degree of determinism at choice points), and the algorithms can be overridden by external plugins. Various errors and warnings are reported in the standard Eclipse way, and double-clicking them brings the focus on the problematic model element. jUCMNav also includes its own MSC viewer, which supports common features such as zooming, scrolling, outlines, and diagram export.

5.2   Related Work

He *et al.* used MSCs generated from a UCM model to synthesize a SDL model for a simple telephony application [8]. They recommended improvements to the UCM traversal semantics and MSC generation that have been addressed here. In particular, the synthetic message names generated for MSCs are used in a consistent way across scenarios, the MSCs now include conditions expressing the selection of plugin maps in dynamic stubs, and the UCM notation now distinguishes between actors (environment) and system components.

UML 2.x activity diagrams share commonalities with UCMs and the type of transformation discussed here could be applicable to the generation of sequence diagrams from activity diagrams. Störrle surveyed several transformations from activity diagrams to different semantic domains [17]. Some are done formally using denotational semantics, some are informal by examples, and others (similar to our approach) are done by algorithm/interpreter. Liang *et al.* surveyed other synthesis approaches for different notations [12]. In contrast with many of these approaches, ours handles path selection based on control variables of different types, scenario models that are hierarchical and/or not well-formed, submodels with multiple input/output segments, and complex component structures.

Bisgaard Lassen *et al.* proposed an approach to generate process descriptions (at the level of UML activity diagrams, Petri Nets, YAWL, or BPEL) from MSCs [4]. In essence, their transformation is the reverse of ours and could easily be adapted to cover UCMs as a target notation. Combining both approaches could enable a round-trip transformation process.

5.3   Analysis of Semantic Variation Points

During the traversal, many Use Case Map concepts could be interpreted in different ways. The semantic variations listed in Table 1 are related to the typical interpretation of the notation in its current form. Conceptually, the traversal pushes tokens along UCM paths. Most of these semantic variation points have a natural solution, often related to the initial implementation in UCMNav. Because no variation points were documented, the implementation was not questioned or re-evaluated. However, given jUCMNav's extensibility and the availability of the Eclipse environment (including the standard *Problems* view), more power can be given to the modeller in terms of precisely defining the expected behaviour and resulting warnings and errors.

The choices made by the default scenario traversal (Table 2) were mainly motivated by intuitiveness and simplicity of implementation; the hardest decisions are related to leaving a plugin map while dealing with concurrency. jUCMNav now supports user-defined preferences for several traversal semantic variations,

Table 1. Identified semantic variations

#	Element	Semantic Variation	Main Alternatives
1	Start Point	Precondition is false	Abort, Pause, Continue
2	Or-Fork Dynamic Stub	Multiple branches evaluate to true	Abort, Pick one (deterministic or not), Follow all
3	Or-Fork Dynamic Stub	No branches evaluate to true	Abort, Pause, follow random
4	And-Join	Not all in-branches arrived	Abort, Continue
5	And-Join	Do they have memory?	Yes, No, Hybrid
6	Multiple	Can block simultaneous instances of a node?	Yes, No
7	Timer	Both continuation and timeout path are enabled	Pick continuation, Pick timeout, Or-Fork Behaviour
8	Timer / Wait	Do they have memory?	Yes, No
9	Timer / Wait	Connected path arrives at unblocked node	Error, Pause, Continue
10	Stub	No plug-in exists	Error, Continue
11	End Point	Multiple different out bindings to fire	All in parallel, All in sequence, Pick one
12	End Point	Same out binding should be fired multiple times	All in parallel, All in sequence, Once
13	End Point	Post-condition is false	Abort, Pause, Continue
14	Scenario	How are start points launched?	In parallel, In sequence, Mixed

and the door is opened to additional options in the formalization of the UCM notation. Interestingly enough, a recent paper [14] evaluates the UCM notation in terms of its expressiveness compared to other workflow notations. The paper identifies a set of workflow patterns [18] that are not currently well-supported by plain UCM constructs. Although many of these patterns can still be modeled using a combination of constructs, they introduce contrived solutions such as in Fig. 2. The relationships between these workflow patterns and the traversal semantic variation points we identified are presented in Table 3.

In summary, there are three main modifications to the UCM notation and its tooling to inherently support a wider breadth of workflow patterns, such as those above. Because these changes are tightly coupled to the traversal algorithm, they provide good insight on the semantic clarifications that are required in UCMs.

- First, two slight notational changes should be made to both Or-forks and And-forks. Conditions should be added on the And-fork branches thus combining the concepts of alternatives and concurrency; this would greatly simplify Fig. 2. Such a feature would also cover non-exclusive Or-forks with multiple **true** branches (semantic variation 2).
- Second, stubs and plugin bindings should be enhanced to support the execution of multiple concurrent plugins and synchronization. This would clear up the main issues brought up by semantic variations 11 and 12 while at the same time greatly increase the expressiveness of Use Case Maps.
- Finally, to properly support these workflow patterns and to clear up issues concerning blocked elements (semantic variations 5, 6 and 8), modifications should be made to the UCM traversal engine in order to support plugin and component instances. Currently, each stub shares the same global plugin

instance, which does have its benefits in terms of simplicity, but greatly limits expressiveness. These changes may require variable instances local to particular components and plugins, as well.

Table 2. Default scenario traversal choices

#	Semantic Variation	Default Implementation
1	Precondition is false	Abort or pause, user-defined preference
2	Multiple branches evaluate to true	Pick one, user-defined preference
3	No branches evaluate to true	Abort or pause, user-defined preference
4	Not all in-branches arrive	Abort
5	Do and-joins have memory?	Hybrid (will soon change to yes)
6	Can block simultaneous instances of a node?	No
7	Both continuation and timeout path are true	Pick continuation
8	Do timers and waiting places have memory?	No
9	Connected path arrives at unblocked node	Error (race condition)
10	No plug-in exists	Continue only if stub has one *in* and one *out*
11	Multiple different out bindings to fire	All in parallel
12	Same out binding should be fired multiple times	Only fire exit path once
13	Post-condition is false	Abort
14	How are start points launched?	In sequence

Table 3. Relationships between workflow patterns and semantic variations

Workflow Pattern	Solution	Related to
Multiple choice	Or-Fork with concurrent branches, And-Fork with conditions on branches. Dynamic Stub with concurrent plug-ins	SV: 2
Synchronizing merge	Synchronizing Dynamic Stub with concurrent plug-ins	SV: 6, 12
N-out-of-M join	Synchronizing (n/m) Dynamic Stub with concurrent plug-ins	SV: 4, 6
Discriminator	Special case (1/m) of above	SV: 4, 6
Multiple Instances without synchronization	Use of replication factor on component or plug-in binding	SV: 2, 6, 11, 12
Multiple Instances with a priori design time knowledge	Synchronizing static stub with replication factor as fixed number	SV: 2, 6, 11, 12
Multiple Instances with a priori runtime knowledge	Synchronizing static stub with replication factor as variable expression	SV: 2, 6, 11, 12
Interleaved parallel routing	Component bindings and specialized traversal	SV: 14
Deferred choice	Specialized traversal	SV: 2, 3
Milestone	Specialized traversal	SV: 2, 3

6   Conclusions and Future Work

Providing an operational traversal semantics for the UCM notation and enabling transformations to MSCs present interesting challenges. In this paper, we have re-engineered and greatly enhanced the pre-existing scenario traversal mechanism, created a scenario traversal listener infrastructure, and identified relevant semantic variation points that will have an impact on the future of the notation and in particular on the traversal semantics. Our enhancements to the jUCMNav tool represent an important step towards a feature-rich, usable, powerful, and maintainable framework to support research and applications based on URN.

The first challenge we foresee is the implementation of the enhancements to the UCM notation described in Section 5.3. By directly supporting a wider variety of workflow patterns, the notation's expressiveness will be greatly enhanced. Once UCM's core is strengthened, the second challenge will be to reinforce URN's characteristic advantage in the niche of early requirement engineering notations: integrated support of goals (via GRL) and scenarios (via UCM) in one model [16]. Having the GRL goal model impact the scenario traversal mechanism (and vice versa) are forthcoming enhancements. Finally, aspect-oriented extensions to URN have recently been proposed [15] and will likely benefit from a good integration with the traversal semantics and MSC generation.

Acknowledgments. This research was supported by the Natural Sciences and Engineering Research Council of Canada, through its programs of Discovery Grants, Strategic Grants, and Postgraduate Scholarships. We are grateful to J.-F. Roy, E. Tremblay, J.-P. Daigle, J. McManus, and G. Mussbacher for various contributions to the jUCMNav tool, and to A. Boyko, T. Boyko, M. Kovalenkov, and T. Abumohammad for their MSC Viewer plugin.

References

1. Amyot, D., Mussbacher, G.: URN: Towards a New Standard for the Visual Description of Requirements. In: Sherratt, E. (ed.) SAM 2002. LNCS, vol. 2599, pp. 21–37. Springer, Heidelberg (2003)
2. Amyot, D., Cho, D.Y., He, X., He, Y.: Generating Scenarios from Use Case Map Specifications. In: (QSIC'03). Third International Conference on Quality Software, Dallas, USA, November 2003, pp. 108–115 (2003)
3. Amyot, D., Echihabi, A., He, Y.: UCMExporter: Supporting Scenario Transformations from Use Case Maps. In: NOTERE'04. NOuvelles TEchnnologies de la RÉpartition, Sadia, Morocco, June 2004, pp. 390–405 (2004)
4. Bisgaard Lassen, K., van Dongen, B.F., van der Aalst, W.M.P.: Translating Message Sequence Charts to other Process Languages using Process Mining. BETA Working Paper Series, WP 207, Dept. Technology Management, Technische Universiteit Eindhoven, The Nederlands (March 2007),
http://ga1717.tm.tue.nl/wiki/publications/beta_207
5. Buhr, R.J.A.: Use Case Maps as Architectural Entities for Complex Systems. IEEE Transactions on Software Engineering 24(12), 1131–1155 (1998)
6. Eclipse: Eclipse Modeling Framework (EMF), http://www.eclipse.org/emf/

7. Gamma, E., Helm, R., Johnson, R., Vlissides, J.M.: Design Patterns: Elements of Reusable Object-Oriented Software. Addison-Wesley, USA (1995)

8. He, Y., Amyot, D., Williams, A.: Synthesizing SDL from Use Case Maps: An Experiment. In: Reed, R., Reed, J. (eds.) SDL 2003. LNCS, vol. 2708, pp. 117–136. Springer, Heidelberg (2003)

9. ITU-T: Recommendation Z.120 (04/04) Message Sequence Chart (MSC). Geneva, Switzerland (2004)

10. ITU-T: Recommendation Z.150, User Requirements Notation (URN) – Language Requirements and Framework. Geneva, Switzerland (2003)

11. java.net: JavaCC^{TM}: JJTree Reference Documentation (2007), https://javacc.dev.java.net/doc/JJTree.html

12. Liang, H., Dingel, J., Diskin, Z.: A Comparative Survey of Scenario-based to State-based Model Synthesis. In: SCESM'06. 5th Int. Workshop on Scenarios and State Machines: Models, Algorithms and Tools, May 2006, pp. 5–12. ACM Press, New York (2006)

13. Miga, A., Amyot, D., Bordeleau, F., Cameron, D., Woodside, M.: Deriving Message Sequence Charts from Use Case Maps Scenario Specifications. In: Reed, R., Reed, J. (eds.) SDL 2001. LNCS, vol. 2078, pp. 268–287. Springer, Heidelberg (2001)

14. Mussbacher, G.: Evolving Use Case Maps as a Scenario and Workflow Description Language. In: 10th Workshop on Requirements Engineering (WER'07), Toronto, Canada (May 2007)

15. Mussbacher, G., Amyot, D., Weiss, M.: Visualizing Early Aspects with Use Case Maps. In: Rashid, A., Aksit, M. (eds.) Transactions on Aspect-Oriented Software Development. LNCS, vol. 4620, Springer, Heidelberg (2007)

16. Roy, J.-F., Kealey, J., Amyot, D.: Towards Integrated Tool Support for the User Requirements Notation. In: Gotzhein, R., Reed, R. (eds.) SAM 2006. LNCS, vol. 4320, pp. 198–215. Springer, Heidelberg (2006)

17. Störrle, H.: Semantics of Control-Flow in UML 2.0 Activities. In: Bottoni, P., Hundhausen, C., Levialdi, S., Tortora, G. (eds.) VL/HCC. Proc. IEEE Symposium on Visual Languages and Human-Centric Computing, Rome, Italy, pp. 235–242. IEEE Computer Society, Los Alamitos (2004)

18. Workflow Patterns website (2007). http://www.workflowpatterns.com

Automated Generation of Micro Protocol Descriptions from SDL Design Specifications

Ingmar Fliege and Reinhard Gotzhein

Computer Science Department, University of Kaiserslautern
Postfach 3049, D-67653 Kaiserslautern, Germany
{fliege,gotzhein}@informatik.uni-kl.de

Abstract. A micro protocol is a ready-to-use, self-contained, distributed component that supports structuring of complex communication systems, and reuse of well proven elementary communication solutions. Micro protocol designs can be formally specified with SDL. For documentation purposes and effective reuse, these SDL designs are augmented by further description elements, for instance, typical scenarios capturing the micro protocol service and the interaction of micro protocol entities. In this paper, we show how these additional description elements can be generated from an augmented micro protocol design specification. We have devised a tool that creates a PDF file, containing the complete micro protocol description with graphical elements and a link to the SDL design specification. Our approach enhances the maintenance of micro protocol libraries, and supports the consistency of micro protocol description elements and SDL designs.

1   Introduction

To master the development and maintenance of communication systems, *structuring* and *reuse* both play a key role. Structuring is essential to controlling complexity; reuse of well proven solutions is crucial to controlling quality and productivity. In [10], we have introduced the structuring concept of *micro protocol*, a communication protocol that encapsulates a single functionality and the required collaboration among micro protocol entities. Micro protocols are ready-to-use, self-contained, distributed components that support both structuring and reuse. They can be composed to form more complex protocols, and, finally, functionally complete, tailored communication systems. In several case studies [3,4,11], we have demonstrated the applicability of micro protocols.

A micro protocol can be defined operationally by specifying architecture, behaviour of protocol entities, and data formats such that functionality and required collaboration are covered. Following good practice in protocol engineering, we model micro protocol entities as asynchronously communicating extended finite state machines. To specify and compose micro protocol entities, we use SDL [6], ITU-T's formal specification and description language. SDL directly supports the specification of design components through SDL type definitions contained

E. Gaudin, E. Najm, and R. Reed (Eds.): SDL 2007, LNCS 4745, pp. 150–165, 2007.
© Springer-Verlag Berlin Heidelberg 2007

in SDL packages. Micro protocol entities are defined by specifying SDL block types, process types, composite state types, and procedures.

For documentation purposes and effective reuse, we have augmented the micro protocol design specification by further description elements:

- *Name* identifies a micro protocol. It refers to the essence of the design problem and its solution, thereby raising the vocabulary of the protocol engineer.
- *Version* identifies a unique state of the micro protocol description, corresponding to the development history.
- *Author* identifies the protocol engineer responsible for this version of the micro protocol description.
- *Intent* provides a short informal description of the micro protocol design problem and its solution.
- *Interface signature* identifies micro protocol entities and their input and output signatures.
- *Interface behaviour* defines scenarios of typical micro protocol entity operation.
- *Service* defines typical scenarios of how this micro protocol interacts with its environment.
- *Architecture* defines the protocol structure and connections between protocol entities.
- *Imported and exported definitions* lists required and provided data types, signal definitions, and agent types, together with syntactical reuse units (e.g., SDL packages).
- *Cooperative usage* describes the usage and composition of this micro protocol with other micro protocols.
- *Checklist* is a list of assumptions that have to be satisfied for the protocol to operate correctly.

These description elements capture design knowledge and support the selection and composition of suitable micro protocols by the protocol engineer. Micro protocol definitions comprising the additional description elements are archived in a repository called *micro protocol library*. In [4], we have introduced a specific development process for the design of communication systems based on micro protocols.

In order to work effectively with micro protocols, all description elements must be consistent with the SDL design. Experience shows that this causes problems, especially if several versions of a micro protocol are to be maintained, and if description elements are spread across several documents. In this paper we propose to use only *one* document – the SDL design specification – and to generate all remaining description elements by analysing this specification. We show that if the SDL design is augmented with specific extra information, this becomes feasible. We have devised a tool that creates a LaTeX file, which is then processed into a complete micro protocol description with graphical elements.

The rest of this paper is structured as follows. In Sect. 2, we show how the SDL design of a micro protocol is augmented to generate the additional description elements, and provide excerpts of the final output. In Sect. 3, we elaborate on the analysis algorithms that we have devised to generate typical scenarios capturing the service of the micro protocol, and the operation of micro protocol entities. Section 4 surveys related work, which is followed by conclusions and outlook in Sect. 5.

2   Micro Protocol Description Elements

In this section, we elaborate on the individual micro protocol description elements, as listed in Sect. 1. The focus here is on the extra information needed by the tool to generate these elements automatically from the SDL micro protocol design, and the results of the generation process. In this section, we will revisit some of the description elements and provide details of analysis algorithms involved. For illustration, we show excerpts of a symmetrical, reduced version of the Initiator Responder (InRes) protocol [4], which—due to its simplicity—can be described as a micro protocol. A manual for the use of our tool, together with the complete InRes example and the generated documentation, can be found in [2].

The tool presented in this paper generates LATEX sources. This has the advantage that layout can be handled separately, and that diagrams can be created

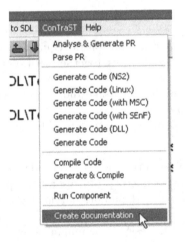

Fig. 1. Tau integration

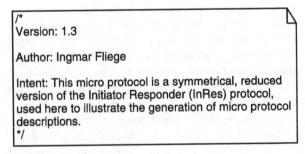

Fig. 2. Formal comments: version, author, intent

from textual output. In the end, a PDF file, containing the complete micro protocol description and a link to the SDL design specification is created.

We have also integrated our tool into the Telelogic Tau SDL Suite [13]. Fig. 1 shows a pull-down menu "ConTraST", which we have added to access functionality of our SDL-to-C++ compiler [5]. The last entry in this menu starts the generation of the micro protocol description.

2.1 Name, Version, Author, and Intent

The SDL design specification of a micro protocol, consisting of SDL type definitions, is collected into an SDL package. Micro protocol entities are defined by SDL block types, process types, composite state types, and procedures. The name of the SDL package is the name of the micro protocol, and used by the tool. Unlike the name, the description elements author, version, and intent can not be derived from the SDL design. Therefore, we provide extra information inserted into the SDL design as comments with keywords. For author, version, and intent, an example of such a comment is shown in Fig. 2. This comment is inserted on top level, i. e., at package level, and triggers the generation of further description elements. The tool extracts the comments from the SDL design specification and produces the output shown in Fig. 3.

InRes-Protocol   1
_____

Name: InRes-Protocol

Version: 1.3

Author: Ingmar Fliege

Intent

This micro protocol is a symmetrical, reduced version of the Initiator Responder (InRes) protocol, used here to illustrate the generation of micro protocol descriptions.

Fig. 3. Tool output: name, version, author, intent

Processing of SDL design specifications is done in several steps. First, a PR file containing all comments is generated, using Telelogic TAU. This PR file is then processed by the SDL parser of our code generator *ConTraST* [5], creating a complete abstract syntax tree. We have extended this parser to preserve the extra information provided by formal comments by adding corresponding attributes to certain nodes of the syntax tree. Our tool for generating micro protocol description elements analyses this syntax tree, and extracts all necessary information.

2.2 Interface Signature

The *interface signature* identifies, for each micro protocol entity type, the incoming and outgoing signals (directed arrows) and attaches them to gates (black

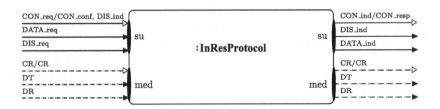

Fig. 4. Tool output: interface signature

ovals) (see Fig. 4). Based on an analysis of the SDL design, a distinction between signals exchanged with the service user (solid arrow lines) and signals exchanged between protocol entities (dashed arrow lines) is drawn. In the InRes example, all interaction with the service user is via gate **su**, whereas interaction between protocol entities is via **med**.

In Fig. 4, the interface signature has been augmented by documentation about used SDL design patterns [9]. In principle, this information can be derived if the application of patterns is supported by the tool chain (for a tool prototype, see [7]). In the current version of our tool, we add formal comments to indicate pattern usage. In the example, the patterns ASYNCHRONOUSNOTIFICATION and SYNCHRONOUSINQUIRY are documented. This is indicated by filled and blank arrow heads, respectively. In case of SYNCHRONOUSINQUIRY, the possilbe replies are listed after the slash. This shows how complementary reuse methodologies can be integrated into a joint documentation.

2.3   Interface Behaviour

The *interface behaviour* is described by a set of *local scenarios*, one per state and transition trigger, documented by message sequence charts (MSCs). Fig. 5 shows an elementary interface behaviour, consisting of the consumption of a signal DIS_req followed by the setting of a timer and the output of a signal CR. Additionally, informal text describing the scenario is generated, which can be generic and/or customized by formal comments in the SDL design specification.

If a transition is more complex, containing, e.g., decisions, loops, and connectors, MSCs with inline expressions are generated. Formal comments that further document decisions may be included in the SDL design; these comments are extracted by the tool, and included in the MSC at the appropriate places. Analysis of the SDL design and the generation of (more complex) MSCs will be treated in Section 3. If, in the state reached by a scenario, there is only one possible input trigger, then this scenario is merged with the subsequent one.

With each graphical symbol of an SDL transition (e.g., states, triggers, actions), an optional comment that explains design decisions or the purpose of certain actions may be associated. These comments are later inserted in the appropriate places of generated description elements. An example of such a comment is shown in Fig. 6. The individual comments are assembled into the informal text describing the scenario (see Fig. 5).

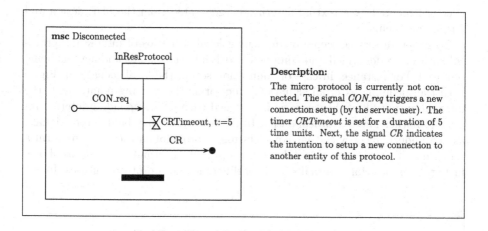

Fig. 5. Tool output: interface behaviour scenario with informal description

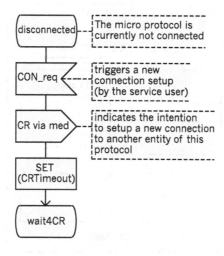

Fig. 6. Formal comments: transition documentation

2.4   Service

A core element of a micro protocol description is the *service* that is provided
by the cooperation of micro protocol entities. In the micro protocol description
the service is captured by a set of *global scenarios*, one per state and external transition trigger, documented by MSCs. A service scenario of the InRes
protocol is shown in Fig. 7. The scenario describes a connection setup, which
is triggered by an external signal CON_req. This is followed by a CON_ind issued to the other service user, who accepts (CON_resp) or rejects (DIS_req) the
connection. Dashed lines indicate internal signal exchanges. The service scenario

is complemented by a textual description, generated from the SDL design and formal comments.

To generate service scenarios, matching local scenarios of interacting protocol entities are identified and composed, with internal signals and actions being removed. For instance, in case of connection setup, the local scenario in Fig. 5 with the incoming external signal CON_req forms the starting point. Next, the internal output CR of this scenario is matched with a corresponding internal input of another micro protocol entity. In general, these may be different signals, as the underlying service that connects micro protocol entities may perform a renaming. To cope with this difficulty, we provide a formal comment as shown in Fig. 8, associating internal signals of different micro protocol entities. In the

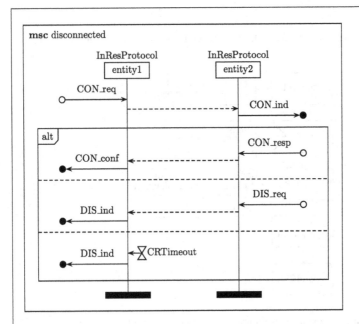

Description:

The signal *CON_req* triggers a new connection setup (by the service user). The signal *CON_ind* notifies the service user about a new connection setup by a remote host. Now, there are three alternatives:

1. The signal *CON_resp* indicates the acceptance during the connection setup. Next, the signal *CON_conf* indicates the successful setup of the connection.

2. The signal *DIS_req* triggers the connection release. The signal *DIS_ind* notifies about the loss of connection.

3. The timer *CRTimeout* indicates the failure of the connection setup. The signal *DIS_ind* is sent.

Fig. 7. Tool output: service scenario

```
/* Interaction:
InResProtocol:CR -> InResProtocol:CR
InResProtocol:DT -> InResProtocol:DT
InResProtocol:DR -> InResProtocol:DR
*/
```

Fig. 8. Formal comment: corresponding signals of interacting protocol entities

example, this is the identical mapping. The selected scenario, which consumes the internal signal CR and outputs a CON_ind to the service user, is appended to the triggering scenario, internal signals and actions are removed. Further scenarios are appended until the service scenario is "complete", which is indicated by additional formal comments (see Sect. 3). In the example, two alternative responses from the service user and a timeout are possible, which are represented by inline expressions in the MSC in Fig. 7.

2.5   Architecture

The *architecture* of a micro protocol is described by a simple diagram, showing protocol entities and their virtual communication structure. Fig. 9 shows the architecture diagram of the symmetrical, reduced version of the InRes protocol. Arrows with solid lines represent service access points, arrows with dashed lines express virtual communication among micro protocol entities. The tool also supports asymmetrical micro protocols, and architectures with more than two protocol entities.

2.6   Required and Provided Definitions

The design specification of a micro protocol consists of SDL type definitions, collected into an SDL package. These type definitions may be used by other SDL packages and/or SDL system specifications. On the other hand, the design specification may require definitions contained in other SDL packages. The required and provided definitions list these dependencies as well as the used SDL packages. Both kinds of information can be derived by analysing the micro protocol design. We omit the tool output, which is purely textual.

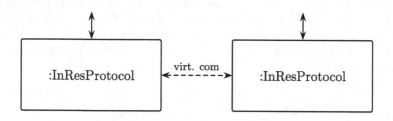

Fig. 9. Tool output: architecture

3   Analysis and Generation Algorithm

The generation of a micro protocol description element is triggered by a formal comment on package level, consisting of version, author, intent, and an optional checklist with assumptions that need to be satisfied for the protocol to operate correctly (see Fig. 2). In Sect. 2, we have elaborated on the tool output, and have pointed out the need for supplying extra information to enable the generation of the description elements. In this section, we will focus on the analysis and generation algorithm for the extraction of local and global scenarios, i.e. on interface behaviour and micro protocol service.

3.1   Interface Behaviour

The analysis of the interface behaviour starts with the transformation of the syntax tree into a simplified and aggregated form, consisting of a set of *Fragments* describing transitions. Fragments are represented by a tuple of origin *state*, an optional *label*, the *input* trigger, *timer* operations, *output* of signals, a list of possible *branches* within a transition and the optional *connector* or *next state*. Further components of this data structure are required for specific decisions and omitted here.

$$Fragment =_{def} \{ \, state, label^{0..1}, input^{0..1}, timer^*, output^*, branch^*,$$
$$connector^{0..1}, nextstate^{0..1} \}$$

Equation 1: Definition of a transition fragment

The set of *Fragments* covers all transitions, free actions and decision branches of the transition graph of a state machine. Details that are not required for the generation of local scenarios (such as expressions and tasks) are omitted.[1]

The simplification and reconstruction of the set of *Fragments* is performed as follows: Elements without signal transfer and without timer operations are removed, and the additional information such as the optional *label*, *nextstate* and comments are shifted to subsequent *Fragments*. The number of decision branches is reduced by merging the comments of branches with the same visible behaviour. Additionally, branches are reordered based on their boolean conditions, to provide a more uniform documentation. Finally, for each element without user-provided comment, a generic comment is created.

The SDL excerpt in Fig. 10(a) is represented by the following set of fragments $f_{1..6}$ (see Equation 1):

$$f_1 := \{ \text{ ``state1'' }, \quad - \quad, \text{ ``sig1'' }, \{t1\}, \{\}, \quad \{\} \quad, - , f_2 \}$$
$$f_2 := \{ \quad - \quad, \text{ ``label1'' }, \quad - \quad, \{\}, \{\}, \{f_3, f_4, f_5\}, - , - \}$$

---

[1] Expressions are analysed when the required definitions are determined.

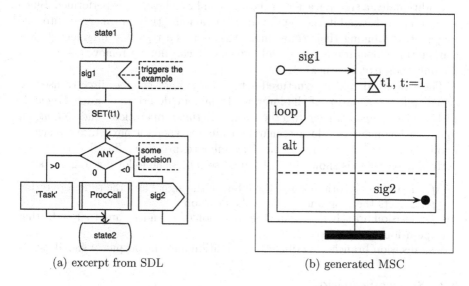

(a) excerpt from SDL   (b) generated MSC

Fig. 10. Example for the simplification and reconstruction

Fragment f_1 contains the origin state "state1", the input of the signal "sig1" and the operation on timer "t1". Due to the label between task and decision, the transition is disrupted at this point, and a reference to the subsequent fragment f_2 is inserted, holding the actual label and the set of further fragments representing decision branches. The comment associated with the decision is also contained in fragment f_2.

$$f_3 := \{ - , \quad - \quad , - , \{\} , \quad \{\} \quad , \{\} , \text{"label2"} , \quad - \quad \}$$
$$f_4 := \{ - , \quad - \quad , - , \{\} , \quad \{\} \quad , \{\} , \text{"label2"} , \quad - \quad \}$$
$$f_5 := \{ - , \quad - \quad , - , \{\} , \{ \text{"sig2"} \} , \{\} , \text{"label1"} , \quad - \quad \}$$
$$f_6 := \{ - , \text{"label2"} , - , \{\} , \quad \{\} \quad , \{\} , \quad - \quad , \text{"state2"} \}$$

Fragments $f_{3..5}$ represent the tree decision branches in Fig. 10(a). f_3 and f_4 describe internal behaviour, no signals are sent[2]. Therefore, only the connector "label2" is inserted. f_5 describes the decision branch with the output of the signal "sig2" and a connector "label1", yielding a loop. f_6 is a free action "label2", terminating the transition and leading to "state2".

By exploiting certain properties, fragments can be simplified and restructured. For example, for a given origin fragment, all branches and connectors can be traced recursively unitl either a next state or the origin fragment are reached, the latter indicating a loop. The same approach is used to determine whether subsequent fragments exhibit the same visible behaviour. For instance, analysis of fragment f_2 will reveal the existing loop.

---

[2] Procedures are currently not part of the analysis.

Additionally, a simplification of the decision branches $f_{3..5}$ is performed. Since f_3 and f_4 both exhibit the same visible behaviour, they are merged into one fragment, combining their comments. Although the resulting fragment f_3 has neither timer operations nor signal outputs, it can not be removed, since it is the only loop exit to a next state.

The simplified and restructured set of *Fragments* can be directly used to generate local scenarios of the interface behaviour description. Each *Fragment* with a given *input* trigger together with all *timer* operations and *outputs* of signals is documented. A local scenario terminates when the next state is reached. Loops and decisions are represented by inline expressions. The local scenario derived from 10(a) is shown in 10(b) and assembles the following fragments:

- f_1: describes the origin state, the input of the signal and the timer operation
- f_2: detects the loop and explains the decision
- f_3: decision branch, describing the condition of f_3 and f_4, and that no further operations are performed
- f_5: decision branch, describing the condition and the output of signal "sig2"

3.2   Service Scenarios

The algorithm for the provided service is more sophisticated, since the interaction of multiple micro protocol entities must be considered. First of all, the algorithm generates the number of required micro protocol entities, each capable of keeping its current state. The trigger for a service scenario is determined in a way similar to interface behaviour scenarios. However, the possibility of already documented transitions and the number of outputs and inputs of a scenario must be taken into account. A major difference between (global) service scenarios and (local) interface scenarios is that internal signal outputs are mapped to internal triggers of other micro protocol entities, with the signal type being hidden in the scenario description. This means that local scenarios are merged into global scenarios and additional language features such as enabling conditions and saves can be taken into account.

The reception of a signal can lead to a signal output to the service user. In this case, there may be a related response from the service user, which is considered to continue the service scenario. The expected reply can be either analysed by the algorithm, or can be indicated by suitable formal comments. The scenario is continued with all possible answers from the service user. Additionally, all possible timeouts in all protocol entities are taken into account. This procedure is repeated until either no further undocumented behaviour is detected or the algorithm reaches the originating protocol entity where only triggers from the service user are possible (see Fig. 7). For each scenario, the number of signal outputs to the service users in other protocol entities is predetermined in order to discard scenarios without visible behaviour.

In order to examine the overall behaviour of the micro protocol, the global state is held as a set of all traversed states of the participating protocol entities. The documentation terminates when all transitions of all states have been documented.

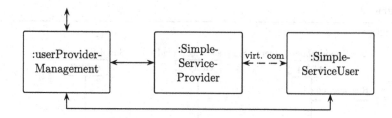

Fig. 11. Architecture of the AmICom service platform

Scenario 1

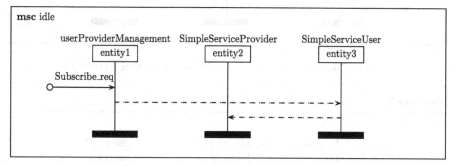

Fig. 12. AmICom: Unsuccessful subscription

Fig. 11 shows the generated architecture of our distributed service platform AMICOM, which consists of several micro protocols, specified as self-contained components in separate SDL packages. They are composed by use of inheritance to describe the two different service roles SimpleServiceProvider and SimpleServiceUser. A ServiceProvider represents an available service in the network, to which multiple ServiceUsers can subscribe. The SDL system of the AMICOM specifies one protocol stack interacting with the environment. The protocol stack is instantiated on each node in the network. Therefore, it is not possible for the documentation algorithm to determine the relationship between ServiceProvider and ServiceUser from the SDL specification. Formal comments (see Fig. 8) provide the necessary information. The process userProviderManagement coordinates the interaction with the applications using this communication platform.

The documentation algorithm extracts typical service scenarios from the SDL specification. In Fig. 12, one of the possible initial actions of an application is presented. The subscription of a service in the network (Subscribe_req) is unsuccessful, since no service has been registered yet.

The second service scenario (Fig. 13) shows the registration of an application service. The signal Register_req is sent to SimpleServiceProvider, which broadcasts the registration request in the network in order to determine whether the same kind of application service has already been registered. This message is processed by all instances of SimpleServiceProvider in the network. If no objection is received

Scenario 2

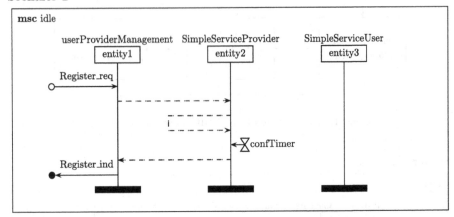

Fig. 13. AmICom: Registration of an application service

Scenario 3

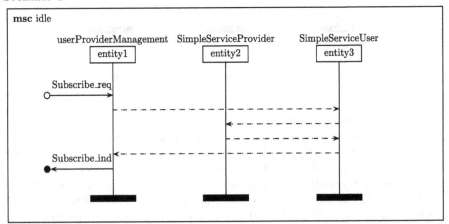

Fig. 14. AmICom: Subscription at an application service

within a certain amount of time, the timer *confTimer* is fired and Register_ind indicates the successful registration to the requesting application.

At this point, the algorithm considers traversed states of the participating protocol entities and can determine that the trigger from the first scenario (Fig. 12) now leads to a different, extended scenario. Therefore, the scenario with different initial states in each protocol instance is recreated (Fig. 14). This time, the Register_req is successful, since an application has registered an application service at SimpleServiceProvider. A confirmation is sent back to the ServiceUser and the application is informed about the successful subscription.

Further scenarios complement the service description of AMICOM, which describe the exchange of data.

4   Related Work

The integration of documentation into software models and the development process has been thoroughly studied in software engineering, and has led to numerous tools supporting the developer in the documentation process. Tools such as JavaDoc and Doxygen [14] examine specific comments in the code, which are then included in automatically generated documentations. However, these documentations only contain descriptions of static elements such as data type definitions, classes, and methods. The algorithms are not powerful enough to analyze the code and thereby find relationships and dependencies of methods or comprehend the behaviour. This originates from the language size and complexity. SDL, in contrast to traditional programming languages, facilitates a trace of the behaviour, due to well-defined semantics and the employment of a state machine model, and therefore allows the generation of abstract behaviour scenarios and descriptions. In [1], a tool for the generation of SDL specifications from MSCs is presented. In the context of our generated documentation, this tool could be used to merge the scenarios of multiple micro protocols, yielding MSCs that represent the interaction of micro protocols.

In [8], a transformation of transition graphs is presented, which generates a semantic interface description of SDL components. The authors address various language features that are involved in the transition selection and present a number of transformations. The transformations include the removal of symbols for internal signal exchange from the transition graph, which leads to a description with the visible behaviour of the components. The reduction of the transition graph tends to result in mistakes in the transition selection, e.g. when transitions are replaced by spontaneous or empty τ-transitions. For this purpose, the authors propose rules that maintain the semantic correctness of the specification (e.g. for the application of save). Furthermore, the removal of identical decision branches and the replacement of timers by spontaneous transitions leads to a reduced transition graph.

The documentation algorithm in this paper does not remove signals from the specification. The simplifications affect tasks, branches, possible loops, and connectors. Besides the simplification of the transition graph, the algorithm has to take all comments in the SDL specification into account and must not remove *Fragments* from the transition graph if they are essential for a meaningful documentation of the behaviour. Timers are also preserved and considered as periodically reappearing events or timeouts for an oberserved operation.

5   Conclusions

In this paper, we have presented an approach and tooling for the automated generation of micro protocol descriptions from augmented SDL design specifications. The approach further emphasizes the central role of the design model in model-driven software development: all relevant information is concentrated in *one* document. From this document, the complete micro protocol description, including interface signature and behaviour, service, and architecture, as well as the simulation and production code (see [12]) are generated. This enhances the maintenance of micro protocol libraries, and supports the consistency and traceability of micro protocol description elements and SDL design specifications.

Currently, the approach and tooling are being applied in several research activities and student assignments. In one project, we are developing a communication middleware for ambient intelligence systems, where several micro protocols are devised and composed. Another research activity deals with complex routing protocols composed from micro protocols, supporting different kinds of addressing mechanisms and topological situations in wireless ad-hoc networks. In further projects, we are devising quality-of-service protocols for ad-hoc networks, with elementary components defined as micro protocols. In all these activities, the automated generation of micro protocol descriptions is a great support.

Certainly, there is still room for improving the tooling presented in this paper. For instance, the algorithms sketched in Sect. 3 can be extended to deal with additional SDL language features, specially procedure calls. Also, a tighter integration of the generated description elements and the SDL design specification by adding further links leading to corresponding excerpts of the SDL design appears feasible. An analysis of the importance of scenarios, together with some heuristics, may improve the value of the generated description elements for the developer. Finally, further description elements to deal with macro protocols resulting from the composition of micro protocols should be considered.

References

1. Khendek, F., Robert, G., Butler, G., Grogono, P.: Implementability of Message Sequence Charts. In: Proceedings of the SDL Forum Society International Workshop on SDL and MSC, Berlin, Germany (June 29 - July 01, 1998)
2. Fliege, I.: Documentation of micro protocols. Technical Report 358/07 (2007), http://vs.informatik.uni-kl.de/publications/2007/F12007/
3. Fliege, I., Geraldy, A., Gotzhein, R.: Micro Protocol Based Design of Routing Protocols for Ad-hoc Networks. In: 7th International Conference on New Technologies of Distributed Systems (NOTERE 2007), Marrakesh, Morocco (June 4-8, 2007)
4. Fliege, I., Geraldy, A., Gotzhein, R., Schaible, P.: A Flexible Micro Protocol Framework. In: Amyot, D., Williams, A.W. (eds.) SAM 2004. LNCS, vol. 3319, pp. 224–236. Springer, Heidelberg (2005)
5. Fliege, I., Grammes, R., Weber, C.: ConTraST - A Configurable SDL Transpiler And Runtime Environment. In: Gotzhein, R., Reed, R. (eds.) SAM 2006. LNCS, vol. 4320, pp. 216–228. Springer, Heidelberg (2006)
6. ITU Recommendation Z.100 (08/02). Specification and Description Language (SDL). Geneva (2002)
7. Dorsch, J., Ek, A., Gotzhein, R.: SPT - The SDL Pattern Tool. In: Amyot, D., Williams, A.W. (eds.) SAM 2004. LNCS, vol. 3319, pp. 50–64. Springer, Heidelberg (2005)
8. Floch, J., Bræk, R.: Using Projections for the Detection of Anomalous Behaviors. In: Reed, R. (ed.) SDL 2001. LNCS, vol. 2078, pp. 251–268. Springer, Heidelberg (2001)
9. Gotzhein, R.: Consolidating and Applying the SDL-Pattern Approach: A Detailed Case Study. Information and Software Technology 45, 727–741 (2003)

10. Gotzhein, R., Khendek, F.: Conception avec Micro-Protocoles. In: Colloque Franco-phone sur l'Ingenierie des Protocoles (CFIP'2002), Montreal, Canada (May 27-30, 2002)
11. Gotzhein, R., Khendek, F., Schaible, P.: Micro Protocol Design - The SNMP Case Study. In: Sherratt, E. (ed.) SAM 2002. LNCS, vol. 2599, pp. 61–73. Springer, Heidelberg (2003)
12. Kuhn, T., Gotzhein, R., Webel, C.: Model-driven development with sdl - process, tools, and experiences. In: ACM/IEEE 9th International Conference on Model Driven Engineering Languages and Systems (MoDELS / UML 2006), Genua, Italy, October 1-6, 2006, pp. 1–6. IEEE Computer Society Press, Los Alamitos (2006)
13. Telelogic AB. Telelogic Tau Generation 1, www.telelogic.com/products/tau/index.cfm
14. van Heesch, D.: Doxygen (2001), http://stack.nl/~dimitri/doxygen/

Synthesizing Components with Sessions from Collaboration-Oriented Service Specifications

Frank Alexander Kraemer, Rolv Bræk, and Peter Herrmann

Norwegian University of Science and Technology (NTNU),
Department of Telematics, N-7491 Trondheim, Norway
{kraemer, rolv.braek, herrmann}@item.ntnu.no

Abstract. A fundamental problem in the area of service engineering is the so-called cross-cutting nature of services, i.e., that service behavior results from a collaboration of partial component behaviors. We present an approach for model-based service engineering, in which system component models are derived automatically from collaboration models. These are specifications of sub-services incorporating both the local behavior of the components and the necessary inter-component communication. The collaborations are expressed in a compact and self-contained way by UML collaborations and activities. The UML activities can express service compositions precisely, so that components may be derived automatically by means of a model transformation. In this paper, we focus on the important issue of how to coordinate and compose collaborations that are executed with several sessions at the same time. We introduce an extension to activities for session selection. Moreover, we explain how this composition is mapped onto the components and how it can be translated into executable code.

1 Introduction

In its early days, reactive software was mainly structured into activities that could be scheduled in order to satisfy real-time requirements. As a result, the rather complex and stateful behavior associated with each individual service session and resource usage was fragmented and the overall behavior was often difficult to grasp, resulting in quality errors and costly maintenance.

The situation was considerably improved by the introduction of state machines modeling stateful behavior combined with *object-based* and later *object-oriented* structuring. By representing individual resources and sessions as state machines, their behavior could be explicitly and completely defined. This principle helped to substantially improve quality and modularity, and therefore became a widespread approach. It also facilitates the separation between abstract behavior specifications and implementation, and enabled model-driven development in which executable code is generated automatically from state machines. SDL [1] was developed as a language to support this approach and, considering its adoption and support, we must say that it has been successful at it.

E. Gaudin, E. Najm, and R. Reed (Eds.): SDL 2007, LNCS 4745, pp. 166–185, 2007.

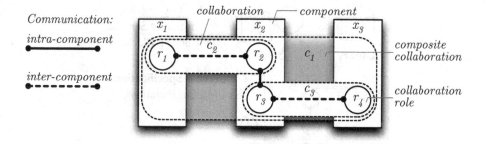

Fig. 1. Relationships between components and collaborations

However, there is a fundamental problem. Service behavior is normally distributed among several collaborating objects, while objects take part in several different services. By structuring according to objects, the behavior of each individual object can be defined precisely and completely, while the behavior of a service is distributed across the objects. This is often referred to as the "crosscutting" nature of services [2,3,4], and is one of the underlying reasons why compositional service engineering is such a challenge. Fundamentally, the behavior of services is composed from partial object behaviors, while object behaviors are composed from partial service behaviors.

A promising step forward to solve this problem is to adopt a *collaboration-oriented* approach, where the main structuring units are formal specifications of services containing both the partial object behavior and the interactions between the objects needed to fulfill the service. These specifications are called collaborations. Albeit many of the underlying ideas have been around for a long time [6,7], the new concept of UML 2.0 collaborations [5] provides a modeling framework that opens many interesting opportunities not fully utilized yet. First of all, collaborations model the concept of a service very nicely. They define a structure of partial object behaviors, the collaboration roles, and enable a precise definition of the service behavior. They also provide a way to compose services by means of collaboration uses and role bindings.

Figure 1 shows a coarse system architecture illustrating the relations between collaborations and objects (referred to as components in the following). A service is delivered by the joint behavior of the components x_1 to x_3, which may be physically distributed. The service described by collaboration c_1 can be composed from the two sub-services modeled by collaborations c_2 and c_3. The necessary partial object behavior used to realize the collaborations is represented by so-called collaboration roles r_1 to r_4. Note how the collaborations cut across the components and define inter-component behavior. Orthogonal to this, component behavior is defined by composition of collaboration roles. Communication between components is assumed to be based on asynchronous message passing only (cf. [8]), while communication within one component may also use shared variables and synchronously executed actions (i.e., an event in one collaboration can cause actions in another collaboration).

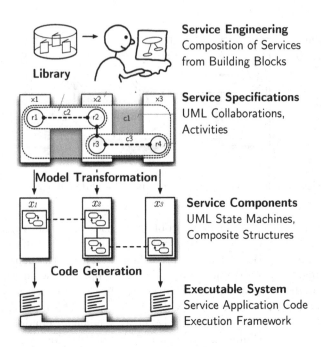

Fig. 2. Service Engineering Approach

We have found that collaboration-oriented decomposition tends to result in sub-collaborations corresponding to interfaces and service features [9] with behavior of limited complexity that may be defined completely and be reused in many different services. This simplifies the task of defining inter-component behavior and separates it from the intra-component composition. It has been shown in [10,11] that collaborations also provide a basis for analysis and removal of errors at a higher level of abstraction than detailed interactions.

A well established approach is to model "horizontal" collaborative behavior using MSCs or UML sequence diagrams. They provide the desired overview, but will normally not be used to define the complete behavior. In this paper, we present our approach (see also [13,14]) in which the complete behavior of collaborations is defined using UML activity diagrams. We offer an extension to UML that enables to compose also behavior that is executed simultaneously in several sessions. This enables a complete and precise definition of the inter-component behavior of each collaboration as well as the intra-component behavior composition of collaborations, without the need to specify interaction details. The approach enables an automatic synthesis of component behaviors in the form of state machines from which executable code is automatically generated, as illustrated in Figure 2. By defining the semantics of activities and state machines using the temporal logic cTLA [12], we are able to verify by formal implication proofs that the transformations of the collaboration-oriented models to the state machines are correct (see [13]). This formal aspect, however, is not the

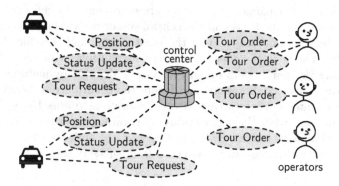

Fig. 3. Illustration of the system

focus of this paper. In the following we first introduce the collaboration-oriented specification approach by means of an example, and show how multiple session instances can be coordinated. Afterwards, we describe the transformation from collaboration to component behavior.

2 Collaborations

In Fig. 3 we introduce a taxi control system. Several taxis are connected to a control center, and update their status (*busy* or *free*) and their current position. Operators accept tour orders from customers via telephone. These orders are processed by the control center which sends out tour requests to the taxis. Taxis may also accept customers directly from the street, which is reported to the control center by a status update to *busy*. Fig. 4 defines this as a UML 2.0

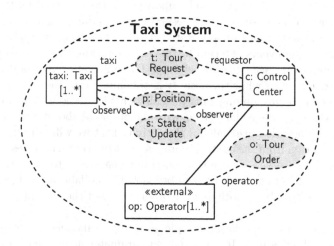

Fig. 4. UML Collaboration

collaboration. Participants in the service are represented by collaboration roles *taxi*, *c*, and *op*. For the taxis and the control center we will later generate components. The operators are part of the environment and therefore labeled as ≪external≫. The control center *c* has a default multiplicity of one, while there can be many taxis and operators in the system, denoted by multiplicity [1..*]. Between the roles, collaboration uses denote the occurrence of behavior: taxis and control center are interacting with collaborations *Status Update*, *Position* and *Tour Request*, while the operators are cooperating with the control center by means of collaboration *Tour Order*. In this way, the entire service, represented as collaboration *Taxi System*, is composed from sub-services.

2.1   Describing Behavior of Collaborations

Besides being a so-called *UML structured classifier* with parts and connectors as shown in Fig. 4, a collaboration is also a *behaviored classifier* and may as such have behavior attached, for example state machines, sequence diagrams or activities. As mentioned in the introduction, we use activity diagrams. They present complete behavior in a quite compact form and may define connections to other behaviors via input and output pins. In [14,15] we showed how service models can be easily composed of reusable building blocks expressed as activities.

The activity *Status Update* (Fig. 5) describes the behavior of the corresponding collaboration. It has one partition for each collaboration role: *observer* and *observed*. As depicted in Fig. 4, these roles are bound to *c* and *taxi*, so that the observer is the control center that observes a taxi. A pleasant feature of our approach is that we can first study and specify the behavior of the control center towards *one* taxi and we later compose this behavior, so that the control center may handle several taxis.

Activities base their semantics on token flow [5, p.319]. Hence, a token is placed into the initial node of the observer in Fig. 5 when the system starts. The token moves through the merge node, upon which the observed party sends its current status to the observer. The observer then updates its local variable *s2*. From then on, the taxi pushes any status change to the control center. As these changes depend on events external to this collaboration, they are expressed by the parameter nodes *set free* and *set busy*. These are *streaming* nodes through which tokens may pass while the activity is ongoing. Later, the parameter nodes (represented by corresponding pins on call behavior actions) will be used to couple the *status update* collaboration with the other collaborations. In addition, we defined an operation *available* for the activity that we will later use to access the status of a taxi from the control center. As this operation accesses variable *s2* localized in the observer, we use the constraint {*observer*} to mark that it may only be accessed from the side of the observer. The collaboration *Position* (not shown) works similarly by notifying the observer about the current geographical position.

The collaboration *Tour Request* depicted in Fig. 6 models the process of notifying a taxi about a tour. It is started via parameter node *request tour*, which starts timer *t* and places a token in waiting decision node *w*. A waiting decision

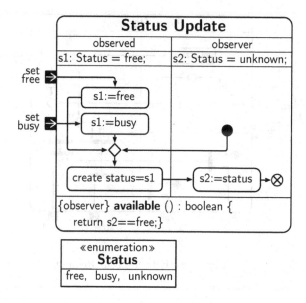

Fig. 5. Activity for Status Update

node is the extension of a decision node with the difference that it may hold a token similar to an initial node, as defined in [13]. w is used in combination with join nodes $j1$ and $j2$ to explicitly model the race between the acceptance of the tour by the driver and the timeout mechanism. Another flow is forwarded to the taxi which first checks its status. This is necessary as the taxi can in fact be busy even if it was available when the requestor started. This is due to the inevitable delay of signals between the distributed components, so that the taxi may have accepted a customer from the street while a request is on its way. In general, the flows between the control center and the taxi (as well as all other flows crossing partitions) are buffered. We describe this in a so-called execution profile (see [5, p. 321]) for our service specifications [16] and model it by implicit queue places, as described in [13]. If the taxi is still free, the control flow is handed over to some external control not part of this collaboration. If the taxi driver accepts the tour, the control flow returns, and a token is offered to join node $j1$. If w still has its token, $j1$ can fire, emit a token on *accepted* on the requestor side, and then terminate the collaboration on the taxi side with an activity final node and output node *accepted*[1]. In case the taxi turned busy or a timeout occurs, a token is offered to $j2$. It fires if w still has its token, so that the collaboration first notifies the requestor upon the cancelation and then terminates the collaboration on the taxi side.

Note that the events *accept tour* and the timeout may both happen, as they are initiated by different parties. This is a so-called mixed initiative [18] that

---

[1] As this ending is alternative to the cancelation of a tour request, it must be expressed by its own UML parameter set, denoted by the additional box around the node.

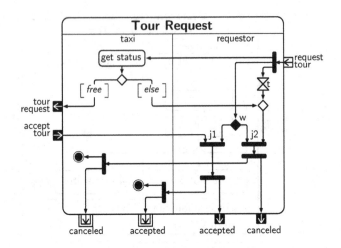

Fig. 6. Activity for Tour Request

must be resolved to prevent erroneous behavior in which one side accepts the request while the other one considers the request as canceled. The taxi therefore sends the acceptance of a tour first to the requestor and waits for a confirmation; if the timer expired in the meantime, the acceptance is intercepted in *j1* and the collaboration terminates consistently with *canceled* on both sides.

2.2 Composing Collaborations with Activities

To generate state machines, components and finally the executable code for the system components, the structural information about how the collaborations are composed (as shown in Fig. 4) is not sufficient. In fact, we need to specify in detail how the different events of collaborations are coupled so that the desired overall behavior is obtained. For this purpose we use UML activities as well, as they allow us to specify *the coordination of executions of subordinate behaviors* [5, p. 318]. Using call behavior actions, an activity can refer to other activities. Like this, the activity of a composite collaboration may refer to the activities of its sub-collaborations and specify how they are coordinated.

Fig. 7 shows the activity for the composed taxi system. Again, each collaboration role is presented by its own activity partition. As the taxi system collaboration is composed from several other collaborations, the activity refers to them via the call behavior actions *s*, *p*, *t* and *o*. Let us first focus on the partition for the taxi on the left hand side. It describes the local coupling between the collaborations a taxi participates in, including some additional logic for the user interface of the taxi, modeled as activities for three buttons and an alarm device that have been fetched from our library of reusable building blocks [17]. When the taxi partition starts, button *busy* is activated. The driver presses it once

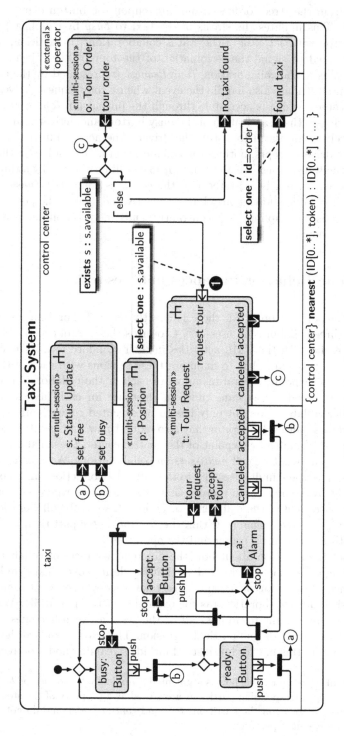

Fig. 7. The Taxi System Activity

a customer from the street orders a tour whereupon the button emits a token at exit *push*. This updates the status of the taxi to *busy* by coupling *push* of the busy button with *set busy* of the status collaboration[2]. In addition, button *ready* is activated to signal the termination of the tour by the driver. As the taxi participates in the collaboration *Tour Request* (represented by the call behavior action *t*), it must also handle the event when a tour request arrives from the control center, which is accessible through the output pin *tour request* of *t*. This event triggers the deactivation of the busy button, and activates the accept button as well as an alarm to notify the driver. The accept button, which is pushed if the driver accepts, notifies the collaboration *t*. Depending on the final outcome of the tour request collaboration (it may still be aborted by a timeout), either the ready button is activated and the status is changed to *busy*, or the taxi remains available and the busy button is activated again. The position collaboration needs no coupling, as it constantly sends the position independently of the other behaviors.

3   Multiple Behavior Instances and Sessions

From the viewpoint of one taxi, there is exactly one collaboration session for each of the three collaboration uses *s*, *p*, *t* towards the control center. This can be handled easily with the UML activities in their standard form. The control center, on the other hand, has to maintain these sessions with each of the taxi cars. From its viewpoint, several instances of each of the collaboration uses *s*, *p* and *t* are executed at the same time; one instance for each taxi. Moreover, the tour order collaboration not only has to be executed concurrently towards several operators, but each operator may also request new tours while others are being processed. From the viewpoint of the control center, the collaborations it participates in, are what we call *multi-session* collaborations. We express this by applying a stereotype «multi-session» to the call behavior actions and represent it graphically by a shadow-like border in those partitions where sessions are multiple[3]. Consequently, the call behavior actions (resp. sub-collaborations) *s*, *t*, and *p* in Fig. 7 have a shadow within the *control center* partition, while *o* is multiple both in the control center and the operators[4].

This raises the question about how the different instances of collaborations may be distinguished and coordinated, so that the desired overall system behavior is obtained. A selection of sessions must take place whenever a token enters a multi-session sub-collaboration (as for example via the pin at ❶). While in some cases we may want to address all of the sessions, in other ones we like to select only a subset or one particular session. The UML standard, however, does not elaborate this matter but instead forbids streaming nodes on reentrant

---

[2] For presentation reasons, this flow is segmented graphically by connector *b*.

[3] Technically, the corresponding partitions are stored as a property of the stereotype.

[4] In this paper we focus on the partitions *taxi* and *control center* and do not further look into the *operator* partition.

behaviors completely, as it *is ambiguous which execution should receive streaming tokens* [5, p. 398]. This is too restrictive, as most systems exhibit patterns with several executions going on at a time, that possibly need coordination. We therefore added the new operators **select** and **exists** to our execution profile.

3.1 Identification of Session Instances

First of all, the different sessions must be distinguished at runtime. This resembles the well-known session pattern (see for example [19, p. 191]) that is found in client/server communication, where the server has some kind of identifier to distinguish different sessions. Accordingly, each collaboration session has an ID. For collaborations having one session instance for a specific participant, the session ID can be chosen to be identical to that of the participant. For example, we can use the ID of the taxi to identify the session instances of the *Tour Request, Status Update* and *Position* collaboration. This is similar to SDL, in which a process identifier *pid* of a communication partner is often used to refer to a session. If there can be more than one session per communication partner (the control center can for instance have several ongoing tour orders from the same operator) any other unique identifier can be used; for collaboration *Tour Order* we can use a unique order number.

3.2 Choosing Session Instances with **Select**

When an operator accepts an order from a customer, a token leaves the output pin *tour order* of *o* in Fig. 7. Let us ignore for the moment the decision and assume it takes the upper branch, towards input pin *request tour* of *t* at ❶. At this point we have to specify into which session instance of *t* the token should enter. We do this by attaching an expression as guard to the edge entering the input pin. If we would like to select all instances (by duplicating the token), we could write **select all**, resulting in an alarm in each taxi, whether busy or free, which is not desired. Instead, we would like to select only one of the free taxis. This means, we want to access properties of the *s: Status Update* sessions. As collaboration uses *s* and *t* have the same set of IDs, we would like to obtain an ID of *s* for which the status is free. To enable the control center to check the status of its taxis, we defined in the activity *Status Update* (Fig. 5) a boolean operation *available* which is executable from the observer side. This operation is used in the select statement. As there may be more than one free taxi, we further specify by adding the keyword **one** that only one of them should eventually be selected. The entire statement is then

select one : s.available.

If none of the taxis is free, no session is selected and the token flow simply stops. We describe later how this situation is ruled out by an alternative behavior using the decision node. If a tour request is canceled, another taxi can be contacted (via connector *c*) by iterating a new tour request.

Once the selected taxi accepts the tour, a token leaves output pin *accepted* and enters *o: Tour Order*. Here we have to select again which of the instances should be chosen. As they are distinguished by the order number, we leave this number as attribute *order* inside the token[5], and extract it by writing

select one : id=order.

The complete EBNF definition for session selection and existence is given in Fig. 8. It allows specifying several filters (e.g., *available*) that are applied in the order of their listing. In this way, we may flexibly use a sequence of filters, for example to call the taxi that is closest to the street address. In this case we would introduce a filter *nearest* which considers the location of the taxis provided by collaboration *p* and computes the taxi which is closest to the customers position.

```
select := 'select' mod ':' [{filter}] ['/' {filter}].
exists := 'exists' name ':' filter ['/' {filter}].
  mod := 'one' | 'all'.
filter := name | 'self' | 'active'
               | 'id=' variable.
```

Fig. 8. EBNF for **select** and **exists**

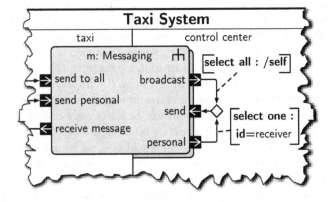

Fig. 9. Messaging service extension

As we still want to select only free taxis, we can apply the available filter before, and write **select one : s**.available nearest, so that an ID has to pass both filters.

To study another form of session selection, we extend the system with a messaging service, where taxi drivers may send messages to each other; either to

---

[5] This implies an UML object flow instead of a simple control flow, which we do not show here to keep the diagrams easier to comprehend.

a specific taxi or to all taxis. Parts of this addition are shown in Fig. 9. Messages are sent via the control center, which maintains one instance of a collaboration *Messaging* with each taxi. As we attach the select statement to the incoming edges and not the nodes directly, a node may be entered with different selection strategies, combined by a merge node. Personal messages arrive from a taxi at pin *personal* and are forwarded by the ID stored as *receiver*, with the known selection statement. Broadcast messages are sent to all other sessions, except the session sending the message, expressed by **select all : /self**. The slash allows to specify negative filters for exclusion. (If for any reason drivers should send broadcasts just to free taxis, we would write **select all : s.available /self**.)

3.3 Reflecting on Sessions with **Exists**

In some cases we have to reason about the status of certain sessions. For example, before we process a request from the tour order collaboration, we check if there are any free taxis available at all. We do this with the operator **exists** that returns a boolean value that can be the guard in a decision. In Fig. 7, we include therefore **exists s : s.available**, where s.available denotes the filter introduced above. Thus, in the example, the selection at ❶ is only reached if at least one taxi is free. If we want to make a decision depending on the fact whether there are any currently ongoing collaboration sessions (which have an active token flow) we may use the standard filter **active**.

3.4 Modeling of Filters

A filter is modeled as an UML operation. Boolean filters only considering one session can be defined as part of the activity describing the collaboration (like *available* in Fig. 5). Filters that need to consider an entire set of sessions or combine data from different collaborations are defined as part of the surrounding activity, such as the filter *nearest*. In contrast to the boolean filter *available*, *nearest* receives and returns an entire set of IDs, from which it can determine the one with the minimal distance to the address given by the token. The address is contained in the token, which is handed over to the filter by the parameter *token*. In principle, the body of operations may be expressed as any kind of UML behavior; in our current tool we use Java, embedded in a language-specific UML *OpaqueBehavior* [5, p. 446], since our code generators create Java code.

4 Mapping to the Component Model and Implementation

In the following, we will discuss how the collaboration models are transformed into the executable component model of our approach. After introducing the component model, we explain the translation of single-session behavior and thereafter the mapping of multi-session behavior to state machines.

4.1 Component Model

Our component model is based on UML 2.0 state machines and composite structures. In [20] we presented an UML profile with constraints ensuring that state machines can be implemented efficiently on different platforms. The internals of such *executable* state machines are similar to SDL processes. They communicate by sending signals, and transitions are triggered by either the reception of a signal or the expiration of a timer. Transitions do not block, so that they can be executed in one run-to-completion step without waiting.

We extend this model with *components* that may contain a number of state machines. Such system components are described by UML classes, and contain one dedicated state machine describing the so-called *classifier behavior*. This state machine typically manages the lifecycle of the component as well as stateless requests arriving from other components, as we shall see later. In addition, a system component can contain further state machines. These are modeled as UML *parts* owned by the structured classifier and have a type referring to a state machine. In contrast to the static state machine expressed by the *classifier behavior*, these parts may have a multiplicity greater than one, so that a system component can hold any number of session instances of different state machine types. A component structure generated by our transformation algorithm is illustrated in Fig. 10 with two taxis and three operators. The taxis have only their default classifier state machines, while the control center component needs additional session state machines, as we will explain in Sect. 4.3.

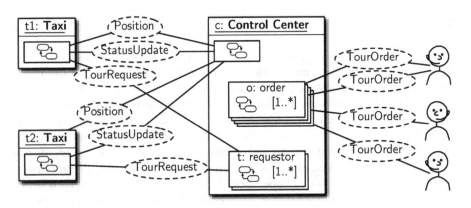

Fig. 10. Component structure and their internal session state machines

A system component keeps track of its state machine instances in a data structure for reflection. Each state machine instance has an ID, so that each of them may be addressed within the component by its part name and ID. State machines may access data of other state machines within the same system component. This is used when behavior in one state machine depends on variables in another ongoing collaboration that is executed by another state machine.

4.2 Mapping of Single-Session Collaborations

In [13] we described an algorithm that transforms activities into executable state machines. One activity partition is translated into at least one state machine. The algorithm scales well since only one partition needs to be considered at a time, not the entire activity. The core idea of this transformation is to map a flow crossing partition borders to a signal transmission between two state machines. Token movements within one partition are translated into state machine transitions. A token starts hereby always at the reception of a signal (where a flow enters a partition) or at a timer node, so that the resulting transitions are triggered by signal receptions or timeouts. A token flow continues traversing the activity graph until the next stable marking is reached, either in form of a join node that cannot yet fire, a waiting decision, a timer node or by leaving the current partition. This stable marking is encoded as control state of the state machine. In this way, the algorithm constructs the entire state machine by a state space exploration of the activity partition corresponding to the state machine.

These basic transformation rules enable a direct mapping of activity flows to state machine transitions as explained and verified in [13]. Moreover, several single-session collaborations composed within the same partition may be integrated within the same state machine by combining their state spaces. Therefore, when we synthesize the component for a taxi, both the behavior for the status update and the tour request collaborations may be implemented by the default state machine, as shown in Fig. 10.

4.3 Mapping of Stateless Multi-session Collaborations

When we analyze the collaboration for the status updates, we find that taxis can send updates at any time, and that the central control has to be prepared at any time to receive them. The behavior on the side of the central control (partition *observer* in Fig. 5) is *stateless*, i.e., an update does not cause a change of behavior, but only modifies data. Our algorithm detects this by looking for partitions to be executed by the central control that do not contain any activity nodes that imply waiting (joins, timers or waiting nodes). The algorithm transforms status updates into one state machine transition that has identical source and target control states. This means for the central control that it does not have to distinguish separate control states for each taxi. Instead, the logic to handle status updates of all taxis may be integrated into one single state machine. The same holds for the behavior of the position collaboration, so that both the status update and the position collaborations may be synthesized into the default classifier behavior of the control center. Fig. 11 depicts the classifier state machine of the control center. The just mentioned behavior for status and position updates are carried out by the two transitions on the left side which are triggered by the external signals *status* and *position* arriving from taxis. The data about position and status has to be stored for each taxi individually, which is done via the the arrays $s2$ and *pos* with the taxi IDs as keys. For stateful behavior towards multiple partners, the state must be kept for each individual session. There are two principal solutions.

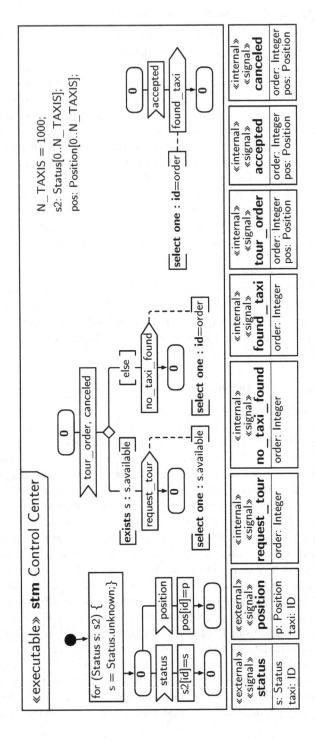

Fig. 11. The classifier behavior state machine for the control center

One solution is to integrate several sessions into one state machine and to distinguish the conversational states by data structures. This, however, leads to state machines with many decisions. The other solution is to use a dedicated state machine instance for each session, such that the state of each session is represented by an individual control state. If state machines are edited manually (for example in TIMe [21]), the second solution is preferred, as the state of conversation towards communication partners can be expressed explicitly by the control state of the state machine, which makes them easier to understand [22]. This may be of minor significance in an approach generating state machines automatically, but it is nonetheless beneficial if results of the transformation shall be read by humans or be validated with existing techniques [18]. We therefore decided to use one state machine for each session. The fact that this solution may lead to many state machine instances is not problematic, as even large numbers of state machines may be implemented efficiently within the same native operating system process by means of a scheduler (see, e.g., [20,22]). A context switch between such state machines just requires to retrieve the current state from a data structure. In a solution integrating all sessions into one state machine, a similar operation would be needed, as we also have to retrieve data belonging to the current state of conversation with a communication partner.

4.4   Mapping and Implementation of select

The instances of stateful multi-session collaborations are represented locally by session state machines, as we discussed above. Directing control flow to a single or a set of collaboration instances means therefore to transfer control flow to the individual session state machines within a component. This is done by notifying the corresponding state machines via internal signals. In order to reduce the possible interleaving of internal and external signals, we apply the design rule given in [22] recommending that internal signals are assigned a higher priority than signals coming from other components. In general, this leads to components that complete internal jobs before accepting external input. In our case, it solves the problem as any **select** signal sent to a session state machine will be handled before an external signal can change its state.

Which state machine(s) should receive the signal(s) is determined by the selection statements from the activities. The transformation therefore copies each selection statement from the edge of the activity and attaches it to the corresponding send signal action. The UML signal is created from the flow. It includes parameters for the data contained in the activity token it represents. The session selection at point ❶ in Fig. 7 is, for example, done by the send signal action *request_tour* in the center of Fig. 11, with the attached selection statement to determine the receiver address.

It is the task of the code generator to create Java statements from the selection expression that compute the actual addresses of the targeted state machine instances. As discussed above, **select** uses a set of positive and negative filters, with an additional flag indicating whether only one matching state machine instance should be returned or all of them. The generated Java method simply sends the set of state machine IDs through all of the filters specified in **select** by using the Java code already expressed in the activity models. The standard filters **self** and **active** are added accordingly. If a collaboration is started (such as at point ❶) the code for the selection includes mechanisms to create new state machine sessions or retrieves instances from a pool, which is not further discussed here.

4.5   Mapping and Implementation of **exists**

In contrast to the select statement, **exists** does not cause a handover of control flow. It is used to get information about properties of the state machines of the system component. As such, it is used in guards of decisions. Decision nodes in activities are mapped directly to choice pseudostates in state machines that have an outgoing transition for each edge leaving the decision node (see [13]). The model transformation simply has to copy the exist guards of the activity edges to the corresponding UML state transitions. The implementation of **exists** for execution in Java is similar to that of **select**, with the difference that a boolean value is returned if one session ID passed all filters.

5   Concluding Remarks

Much research effort has been spent on the problem of deriving component behaviors from service specifications [23,24]. In many approaches, the service behavior is specified in terms of sequence diagrams or similar notations, which are translated into component behaviors defined as state machines (see [25] for a survey). It is also possible to derive message sequence scenarios from higher-level specifications in the form of activity diagrams or Use Case Maps [26], and then derive component behaviors in a second step. A direct derivation from Use Case Maps was demonstrated in [27]. In this paper, however, we consider the direct and fully automated derivation of component behavior from the specification of collaboration behavior expressed as activities. While we presented the transformation from single-session collaborations to state machines in [13], we have extended the notation of activities and our transformation algorithm to handle also collaborations executed in several sessions at the same time, as presented in this paper. The advantage of our notation with **select** and **exists** is that they can express the relations between sessions explicitly on an abstract level and are still straight-forward to map to state machines that can be implemented by our code generators [28]. The transformation algorithm is implemented as an Eclipse plug-in and works directly on the UML 2.0 repository of the Eclipse UML2 project.

We consider the specification of services in a collaboration-oriented way as a major step towards a highly automatic model-based software design approach. As depicted in Fig. 1, we hide the *inter-component* communication in the collaborations and activities while the *intra-component* communication is carried out by linking activities with each other in partitions of surrounding activities.

This makes it possible to express sub-services in separation, which facilitates the general understanding of their behavior. Moreover, each collaboration models a clear, separate task such that interaction-related problems like mixed initiatives can be detected and solved more easily since only the problem-relevant behavior is specified. The composition of collaborations profits from the input and output nodes of activities which form the behavioral interfaces of the collaboration roles. Different collaborations can be suitably composed by connecting their nodes using arbitrary activity graphs.

Another advantage of collaboration-oriented specifications is the higher potential for reuse. Usually, the sub-services modeled by collaborations can be used in very different applications (such as for example the distributed status update expressed by the collaboration *Status Update*). These sub-services can be modeled once by a collaborations which can be stored in a library. Whenever such a sub-service is needed, its activity is simply taken from the library, instantiated and integrated into an enclosing collaboration. In our example, *Status Update*, *Button*, *Alarm* and *Position* are good candidates for reuse.

An ongoing research activity is the development of suitable tools for editing, refining, analyzing, proving and animating collaboration-based models. This will be performed within the research and development project ISIS (Infrastructure of Integrated Services) funded by the Research Council of Norway. The concept of our approach will be proven by means of real-life services from the home automation domain. We consider collaboration-oriented service engineering as a very promising alternative to traditional component-centered design and understand the extensions for modeling and transforming sessions, presented in this paper, as an important enabler.

References

1. ITU-T: Recommendation Z.100: Specification and Description Language (SDL)
2. Krüger, I.H., Mathew, R.: Component Synthesis from Service Specifications. In: Leue, S., Systä, T.J. (eds.) Scenarios: Models, Transformations and Tools. LNCS, vol. 3466, pp. 255–277. Springer, Heidelberg (2005)
3. Rößler, F., Geppert, B., Gotzhein, R.: Collaboration-Based Design of SDL Systems. In: Reed, R., Reed, J. (eds.) SDL 2001. LNCS, vol. 2078, pp. 72–89. Springer, Heidelberg (2001)
4. Fisler, K., Krishnamurthi, S.: Modular Verification of Collaboration-Based Software Designs. In: 8th European Software Engineering Conference, pp. 152–163. ACM Press, New York (2001)
5. Object Management Group: Unified Modeling Language: Superstructure, version 2.1.1 formal/2007-02-03 (2007)
6. Reenskaug, T., Wold, P., Lehne, O.A.: Working with Objects, The OOram Software Engineering Method. Prentice-Hall, Englewood Cliffs (1995)
7. Reenskaug, T., Andersen, E.P., Berre, A.J., Hurlen, A., Landmark, A., Lehne, O.A., Nordhagen, E., Ness-Ulseth, E., Oftedal, G., Skaar, A.L., Stenslet, P.: OORASS: Seamless Support for the Creation and Maintenance of Object-oriented Systems. Journal of Object-oriented Programming 5(6), 27–41 (1992)

8. Bræk, R., Floch, J.: ICT Convergence: Modeling Issues. In: Amyot, D., Williams, A.W. (eds.) SAM 2004. LNCS, vol. 3319, pp. 237–256. Springer, Heidelberg (2005)

9. Sanders, R.T., Bræk, R., von Bochmann, G., Amyot, D.: Service Discovery and Component Reuse with Semantic Interfaces. In: Prinz, A., Reed, R., Reed, J. (eds.) SDL 2005. LNCS, vol. 3530, pp. 85–102. Springer, Heidelberg (2005)

10. Castejón, H.N., Bræk, R.: Formalizing Collaboration Goal Sequences for Service Choreography. In: FORTE 2006. LNCS, vol. 4229, Springer, Heidelberg (2006)

11. Castejón, H.N., Bræk, R.: A Collaboration-based Approach to Service Specification and Detection of Implied Scenarios. In: ICSE's 5th Workshop on Scenarios and State Machines: Models, Algorithms and Tools (SCESM'06) (2006)

12. Herrmann, P., Krumm, H.: A Framework for Modeling Transfer Protocols. Computer Networks 34(2), 317–337 (2000)

13. Kraemer, F.A., Herrmann, P.: Transforming Collaborative Service Specifications into Efficiently Executable State Machines. In: 6th International Workshop on Graph Transformation and Visual Modeling Techniques (GT-VMT) (2007)

14. Kraemer, F.A., Herrmann, P.: Service Specification by Composition of Collaborations — An Example. In: 2nd International Workshop on Service Composition (Sercomp), Hong Kong (2006)

15. Herrmann, P., Kraemer, F.A.: Design of Trusted Systems with Reusable Collaboration Models. Joint iTrust and PST Conferences on Privacy, Trust Management and Security, IFIP (to appear, 2007)

16. Kraemer, F.A.: UML Profile and Semantics for Service Specifications. Avantel Technical Report 1/2007, Department of Telematics, NTNU, Trondheim, Norway (2007), ISSN 1503-4097

17. Kraemer, F.A.: Building Blocks, Patterns and Design Rules for Collaborations and Activities. Avantel Technical Report 2/2007 ISSN 1503-4097, Department of Telematics, NTNU, Trondheim, Norway (2007)

18. Floch, J.: Towards Plug-and-Play Services: Design and Validation using Roles. PhD thesis, Norwegian University of Science and Technology (2003)

19. Rising, L. (ed.): Design Patterns in Communications Software. Cambridge University Press, Cambridge (2001)

20. Kraemer, F.A., Herrmann, P., Bræk, R.: Aligning UML 2.0 State Machines and Temporal Logic for the Efficient Execution of Services. In: Meersman, R., Tari, Z. (eds.) On the Move to Meaningful Internet Systems 2006: CoopIS, DOA, GADA, and ODBASE. LNCS, vol. 4276, Springer, Heidelberg (2006)

21. Bræk, R., Gorman, J., Haugen, Ø., Melby, G., Møller-Pedersen, B., Sanders, R.T.: Quality by Construction Exemplified by TIMe — The Integrated Methodology. Telektronikk 95(1), 73–82 (1997)

22. Bræk, R., Haugen, Ø.: Engineering Real Time Systems: An Object-Oriented Methodology Using SDL. The BCS Practitioner Series. Prentice-Hall, Englewood Cliffs (1993)

23. von Bochmann, G., Gotzhein, R.: Deriving Protocol Specifications from Service Specifications. In: ACM SIGCOMM Conf. on Communications Architectures & Protocols, pp. 148–156. ACM Press, New York (1986)

24. Yamaguchi, H., El-Fakih, K., von Bochmann, G., Higashino, T.: Protocol Synthesis and Re-Synthesis with Optimal Allocation of Resources based on Extended Petri Nets. Distrib. Comput. 16(1), 21–35 (2003)

25. Liang, H., Dingel, J., Diskin, Z.: A Comparative Survey of Scenario-Based to State-Based Model Synthesis Approaches. In: Int. Ws. on Scenarios and State Machines: Models, Algorithms, and Tools, ACM Press, New York (2006)

26. Amyot, D., He, X., He, Y., Cho, D.Y.: Generating Scenarios from Use Case Map Specifications. qsic 00, 108 (2003)
27. Castejón, H.N.: Synthesizing State-machine Behaviour from UML Collaborations and Use Case Maps. In: Prinz, A., Reed, R., Reed, J. (eds.) SDL 2005. LNCS, vol. 3530, Springer, Heidelberg (2005)
28. Kraemer, F.A.: Rapid Service Development for Service Frame. Master's thesis, University of Stuttgart (2003)

Experiences in Using the SOMT Method to Support the Design and Implementation of a Network Simulator

Manuel Rodríguez[1] and José María Parra[2]

[1] University of Valladolid, Spain
manuel.rodriguez@tel.uva.es
[2] INSA, Ingeniera de software avanzado, S.A., Spain
jmparra@insags.com

Abstract. This paper deals with the analysis and design of a computer network simulator for educational purposes. The SOMT method based on object-oriented analysis and SDL design has been used for that purpose. The simulator developed allows protocol descriptions independent of event management mechanisms and run-time network topology configuration without modifying the SDL description of the system developed.

1   Introduction

The research and teaching of protocols for communication networks requires simulation as a means for understanding and debugging their behavior. Simulation is also required for protocol performance evaluation.

To develop a network simulator, notations for high-level behavior description would be desirable, specially for the description of the protocols to be simulated. These notations should allow the use of the same protocol description for simulation, testing and automatic code generation of the network simulator.

Formal description techniques offer numerous advantages for the design and evaluation of systems: a) well-defined set of constructs for an unambiguous system description; b) support of hierarchical structuring of systems; c) a basis for simulation, verification and implementation.

SDL [1] as an FDT further offers a graphical representation of the system behavior, increasing the understandability of the system specification. Behavior description is based on the concept of extended finite state machines (EFSM), that form the basis of other notations in widespread use like UML statecharts [2].

Despite the advantages of SDL for the formal description of system behavior and structure, it is not the ideal notation for all the phases of system development, specially the analysis phase. SDL requires the specification of many details, even for the simple models needed in the early phases of development, and does not support the specification of relations (associations) between objects.

Object-oriented analysis is a well-known and popular technique for understanding a problem and analyzing a system. There are many different versions of object-oriented analysis published as different methods in various books. The

E. Gaudin, E. Najm, and R. Reed (Eds.): SDL 2007, LNCS 4745, pp. 186–202, 2007.

Object Management Group (OMG) has agreed upon a standard language for object-oriented methods and tools, the Unified Modeling Language (UML) [2]. In spite of the advantages of UML for system analysis, the current version of this language is not formally defined. Thus, UML system descriptions are not completely unambiguous (see [3] for the current state of the development of a mathematically formalized semantics definition for UML).

There are several software development methods that integrate object-oriented analysis and SDL design. Among them are TIMe (*The Integrated Method*) [4] and SOMT (*SDL-oriented Object Modeling Technique*) [5]. The intention is, of course, to provide developers with the best of both worlds: the high-level description of structure and behavior and ease of use of the object oriented analysis in the early phases, together with the formal behavior description provided by SDL (that cannot currently be obtained using UML) with simulation and validation facilities provided by SDL tools.

This paper presents the experiences during the development of a network simulation for educational purposes using the SOMT method. The rest of the paper is organized as follows. Section 2 gives an overview of the SOMT method. Section 3 is devoted to the analysis and design phases of the network simulation. In Sect. 4 we discuss some aspects of the SOMT and other software development methods. Finally, in Sect. 5 we discuss the conclusions of the paper.

2   The SOMT Method

The SOMT method [5] provides a framework that shows how to use object-oriented analysis and SDL-based design together in a coherent way. The framework is based on describing the analysis and design of a system as a number of activities. Each activity deals with some specific aspects of the development process. The work done in the activities is centered around a number of models, that document the result of the activities. As an integral part of the SOMT method, guidelines are given for the transition between the different models. The activities and the main models used in SOMT are illustrated in Fig. 1.

The current version of the SOMT method and the tool that supports it (Telelogic SDT) are based on SDL-96. Due to this fact, none of the SDL-2000 features (such as UML class diagrams as part of an SDL system description) can be used. This restriction affects the mapping of UML to SDL used in the activities of the system and object design phases (see [5] for details). Anyhow, the UML extensions of SDL-2000 are compatible with the mappings from UML to SDL-96 defined in the SOMT method.

ITU-T recommendation Z.109, SDL combined with UML [6], defines an extended subset of UML that maps directly to SDL and that can be used in combination with SDL. This recommendation also includes the restricted subset of UML to SDL mapping. The approach used in this Recommendation is based on a subset of UML while the SOMT method is based on standard UML. This way the SOMT method mappings are applicable to any UML class diagram and not only to diagrams specifically designed for the Z.109 restricted subset of UML.

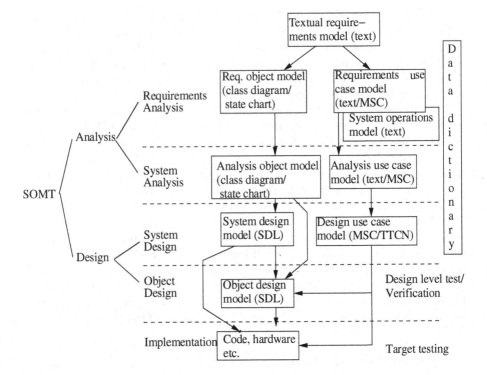

Fig. 1. SOMT activities and main models

3   The SDL Network Simulator

This section presents the development process of a network simulator using the
phases and activities described in the SOMT method (see Sect. 2).

3.1   Requirements Analysis

In this phase, a textual requirement model is used as a source of information
about the problem to be solved and its domain. This information is usually
completed using other sources like books about the specific domain (for our
problem the references [7,8,9] have been used). This information is used to obtain
the rest of the models (use case model, requirements object model and data
dictionary).

The main features of the network simulator included in the textual requirements model are the following:

- simulator for educational purposes, mainly used for behavior and performance analysis of data link layer protocols
- the protocol description used should be valid for both simulation and production code generation

- the protocol stack is composed of three layers: application, data link and physical, but it could be easily extendable to include more layers
- the physical medium used should be a point-to-point link, but the simulator must support other media without the need of modifications in the protocol stack description
- the application layer is responsible for generating traffic for lower layers and consuming data from them
- the data link layer protocols that can be selected for simulation are stop and wait, sliding window without reject, sliding window go back n and sliding window with selective reject
- the simulation modes are step by step (simulator stops after each event) and continuous (simulator runs until user stops it)

From these requirements and the knowledge of the problem domain, the requirements object model, as shown in Fig. 2, is obtained.

This model includes all the classes related to concepts external to the simulator (*user* class) and internal but visible in the system boundary (*simulatorInterface* class and classes related to the layers and protocols being simulated).

The *simulationInterface* class is the interface between the user and the simulator, and allows the user to configure the simulation parameters and start, stop, continue and abort a simulation. Furthermore, all the events produced during the simulation and the values of the performance evaluation parameters are sent to the user.

As a result of the activities of this phase, several message chart diagrams showing scenarios of system element interactions are also obtained. One of these interactions, corresponding to the simulation configuration, is shown in Fig. 3.

Note that the user is not aware of the communications among the internal modules of the simulator. Thus, from a requirements analysis point of view, the user and the simulatorInterface are the only classes involved in the simulator configuration scenario.

3.2 System Analysis

One of the main goals of this phase is to obtain the internal structure description of the system. This structure is described in the analysis object model, as shown in Fig. 4.

In the analysis object model all the classes visible in the system boundary of the requirement object model are completed by including attributes and methods. Furthermore, all the external classes are not included (*simulator_interface* and *user* classes) and some new classes needed for the simulation to fulfill its requirements are included (*timing* class).

The *timing* class is responsible for receiving events (and their timestamps) from the stack protocol layers and the physical medium, ordering them by timestamp and controlling the simulation clock. Another function of this class

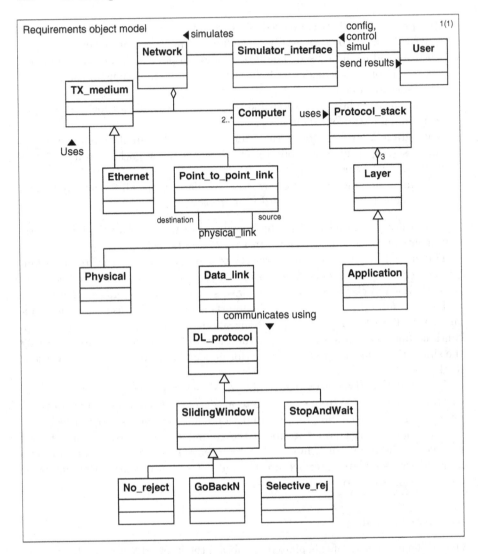

Fig. 2. Logical structure for the requirements analysis phase

is to notify that a protocol event has been produced (the simulation clock has been advanced to the value of the event timestamp).

In the analysis object model some system structure simplifications can also be observed: *protocolStack* and *computer* classes have been merged into one class (*protocolStack*) because of the fact that every computer simulated only uses one protocol stack according to the simulator requirements. This simplification leads to a simpler SDL system structure (see Sect. 3.3).

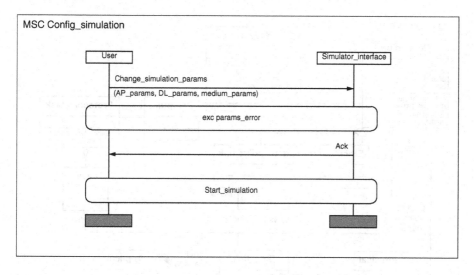

Fig. 3. Example of a scenario: Simulator configuration

3.3 System Design

In this phase the SDL system structure and the interfaces among the system parts are defined using mainly the information described in the analysis object model.

The rules described in [5] are used to obtain a description of the application architecture using SDL system and/or block diagrams. These rules can be automatically applied by using the *paste* as concept of the CASE tool used. This way, a UML concept, for example a class in the analysis object model, can be pasted as the corresponding SDL concept according to the rules (in this case, a block type, a process type or a signal definition for the class operations). With this concept, block types and process types structure, and signal definitions can be automatically obtained.

Applying the aforementioned rules to the analysis object model of Fig. 4, the class *protocolStack* is translated into a block type *protocolStack* containing three process types, corresponding to the classes *application*, *datalink* and *physical*. The process types corresponding to *PHY_Protocol*, *DL_Protocol* (and its subclasses) and *AP_Protocol* classes should also have to be defined inside the same block type as the process types modeling layers because of the relationships (which imply communications) among them. There is also a control process type responsible for instantiating the process type corresponding to the selected data link protocol.

To simplify the SDL system structure we have added some new rules to the mapping rules proposed in the SOMT method. According to SOMT rules, two associated classes (A and B) are translated into two SDL process types (PT_A and PT_B) connected by routes and defined inside the same block type. If one of

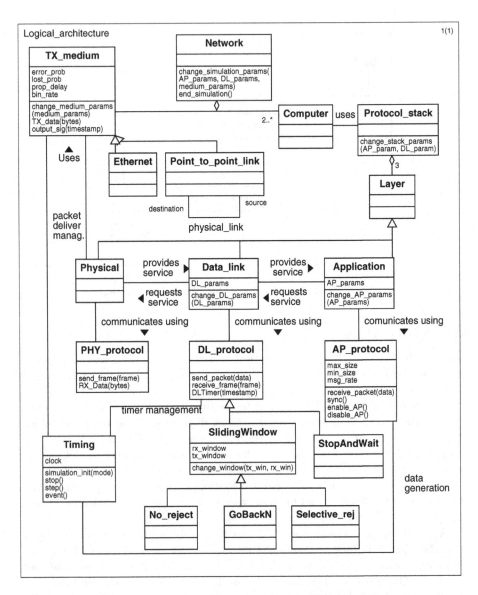

Fig. 4. Logical structure for the system analysis phase

the associated classes (B) has subclasses (Bi, i=0,1, ...) this rule will lead to a block type structure with several interconnected process types: one process type (PT_Bi) for each subclass, one control process type (PT_Control_B) responsible for instantiating the PT_Bi process types, and one process type for the A class (PT_A).

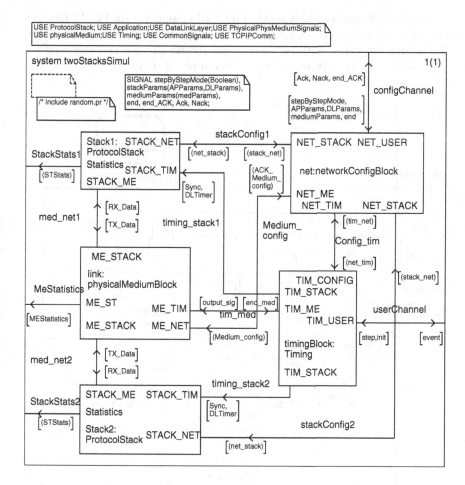

Fig. 5. SDL system structure: simulator with static structure

If the multiplicity of the association is "one" for the superclass (B), only one of the process types corresponding to the subclasses will be instantiated.

In this case, the SDL structure will be simplified if the process types modeling the superclass (B) and the subclasses (Bi) are converted into procedures (Proc_B and Proc_Bi, respectively), and the union of the signals of their signal sets are added to the control process PT_Control_B. This process type will also be responsible for calling the procedure corresponding to the instantiated subclass (according to the system configuration). The procedures modeling the subclasses include the same finite state machine description as the previous process types PT_Bi, and with the same signal handling, thus, there are no differences in the behavior of the PT_Bi process types and the behavior of the control process type that includes the procedures. This simplification is valid for every system fulfilling the aforementioned conditions.

194   M. Rodríguez and J.M. Parra

The system obtained by applying the proposed mapping of the SOMT method and the new rules added can be seen in Fig. 5 (system structure for a simulator configured for a network with two computers communicating through a point-to-point link) and Fig. 6 (protocolStack block internal structure).

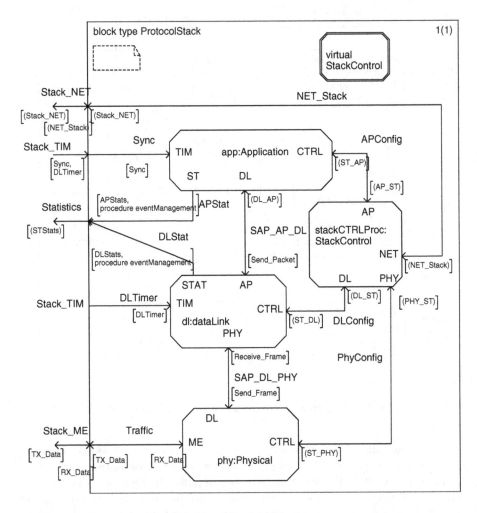

Fig. 6. protocolStack block structure

This first version of the simulator consists of one SDL system including blocks for the protocol stacks, physical medium and timing module. Due to the lack of dynamic block instance creation and connection of their channels to the environment in SDL-96 (the version supported by the SDL CASE tool used), the simulator network topology is fixed when the SDL system structure is defined in this version of the simulator (see Fig. 5).

The simulator system consists of several blocks:

- one *net* block, containing a process in charge of the configuration of the protocol stacks (data link protocol selected, for example), physical medium (propagation delay, for example) and timing module;
- one *timing* block containing a process for management of simulator events;
- one *link* block, containing a process that models the physical medium;
- two blocks of type *ProtocolStack*, each one including processes modeling the three protocol layers used in every computer of the network.

The application of the modified rules of the UML-SDL mapping to the system structure cause the process types modeling protocols to be converted into procedures. These procedures are called from the corresponding control process type.

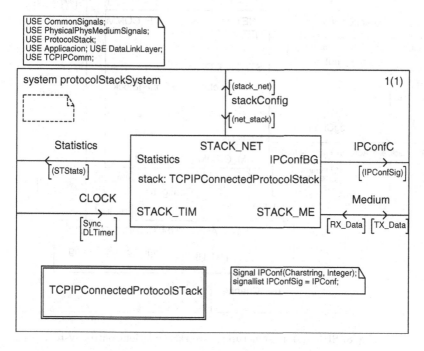

Fig. 7. SDL system structure: protocolStack system

Due to the fact that process types corresponding to layer classes are only responsible for configuring layer protocols, each of these has been merged with the control process type in charge of instantiating the layer protocol to be executed. The structure of the block type protocolStack resulting from applying these simplifications can be see in Fig. 6. A brief description of the functions of the main process types can be see in Sect. 3.4.

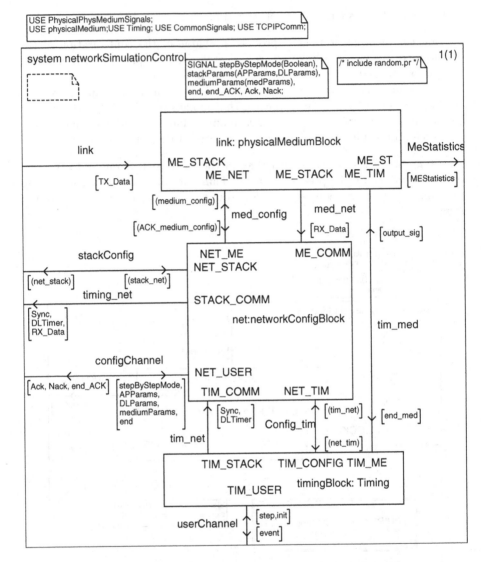

Fig. 8. SDL system structure: networkSimulationControl system

To allow a dynamic network topology configuration the SDL system has to be decomposed into two SDL systems. This second version of the simulator consists of two types of SDL systems: *protocolStackSystem*, shown in Fig. 7, that contains an instance of the protocolStack block type (in fact, a modified version of the block type that includes the aspects related to the TCP/IP communication with other SDL systems), and *networkSimulationControl*, shown in Fig. 8, that contains instances of the *physicalMedium*, *timing* and *network* (used for configuration and signal exchanging with other systems using TCP/IP) block types.

With the new structure for the simulator, the user (through the graphical interface) executes the *networkSimulationControl* system which is responsible for the execution and communication with the *protocolStack* systems (there will be as many *protocolStack* systems as computers in the network topology simulated).

For the communications among the SDL systems the TCP/IP communication module of the Telelogic SDT 4.6 tool has been used. To encapsulate the details of these communications and avoid changes in the protocol description a new version of the *protocolStack* block type (*TCPConnectedProtocolStack*) has been developed. This block includes a new version of the control process type that sends, during the initialization phase, the (dynamically assigned) IP address and port used by the protocolStack system to the control system. The IP address and port of the control system are read from a configuration file and are used for routing every signal sent to the environment of the *protocolStack* system.

Furthermore, the control process type of the *networkConfigBlock* have been redefined to be also in charge of storing the mappings among *protocolStack* system identifiers and their IP address and port, and for routing every signal sent to the control system environment using these mappings. The routing is done by adding the IP address and port of the destination system to every signal, and using the internal routing functions of the Telelogic tool.

3.4 Object Design

The main task of this phase is to define completely and unambiguously the SDL system, including the behavior description of all the process types. For this description the information included in the state charts related to the corresponding process types (if defined) can be used. Another source of information is the MSCs descriptions of scenarios. The complete process type behavior should be defined as the union of the behaviors of the corresponding class in all the scenarios it belongs to.

Process type behavior will also be affected by the textual requirements of the requirements analysis phase. For example the requirement "the protocol description used should be valid for both simulation and production code generation" will affect the behavior description of the protocol procedures (aspects related to simulation event management should be isolated from the protocol behavior). To fulfill this requirement, auxiliary procedures for event and clock management (*addEvent*, *eventManagement* and *releaseEvenList*) have to be used in the protocol description (different versions of these procedures will be used for simulation and production code generation without the need to modify the protocol description).

Every process modeling a protocol stack layer (or the physical medium) sends its events to the *Timing* block type using the remote procedure *eventManagement* (exported by the process of this block type).

In the case of production code generation, the *eventManagement* procedure should be modified to use timers that trigger the appropriate signals (*sync, timeout* or *output_sig*) instead of a simulated clock, and to be a local called procedure in every protocol stack block. Furthermore, the real physical medium should be substituted for a physicalMedium block, every protocol stack system will be directly connected to this medium, a local configuration procedure in every protocol stack block should be substituted for block type *networkConfigBlock* and the *Timing* block type will not be needed.

The main functions of the processes obtained in this phase are described in the following sections.

Clock and event management: the timing module. The timing module, modeled by the *TimingBlock* block type and its *eventMonitor* process type is mainly responsible for:

- simulation clock management;
- receiving the events (including their timestamp, present or future time) from other processes and sending the appropriate associated signal (if any) when the clock is advanced to the timestamp value;
- sending the *sync* signal to the application layer – this signal triggers the packet generation;
- sending the *timeout* signal to the data link layer – this signal triggers the frame retransmission
- sending the *output_sig* signal to the physical medium – this signal triggers the sending of frame bytes to the destination stack physical layer;
- notifying the events to the user.

To fulfill these requirements this module has to receive all the events of the layers and physical medium, order them by timestamp, advance the simulation clock to the earliest event and send the signal corresponding to that event (if any) to the corresponding layer or physical medium.

The application layer. The process modeling the application layer is responsible for generating packets for the data link layer according to the configuration (minimum and maximum size and message rate). The generation of one packet and its sending to the data link layer (using the *send_packet* output signal) is triggered by the input of *sync* signal from the *timingBlock* block type.

This process is also responsible for receiving packets from the data link layer (using the *receive_packet* input signal).

The data link layer. The process modeling the data link layer is responsible for configurating the parameters of the selected protocol and call the procedure corresponding to this protocol. The main signals used by this process are:

- output signals:
    - *send_frame* for sending a frame to the physical layer;
    - *receive_packet* for sending a packet to the application layer;
- input signals:
    - *send_packet* for receiving a packet from the application layer;
    - *receive_frame* for receiving a packet from the physical layer;
    - *DLTimer*: sent to this layer by the *timingBlock* block type when a frame timer timeouts.

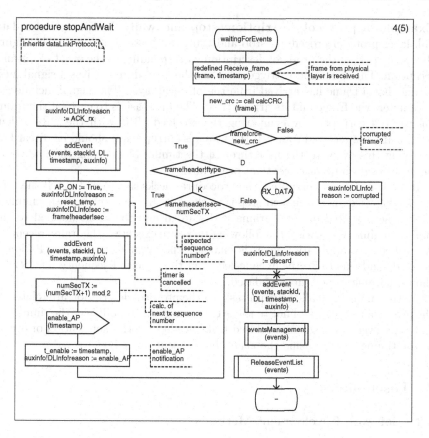

Fig. 9. Stop and wait procedure

The physical layer. The process modeling the physical layer is responsible for receiving frames from the data link layer (using the input signal *send_frame*) and sending them to the physical medium (using the output signal *TX_data*). It is also responsible for receiving frames from the physical medium (using the input signal *RX_data*), checking if the frames have a destination address corresponding to the computer the layer belongs to (otherwise they are discarded), and sending them to the data link layer (using the output signal *receive_frame*).

The physical medium. The process modeling the physical medium is in charge of the following functions:

– receiving frames from a physical layer (using the input signal *TX_Data*);
– calculating the frame arrival time to the destination computer and notifying this event to the timing module;
– sending frames to a physical layer (using the output signal *RX_Data*) when the input signal *output_sig* is received from the timing module (indicating that the clock value equals the arrival time of the frame).

Example of protocol description: stop and wait. An example of a data link layer protocol procedure, stop and wait, can be seen in Fig. 9. This figure shows the part of the protocol description corresponding to the event of a frame reception. The transition is triggered when the procedure receives a signal indicating that a frame has arrived from the physical layer. This signal includes as parameters the frame and its arrival time. The first task is to check if the frame has arrived corrupted by comparing the received CRC with the CRC calculated using the received frame. If the frame is corrupted, it should be discarded, notifying this event to the user through the timing block using the *addEvent*, *manageEvent* and *relaseEventList* procedures.

If the frame is not corrupted, the procedure checks the frame type. If the type is an acknowledgment the next step is to check its frame number. If this number is not the expected one, the frame is discarded and the event notified to the timing module. Otherwise, the following tasks are executed: the frame reception is notified, the application layer is enabled, the event of timer cancellation is notified (and timer effectively canceled) and the expected sequence number for the next frame to be sent is updated.

As shown in Fig. 9 all the main tasks in the protocol description are related to the protocol behavior and not to the event management module of the simulator. The only event management related tasks needed are the notification of events to the timing module using the *eventManagement* procedure.

4   Discussion

4.1   Software Development Methods

For the development of complex telecommunications, (soft) real-time or reactive systems in general, a promising combination is to use [4]:

- object orientation as a common approach to analysis, design and implementation, with concurrent processes as objects;
- interaction scenarios for the specification of communication between users and systems (use cases) and between objects of systems;
- state/transition based specification of behavior of individual objects.

There are software development methods that support this combination by using the OMG standardized language UML, like the Unified Process Model [10]. The main drawback of these methods is the lack of formal semantics definition of UML.

Another group of methods supports the same combination by the integrated use of UML for object model analysis, MSC for interaction scenarios, and SDL for specification and design of behavior. Among this group of methods the SOMT method [5], and the TIMe method [4] can be found.

Both methods distinguish between analysis and design activities but the internal sub-activities are different. In the TIMe method, analysis activity consists of two main activities: domain analysis (for identifying concepts of the domain) and requirements analysis (for identifying properties of the system to be developed). These activities are included in the requirements analysis activity of the SOMT method (and in part of the system analysis activity), but without a clear difference.

Roughly speaking, the TIMe design activity corresponds to the SOMT system design (for specifying system structure) and object design (for specifying system objects' behavior), and the TIMe implementation and instantiation activities to the SOMT implementation activity (without a clear difference between implementation and instantiation concepts).

In a general sense, the TIMe method describes the activities and concepts involved in system development in a more rigorous way than the SOMT method, and introduces useful mechanisms for system development (e.g. frameworks to simplify the reutilization of designs). Despite all these advantages, we think it is more complex and difficult to apply the TIMe method to projects of small size, than the SOMT method.

The main drawback of the TIMe method is the lack of tool support for applying it to a project (the SOMT method is supported to a great extent by Telelogic's SDT tool).

4.2   Experiences in Using the SOMT Method

In this section we present our experiences in using the SOMT towards the development of the network simulator.

The use of the method has proven to be useful to force the developers to think about what is the problem to be solved and its domain, and to represent this knowledge with an appropriate notation, before thinking how to solve it.

The main problems we have found in using the method are due to the change of notations from UML to SDL between analysis and designs activities (though this change is partially supported by the CASE tool used).

Associations between active objects in UML can not be directly expressed in SDL, and usually are only translated into routes communicating the SDL process modeling the objects. Although this is the translation proposed by the SOMT method, it is not supported by the CASE tool.

The application of translation rules from UML to SDL is supported in Telelogic SDT by the *paste as* concept (a UML element is copied and pasted as an SDL concept, and only the valid options for this translation can be selected). Nevertheless, the paste as mechanism can only be applied element by element and not to a group of elements simultaneously. This drawback limits the number of UML-SDL translation rules that can be applied automatically (for example, the gate definition of a block type corresponding to an aggregation can not be obtained automatically).

It is not clear what is the best structure in SDL to represent a UML aggregation in which some of the part classes are associated with other classes. There are several options: a) trying to keep the aggregation structure; in this case, we have to define one block type to model the aggregation (containing the process types corresponding to the part classes) and another one containing the associated classes; b) include the associated classes in the block type modeling the aggregation. The first approach is closer to the structure of the UML model while the second one allows a simpler SDL structure.

5 Conclusions

In this paper we have described the analysis and design of a network simulator for educational purposes using the SOMT method, that integrates object-oriented analysis with SDL design.

The simulator developed fulfills all the initial requirements, including the need of protocol behavior description independent of the simulator event management mechanism. This requirement has been fulfilled using auxiliary procedures to notify events to the timing module. This procedures can be adapted for generating production code of the protocols without the need of modifying the protocol description.

Furthermore, a new rule for the UML analysis model to SDL system structure mapping has been proposed, based on the use of procedures instead of process types. This rule simplifies the SDL system structure by reducing the number of processes and signal routes.

Due to the lack of dynamic block creation in the SDL version used, a new structure for the simulator has been proposed, consisting of one SDL system for simulation control and physical medium management, and several SDL systems modeling the protocol stack of every computer belonging to the network. The new structure allows different network topologies without the need of modifying the SDL system definitions.

References

1. ITU-T: ITU-T Recommendation Z.100. SDL: Specification and Description Language (2002)
2. Object Management Group: Unified Modeling Language 2.0 (2004)
3. Broy, M., Crane, M.L., Dingel, J., Hartman, A., Rumpe, B., Selic, B.: 2nd UML 2 Semantics Symposium: Formal Semantics for UML. In: Kühne, T. (ed.) MoDELS 2006. LNCS, vol. 4364, pp. 318–323. Springer, Heidelberg (2007)
4. SINTEF: TIMe: The Integrated Method (1999)
5. Telelogic, A.B.: Telelogic TAU 4.6 User's Manual: SOMT Method (2004)
6. ITU-T: ITU-T Recommendation Z.109. SDL combined with UML (1999)
7. Tanenbaum, A.S.: Computer Networks. 4 edn. Pearson Education (2003)
8. Stallings, W.: Data and computer communications, 7th edn. Prentice-Hall, Englewood Cliffs (2005)
9. Law, A.M., Kelton, W.D.: Simulation modeling and analysis. McGraw-Hill, New York (2000)
10. Object Management Group: The Unified Process Model (2000)

Consistency of UML/SPT Models

Abdelouahed Gherbi and Ferhat Khendek

Electrical and Computer Engineering Department
Concordia University
1455 de Maisonneuve Blvd. W.
Montreal, Quebec H3G 1M8 Canada
{gherbi,khendek}@ece.concordia.ca

Abstract. UML supports a multi-view modeling approach for overcoming software complexity. It consists of several diagrams, which allow for considering software systems from different perspectives: structure, behavior and deployment. However, this multi-view approach faces the challenging issue of consistency. Moreover, when UML is used for real-time systems, through its specialized profiles such as UML/SPT for instance, the consistency issue becomes more complex. New aspects, relevant for real-time systems design, should be taken into consideration. These include concurrency, time constraints and schedulability. In this paper, we present a consistency framework for UML/SPT models. This framework addresses incrementally the various aspects of consistency including syntactic, semantic, concurrency-related and time consistency. In this framework, we introduce an approach for checking time consistency between statecharts and sequence diagrams using schedulability analysis.

1 Introduction

UML [16] is nowadays seen as the *de facto* standard software modeling language. UML consists of a multitude of diagrams used to model the structure, the behavior and the deployment of the system under consideration. It is well known that these different views may lead to inconsistencies. Moreover, UML is also used to model real-time systems. This can be done using the UML profile for real-time such as the OMG standard UML/SPT [15] or the upcoming standard MARTE [14]. In the case of real-time system modeling, new aspects need to be taken into account, namely concurrency, time constraints and schedulability. These aspects may contribute to worsen the consistency issue.

UML's built-in consistency mechanisms are limited to a set of well-formedness rules expressed in OCL in the metamodel. Higher level consistency concepts are, however, not accounted for at the language level. Considering the complexity of a UML/SPT model, which is composed of several UML diagrams and which captures in addition aspects such as concurrency and time constraints using appropriate stereotypes defined in the profile, it is difficult to provide one definition of consistency. An incremental approach to consistency of UML/SPT models that distinguishes the syntactic and semantic levels is more appropriate.

E. Gaudin, E. Najm, and R. Reed (Eds.): SDL 2007, LNCS 4745, pp. 203–224, 2007.
© Springer-Verlag Berlin Heidelberg 2007

In this paper, we are interested in inter-diagram consistency in a UML/SPT model. The contributions are twofold. First, we present a consistency framework for UML/SPT models. In this framework, we define the consistency of UML/SPT models in terms of syntactic consistency and semantic consistency. The latter is defined further in terms of behavioral consistency, concurrency-related consistency and time consistency. Second, we focus on time consistency of behavioral diagrams of UML/SPT models, namely statecharts and sequence diagrams. We introduce an approach that relies on schedulability analysis. In order to do so, we show how a UML/SPT-based schedulability analysis model is generated from statecharts and sequence diagrams. Our transformation approach initially presented in [6] is then used to enable appropriate schedulability analysis techniques and consequently check time consistency of the model.

The rest of this paper is organized as follows. In Sect. 2, we provide a brief overview of the UML profile for real-time systems and we illustrate it with a model of the generalized railroad crossing system. In Sect. 3, we introduce a framework for an incremental definition of consistency for UML/SPT models. In Sect. 4, we provide formal notations and definitions of UML sequence diagrams, statecharts and behavioral consistency of UML/SPT models. In Sect. 5, we present an approach for checking time consistency of UML/SPT models using schedulability analysis. We review the related work in Sect. 6 and conclude in Sect. 7.

2   Overview of UML/SPT

UML/SPT [15] is an OMG standard UML profile for the modeling and analysis of real-time systems. It enables the modeling of resources, time, and concurrency. In addition, UML/SPT supports schedulability and performance analysis. UML/SPT provides a set of stereotypes that can be used to annotate UML diagrams with quantitative information. This enables the prediction of key properties at early stages of a development process using quantitative analysis.

The structure of the UML/SPT profile, illustrated in Fig. 1, is composed of a number of sub-profiles. The core of the profile represents *the General Resource Model* framework. This is further partitioned into three sub-profiles: *RTresourceModeling* for the basic concepts of resource and quality of service; *RTconcurrencyModeling* for concurrency modeling; and *RTtimeModeling* for the time concept and time-related mechanisms. Furthermore, UML/SPT is composed of extensible analysis

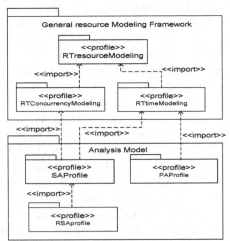

Fig. 1. The Structure of UML/SPT Profile

sub-profiles, including: *PAprofile* for the performance analysis modeling and *SAprofile* for the real-time schedulability analysis modeling.

UML/SPT defines for each of these sub-profiles a domain model encapsulating the main concepts involved in time, concurrency, performance and schedulability modeling. These domain models are then mapped to UML through a set of stereotypes. In the following, we illustrate UML/SPT with a model for the Generalized Railroad Crossing System (GRCS) [7].

This system controls a gate in a critical region to protect a railroad crossing as depicted in Fig. 2. A set of trains can traverse the crossing in parallel using different tracks. The system uses sensors to detect an entering/exiting train to/from the critical region. The GRCS should satisfy certain time requirements as depicted in Fig. 3. The fastest train takes $t_{approach}$ to reach the gate after entering the critical section and it takes $t_{crossing}$ to cross the gate section. A closed gate takes t_{up} to open fully while an open gate takes t_{down} to close completely.

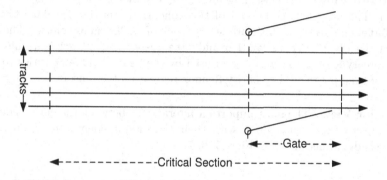

Fig. 2. Generalized Railroad Crossing System

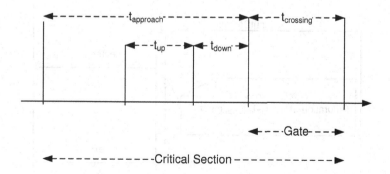

Fig. 3. Generalized Railroad Crossing Time Constraints

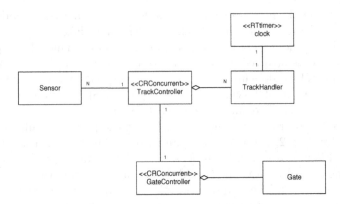

Fig. 4. Generalized Railroad Crossing Structure View

Structure View: The class diagram in Fig. 4 shows the static structure of the design. The system is composed of two concurrent entities `TrackController` and `GateController`, which are stereotypes of ≪CRconcurrent≫. They use the passive objects, `TrackHandler` and `Gate`, respectively. `Clock` is a timer that is a stereotype of ≪RTtimer≫ and used by the `TrackHandler` entities to keep track of time progress. The entity `Sensor` represents the sensors.

Behavior View: The most important interactions between the entities defined in the system structure along with their time requirements are given in the sequence diagrams shown in Figs. 5, 6, 7 and 8.

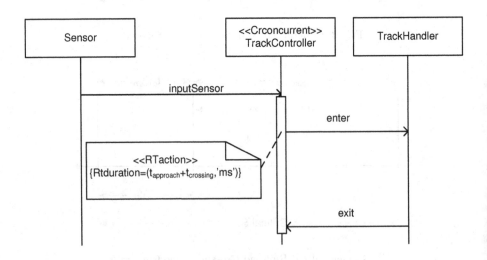

Fig. 5. Entering Train Scenario

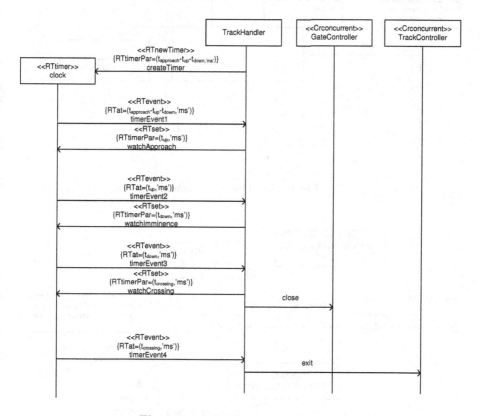

Fig. 6. TrackHandler Timed Behavior

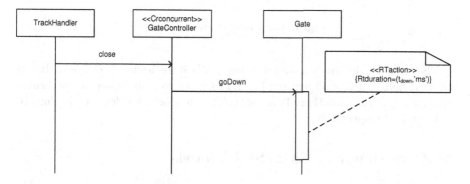

Fig. 7. Gate Closing Scenario

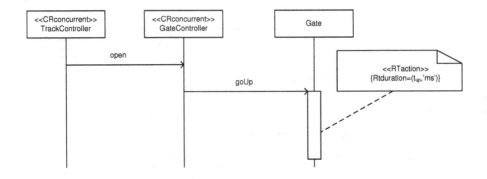

Fig. 8. Gate Opening Scenario

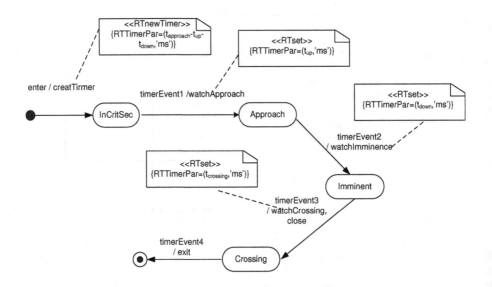

Fig. 9. TrackHandler State Machine

The detailed design is modeled using UML statecharts. These describe the internal behavior of each entity. The statecharts corresponding to the **Track-Controller**, **TrackHandler**, **GateController** and **Gate** are depicted in Figs. 10, 9, 11 and 12 respectively.

3 Consistency of UML/SPT Models

An UML/SPT design model of a real-time system is an UML model that captures in addition concurrency and time constraints. As such, it is composed of several UML diagrams annotated with stereotypes to describe concurrency and

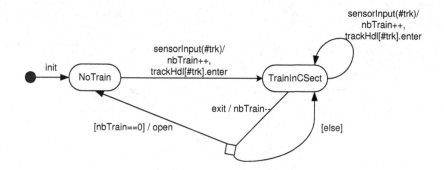

Fig. 10. TrackController State Machine

Fig. 11. GateController State Machine

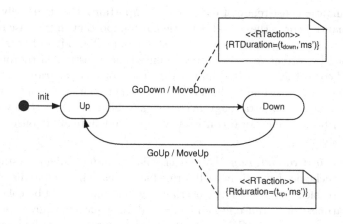

Fig. 12. Gate State Machine

time constraints. It is not straightforward to provide a single and comprehensive definition for consistency of UML/SPT models. The consistency issue of these models can be summarized as shown in Fig. 13. We distinguish between intra-diagram and inter-diagram consistencies.

Intra-diagram consistency concerns one type of diagrams, also called one view of the system. For such kind of consistency we are concerned for instance with the well-formedness of the diagrams, which can be checked using UML well-formedness rules expressed in OCL in the metamodel. These rules help in obtaining UML diagrams that are well-formed with respect to the abstract syntax.

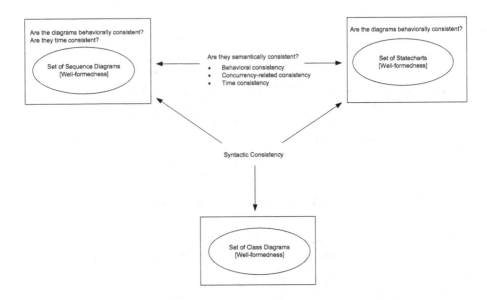

Fig. 13. Consistency of UML/SPT Models

The semantic consistency of each view is important. This is usually referred to as (semantic) correctness, and is particularly important in the case of behavioral diagrams like sequence diagrams or statecharts. This kind of consistency is well studied by formal verification community that investigated thoroughly the behavioral correctness and the timing correctness of such diagrams.

Inter-diagram consistency (the focus of this paper) can be syntactic or semantic, in a similar way to intra-diagram consistency. Semantic consistency includes, in addition to the behavioral consistency, concurrency-related consistency and time consistency.

- **Syntactic Consistency:** This consistency is an inter-diagram static property, which goes beyond the well-formedness of each individual diagram. The syntactic elements used in the overlapping diagrams should be coherent and compatible. For instance, it can be defined for sequence diagrams and statecharts composing a UML model [10]. Several approaches in the literature [8] address the consistency of a UML model at the syntactical level.

    As an example, the model described in Sect. 2 is not syntactically consistent. In the sequence diagram depicted in Fig. 7, TrackHandler sends a message close to GateController. This requires a link between two instances of these classes to enable this communication. There is no association between these classes in the class diagram. Consequently, the class diagram and the sequence diagram in Fig. 7 are syntactically inconsistent.
- **Semantic Consistency:** The semantic consistency is a dynamic property. We distinguish the behavioral consistency for general-purpose UML models from concurrency-related consistency and time consistency, which are specific to UML/SPT models.

- *Behavioral Consistency* is defined for the diagrams used to describe the dynamic behavior of systems. These are mainly the sequence diagrams and statecharts, which capture two different perspectives of the system behavior. Indeed, a sequence diagram describes a partial behavior of the system, which is a particular run/execution of the system. On the other hand, a statechart is a comprehensive description of the behavior of a single object/class. Consequently, a set of sequence diagrams and statecharts model a consistent behavior if the interactions modeled by each sequence diagram can be generated by a particular run of the statecharts associated with the objects involved in the sequence diagram. This can be checked for example by mapping the statecharts and the sequence diagrams to a timed automata formalism [9].
- *Concurrency-related Consistency* comes on top of behavioral consistency to capture issues specific to concurrency in UML/SPT models. It is related to the concurrency choices that are expressed in UML/SPT models. Concurrency design choices are important to use system resources efficiently in order to satisfy time constraints. However, concurrency is likely to lead to issues such as deadlock and other race conditions. Concurrency modeling with UML/SPT is done with stereotypes defined in the *RTConcurrencyModeling* package. The semantics of these stereotypes is defined by the concurrency domain model. We provided a formal definition for this domain model using timed automata in [5]. This enables the usage of model checking techniques for detecting concurrency related problems in UML/SPT models.

  For instance, let us consider the model discussed in Sect. 2 with two tracks. Figure 14 shows the timed automaton corresponding to the class `TrackController`. This timed automaton is generated using the techniques introduced in [5]. UPPAAL [11] shows that the CTL expression (1) is satisfied. This expression models the possibility that a train is crossing the gate section while the gate is open.

  $$\exists\Diamond((\text{TrkHdl1.Crossing or TrkHdl1.Crossing}) \text{ and gt.Up}) \quad (1)$$

  This problem is due to a flawed concurrency design choice where the entities `TrackHandler` are passive objects. They use the thread of control of their associated concurrent unit, `TrackController`, to proceed and meanwhile the latter is blocked (i.e. in the wait state). Any *inputsensor* received is then missed and consequently the train can cross the gate after the `TrackController` has send an *open* message to the `GateController`. `TrackHandler` should then be concurrent.
- *Time Consistency* comes on top of behavioral and concurrency related consistencies. It is related to time constraints expressed using UML/SPT time stereotypes. We distinguish two kinds of time consistency in UML/SPT models: The logical time consistency of sequence diagrams, and system's time consistency including sequence diagrams, statecharts and deployment constraints. We elaborate on time consistency in Sect. 5.

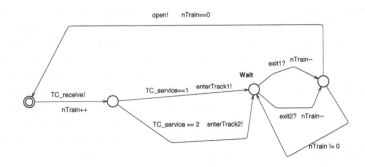

Fig. 14. Track Controller with Sequential Track Handlers

4   Formal Notation and Definitions

We present in this section a formal notation for the UML behavioral diagrams, sequence diagrams and statecharts. Similar ones have been presented in the literature [10,12]. We use this notation to define formally the behavioral consistency between a set of sequence diagrams and a set of statecharts.

Definition 1. *A sequence diagram SeqD is a tuple $<O, E, V, Label>$ where:*

- O *is the set of objects.*
- $E = S \cup R$ *is the set of events.*
- $V \subseteq S \times R$
- $Label : V \to MNames$ *is a labeling function and MNames is a set of messages names.*

A sequence diagram describes a sequence of message events. Each message m is associated with two causally ordered events, a send event, $send(m) \in S$, and a reception event, $receipt(m) \in R$, respectively. Semantically, a sequence diagram is seen as a partially ordered set of events. In the following $Object : E \to O$ is a function mapping an event to the object on which its occurs.

Definition 2. *The semantics of a sequence diagram SeqD $<O, E, V, Label>$ is defined by the structure $(E, \preceq)$ where $\preceq$ is defined as follows:*

- $\forall\ (e_i, e_j) \in V \Rightarrow e_i \preceq e_j$
- $\forall e_i, e_j \in E$ *and* $Object(e_i) = Object(e_j)$ *and* $t(e_i) \leq t(e_j) \Rightarrow e_i \preceq e_j$

We define the function $\Pi_o^{SeqD} : E^* \times O \to E^*$ as the projection of the sequence of events induced by a sequence diagram $SeqD$ on an object $o \in SeqD.O$. This function yields a totally ordered set of events because all the events associated to one object are ordered.

In the following, we consider a formal definition of a simple statechart. This definition omits, for the sake of simplicity, other features of statecharts such as sub-states, pseudo-states.

Definition 3. *A statechart SC is a tuple $<S, E, A, T>$ where:*

- *S is the set of states.*
- *E is the set of events.*
- *A is a set of actions.*
- *$T : S \times E \times A \rightarrow S$ a transition relationship.*

The operational semantics of a statechart is defined informally in the UML meta-model [16]. Moreover, there are several proposals in the literature for the formal description of the UML statechart semantics [17]. In the following, we assume that the predicate $IsARun(sc, se)$ is true if the events sequence se corresponds to a valid transition sequence of the statechart sc.

Using the previous notation, we can define the behavioral consistency between a sequence diagram and a set of statecharts as follows:

Definition 4. *A sequence diagram SeqD and set of statecharts $SC = \{o.sc|o \in SeqD.O\}$ model a consistent behavior if and only if:*

$$\forall \ o \in SeqD.O, \ IsARun(o.sc, \Pi_o^{SeqD}) = True$$

Consequently, the behavioral consistency between a set of sequence diagrams and a set of statecharts can be defined as follows:

Definition 5. *A set of sequence diagrams $SEQD = \{SeqD_1, SeqD_2, .., SeqD_n\}$ and a set of statecharts $SC = \{Sc_1, Sc_2, ..., Sc_m\}$ define a consistent behavior if and only if each sequence diagram $SeqD_i \in SEQD$ and the set of statecharts $SC' = \{o.sc \in SC|o \in SeqD_i.O\}$ define a consistent behavior.*

5 UML/SPT Time Consistency

In this section, we present an approach for checking the time consistency of UML statecharts against a set of sequence diagrams capturing the time constraints. We assume that each sequence diagram models a system end-to-end transaction in response to an external event. The main idea underlying our approach is to use schedulability analysis as a means to check the time consistency. Indeed, a sequence diagram captures a specific interaction subject to a specific time constraint. As a result, a sequence diagram induces a sequence of state transitions in each statechart. This transition sequence involves a sequence of computations/actions. The statecharts are consistent with a set of sequence diagrams if and only if all the computations executed by the statecharts and induced by the different sequence diagrams are schedulable in the context of a particular deployment environment. This means that in a such deployment environment, in the worst-case scenario, all these computations can be completed within the deadlines resulting from the time constraints.

Our approach relies on using an appropriate schedulability analysis technique. In order to do so, we generate a UML/SPT-based schedulability analysis model from the statcharts, the sequence diagrams and a deployment model. The latter describes platform-dependent information such as CPU characteristics, shared resources, threads, priorities, etc. This information allows the determination of the worst case execution time (WCET) of the different actions in the deployment environment using techniques such as [2]. The generated UML/SPT model is an instance of the schedulability analysis domain model defined in the *SAprofile* package of UML/SPT. This model captures the system external events and the corresponding system responses. These are composed of the actions executed by the different objects and that are allocated to the different available threads. This model can then be supplied for schedulability analysis. We have defined in [6] an approach for transforming UML/SPT models into task models suitable for schedulability analysis. In the following, we elaborate on the main parts of our approach outlined in Fig. 15.

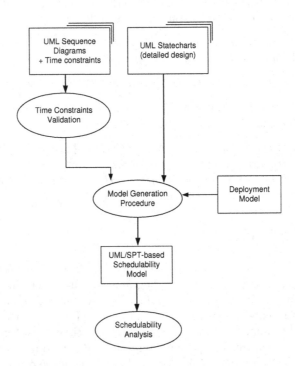

Fig. 15. UML/SPT Model Time Consistency

5.1   Logical Time Consistency Validation

The time constraints captured using sequence diagrams should be logically consistent. This is necessary otherwise no behavior would satisfy contradictory time constraints and hence no possible implementation. The techniques proposed in [19] are used for this step. These techniques allow for checking time consistency in MSC specifications. These are adapted to check the consistency of UML/SPT time constraints modeled with UML sequence diagrams.

5.2   UML/SPT Model Generation

In this section, we focus on the step of UML/SPT-based schedulability model generation. The generated model is an instance of the domain model illustrated in Fig. 16. We have compiled this domain model from the dynamic usage model,

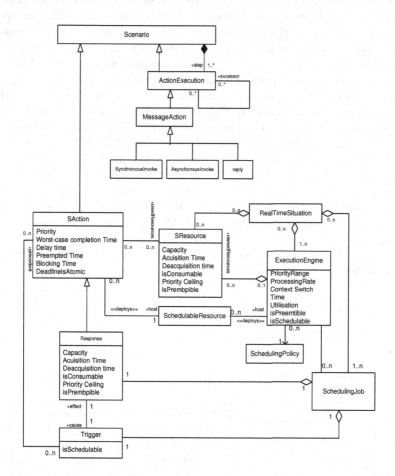

Fig. 16. Compiled Domain Model supporting Schedulability Analysis from UML/SPT

the concurrency model and the schedulability analysis domain model defined in UML/SPT standard [15]. Our general procedure to generate this model is outlined in Algorithm (1). The objective of Step 1 is to determine the set of computation units executed by the statecharts and triggered by the reception of an event. These computation units are composed of all the actions executed by the statechart in a run to completion step. These actions include those executed in entry of a state, the exit of a state and the transition. In order to do so, the set of events in the sequence diagram is partitioned using the projection function $\Pi_{o_i}^{SeqD}$ defined earlier. This yields a totally ordered set of events per object, tr_{o_i}. This set is then restricted to the reception events as these are the computations triggering events, $tr_{o_i}^R$. The set of computations units per object, $Action_{o_i}$, is then determined using these reception events by a function $getR2C(Statechart, event)$, which computes for each statechart the different actions executed at the reception of an event. These computation units correspond to the class $SAction$ in the domain model shown in Fig. 16. The corresponding stereotype provided by UML/SPT is ≪SAction≫. In Step 2 and Step 3, the relationship between the determined computation units is established. This relationship is either a sequentiality or a causality relationship. The sequentiality relationship captures the sequence of $ActionExecutions$ within a $Scenario/SAction$ as shown in the domain model in Fig. 16. This is determined using the order of the reception events associated to one object $tr_{o_i}^R$. The causality relationship corresponds the causality domain model defined in UML/SPT and shown in Fig. 17. This is determined using the order relation between the send event and reception event. We assume that the predicate $gen(a, e)$ is true when the execution of the action a generates the event e and the predicate $trigger(e, a)$ is true when the event e triggers the execution of the action a. The final step, Step 4, in this procedure integrates the deployment information in the generated model. This information is provided by a deployment model and includes for example the worst case execution time, the priority of each action, the deployment of the actions on the available threads.

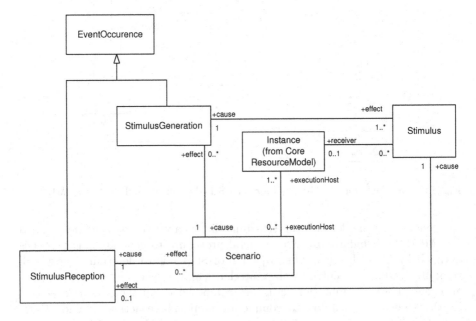

Fig. 17. UML/SPT Causality Domain Model

Algorithm 1. UML/SPT-based Schedulability Model Generation

Input:

    let $SeqD$ <O, E, V,Label> be a sequence diagram

    let $SC = \{o_i.sc | \forall o_i \in O\}$ be a set of associated statecharts

Step 1: Actions determination

for all $o_i \in O$ **do**

    Step 1.1: Event partition

        let $tr_{o_i} \leftarrow \Pi_{o_i}^{SeqD} = \{e_{o_{i1}}, e_{o_{i2}}, .., e_{o_{im}}\}$

    Step 1.2: Event restriction to receptions

        let $tr_{o_i}^R \leftarrow tr_{o_i} \cap R = \{e_{o_{i1}}^r, e_{o_{i2}}^r, .., e_{o_{ik}}^r\}$

    Step 1.3: Run to completion steps

        let $Action_{o_i} \leftarrow \cup_{j \leq k} \{getR2C(o_i.sc, e_{o_{ij}}^r)\}$

end for

    let $Actions = \cup_{o_i \in O} Action_{o_i}$

Step 2: Sequentiality relation

$\xi = \{(a_j, a_k) | a_j, a_k \in Actions \wedge \exists o_i \in O \wedge \exists e_{o_{ij}}^r, e_{o_{ik}}^r \in tr_{o_i}^R \wedge e_{o_{ij}}^r \preceq e_{o_{ik}}^r\}$

Step 3: Causality relation

$\zeta = \{(a_i, a_j) | a_i, a_j \in Actions \wedge \exists e, e' \in E \wedge (e, e') \in V \wedge gen(a_i, e) \wedge trigger(e', a_j)\}$

Step 4: Deployment information integration

for all $a_i \in Actions$ **do**

    let $(a_i.wcet, a_i.priority, a_i.thread, ...) \leftarrow deploys(a_i)$

end for

5.3 Schedulability Analysis Phase

In previous work [6], we defined a metamodel based transformation. This transformation allows to derive a task model expected by the schedulability analysis technique defined in [18] from a UML/SPT model. For this step of our approach, we use this model transformation to enable the schedulability analysis. The analysis allows for computing the worst case response time for each action in each system-wide transaction. The design model is schedulable if all the response times satisfy the deadlines. In such a case the statecharts are consistent with the time constraints expressed in the sequence diagrams assuming the deployment environment provided by the deployment model.

5.4 Example

As an example of application of Algorithm (1), we consider three important scenarios, which are the arrival of a train to a critical section (sequence diagram $SeqD1$), a train reaching a point where the gate has to be closed ($SeqD2$) and a train exiting the section ($SeqD3$). Figures 18, 19 and 20 respectively show the process of determining the actions executed by the different statecharts and induced by the sequence diagrams. Figure 21 shows the results of the causality and sequentiality relationships and the obtained end-to-end transactions in the system. The obtained UML/SPT model after integration of deployment information is shown in Fig. 22. This model is then supplied for schedulability analysis [18], after its transformation into an suitable task model using the approach defined in [6], in order to check the time consistency of the design model.

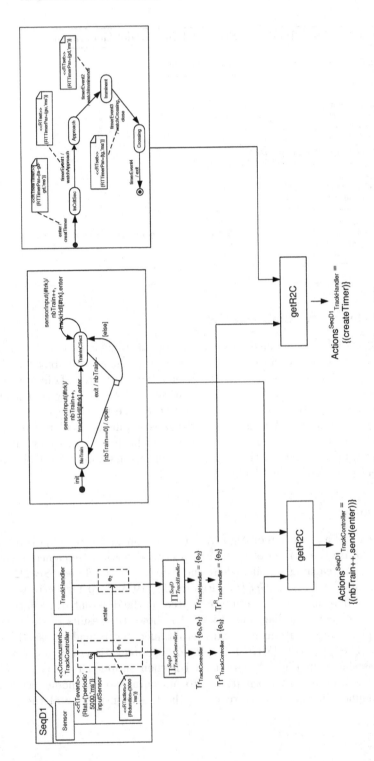

Fig. 18. Actions Induced by SeqD1

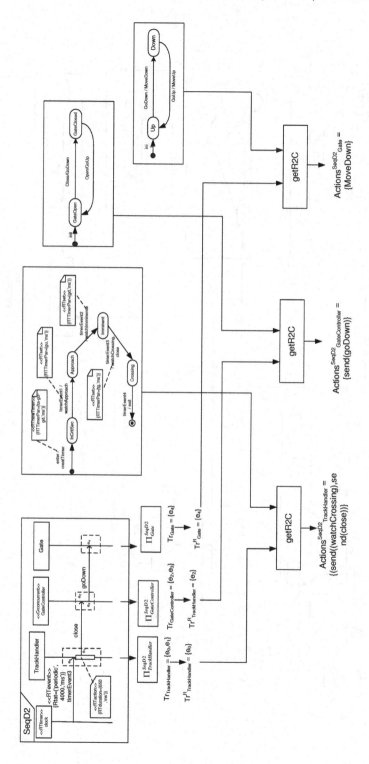

Fig. 19. Actions Induced by SeqD2

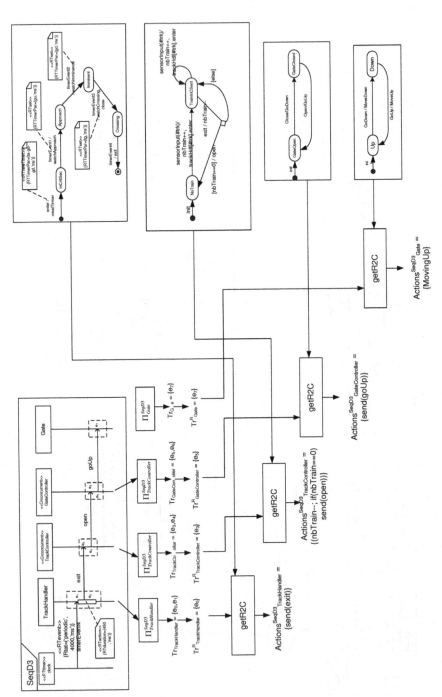

Fig. 20. Actions Induced by SeqD3

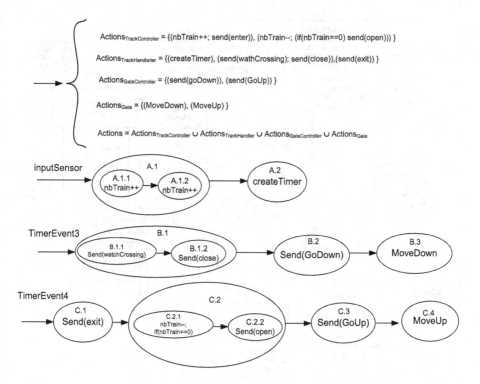

Fig. 21. End-to-End Transactions Induced by the Sequence Diagrams

6   Related Work

Consistency is an important issue in the context of UML modeling. This led to extensive research work [1,8]. A classification of the consistency issues in terms of horizontal/intra-model and vertical/inter-model in UML modeling has been pointed out in [4] and in [8]. The closest work to ours is probably [10]. In this paper, syntactic and semantic consistency were distinguished and temporal consistency was singled out as particular case of semantic consistency. The focus was put on the time constraints although the modeling language considered, UML-RT, does not have any provision for expressing time constraints. In [13], an approach was presented to check the consistency of real-time system specifications using sequence diagrams. This approach is based on a linear programming algorithm to check the consistency of timing constraints in a sequence diagram and a composition of sequence diagrams. Time consistency in MSC based on a formal semantics for MSC has been investigated in [19].

The transformation of UML artifacts used to model dynamic behavior into timed automata for purposes of verification and consistency checking has been the focus of several research works including [3,9]. Firley et al. consider in [3] an approach to transform sequence diagrams with time constraints to observer

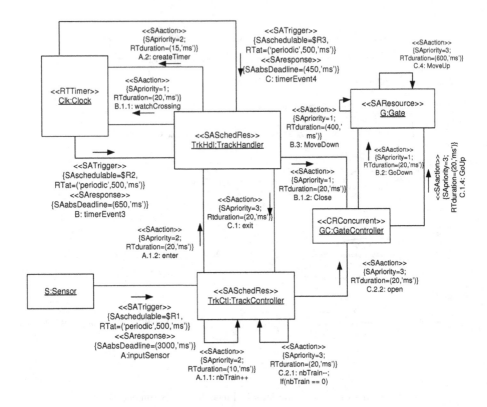

Fig. 22. Generated UML/SPT-based Schedulability Model

timed automata. Knapp et al. address in [9] the issue of consistency between the main UML artifacts used to model the real-time system dynamic behavior: timed state machines and sequence diagrams with time constraints. The former express the detailed design of the system and the latter specify the main scenarios. This work proposed a technique for the verification of the consistency between the two views based on UPPAAL timed automata. The timed state machines are compiled into timed automata and the sequence diagrams annotated with time constraints are transformed into observer timed automata. The latter transformation is a slight extension to the technique proposed in [3]. The model checker UPPAAL is then used to verify the timed automata with respect to the observer timed automata. This technique is embodied in a prototype tool called HUGO/RT.

7 Conclusions

UML model consistency is a challenging issue. It becomes worse when aspects such as concurrency and time constraints are taken into account. We presented in this paper a framework for an incremental definition of the consistency in

UML/SPT models. Within this framework, we address respectively the syntactic and semantic consistency, which includes in addition to behavioral consistency, the concurrency-related consistency and time consistency as these are important features of UML/SPT models. Considering the time consistency of UML/SPT models, we focused on the consistency of a set of statecharts with respect to time constraints modeled using sequence diagrams. Our approach to address this issue is to use schedulability analysis techniques. We showed how to generate UML/SPT model supporting such schedulability analysis techniques from statecharts and sequence diagrams. This model can then be further transformed into appropriate task model using techniques such as those presented in our previous work [6].

The approach based on schedulability analysis for checking time consistency between statecharts and sequence diagrams provides, however, a limited feedback to the designer. There are other important questions that need to be addressed in future work. Indeed, when the analysis shows that a design model is not time consistent, what can be done to fix the inconsistency? Is it possible to provide more fine-grained feedback in pointing out the origin of the inconsistency? What changes can be made to the design model and/or the deployment environment that might fix the problem?

Acknowledgments. This work has been partially supported by the Natural Sciences and Engineering Research Council of Canada (NSERC).

References

1. Astesiano, E., Reggio, G.: An Attempt at Analysing the Consistency Problems in the UML from a Classical Algebraic Viewpoint. In: Wirsing, M., Pattinson, D., Hennicker, R. (eds.) Recent Trends in Algebraic Development Techniques. LNCS, vol. 2755, pp. 56–81. Springer, Heidelberg (2003)
2. Erpenbach, E.: Compilation, Worst-Case Execution Times and Schedulability Analysis of Statecharts Models. Phd thesis, Department of Mathematics and Computer Science of the University of Paderborn (April 2000)
3. Firley, T., Huhn, M., Diethers, K., Gehrke, T., Goltz, U.: Timed Sequence Diagrams and Tool-Based Analysis - A Case Study. In: France, R.B., Rumpe, B. (eds.) UML'99 - The Unified Modeling Language. Beyond the Standard. LNCS, vol. 1723, pp. 645–660. Springer, Heidelberg (1999)
4. Groenewegen, L., Engels, G., Küster, J.M., Heckel, R.: A Methodology for Specifying and Analyzing Consistency of Object-oriented Behavioral Models. In: Gruhn, V. (ed.) ESEC. Proceedings of the 8th European Software Engineering Conference, pp. 186–195. ACM Press, New York (2001)
5. Gherbi, A., Khendek, F.: Timed-automata Semantics and Analaysis of UML/SPT Models with Concurrency. In: Proceedings of 10th IEEE International Symposium on Object/component/service-oriented Real-Time Distributed Computing (ISORC, 7-9 Mai 2007, Santorini Island, Greece (2007)
6. Gherbi, A., Khendek, F.: From UML/SPT Models to Schedulability Analysis: a Metamodel-Based Transformation. In: ISORC 2006. 9th IEEE International Symposium on Object-Oriented Real-Time Distributed Computing, Gyeongju, Korea, 24-26 April 2006, pp. 343–350. IEEE Computer Society Press, Los Alamitos (2006)

7. Heitmeyer, C.L., Lynch, N.A.: The Generalized Railroad Crossing: A Case Study in Formal Verification of Real-Time Systems. In: RTSS '94. Proceedings of the 15th IEEE Real-Time Systems Symposium, San Juan, Puerto Rico, pp. 120–131. IEEE Computer Society Press, Los Alamitos (1994)

8. Huzar, Z., Kuzniarz, L., Reggio, G., Sourrouille, J.-L.: Consistency Problems in UML-Based Software Development. In: Nunes, N.J., Selic, B., Rodrigues da Silva, A., Toval Alvarez, A. (eds.) UML Modeling Languages and Applications. LNCS, vol. 3297, pp. 1–12. Springer, Heidelberg (2005)

9. Knapp, A., Merz, S., Rauh, C.: Model Checking - Timed UML State Machines and Collaborations. In: Damm, W., Olderog, E.-R. (eds.) FTRTFT 2002. LNCS, vol. 2469, pp. 395–416. Springer, Heidelberg (2002)

10. Küster, J.M., Stroop, J.: Consistent Design of Embedded Real-Time Systems with UML-RT. In: ISORC 2001. 4th International Symposium on Object-Oriented Real-Time Distributed Computing, Magdeburg, Germany, 2-4 May 2001, pp. 31–40. IEEE Computer Society Press, Los Alamitos (2001)

11. Larsen, K.G., Pettersson, P., Yi, W.: UPPAAL in a Nutshell. International Journal on Software Tools for Technology Transfer 1(1-2), 134–152 (1997)

12. Li, X., Lilius, J.: Timing Analysis of UML Sequence Diagrams. In: France, R.B., Rumpe, B. (eds.) UML '99 - The Unified Modeling Language. Beyond the Standard. LNCS, vol. 1723, pp. 661–674. Springer, Heidelberg (1999)

13. Li, X., Lilius, J.: Checking Compositions of UML Sequence Diagrams for Timing Inconsistency. In: APSEC 2000. 7th Asia-Pacific Software Engineering Conference, Singapore, 5-8 December 2000, pp. 154–161. IEEE Computer Society Press, Los Alamitos (2000)

14. OMG. UML Profile for Modeling and Analysis of Real-Time and Embedded systems (MARTE). Document: realtime/05-02-06 (February 2005)

15. OMG. UML Profile for Schedulability, Performance, and Time Specification. OMG Adopted Specification Version 1.1, formal/05-01-02 (January 2005)

16. OMG. Unified Modeling Language: Superstructure. version 2.0 formal/05-07-04 (August 2005)

17. Paltor, I., Lilius, J.: Formalising UML State Machines for Model Checking. In: France, R.B., Rumpe, B. (eds.) UML '99 - The Unified Modeling Language. Beyond the Standard. LNCS, vol. 1723, pp. 430–445. Springer, Heidelberg (1999)

18. Saksena, M., Kervelas, P.: Designing for schedulability: Integrating schedulability analysis with object-oriendted design. In: The 12th Euromicro Conference on Real-Time Systems (June 2000)

19. Zheng, T., Khendek, F.: Time Consistency of MSC-2000 Specifications. Computer Networks 42(3), 303–322 (2003)

Formal Verification of Use Case Maps with Real Time Extensions

Jameleddine Hassine[1], Juergen Rilling[1], and Rachida Dssouli[2]

[1] Department of Computer Science, Concordia University, Montreal, Canada
{j_hassin,rilling}@cse.concordia.ca
[2] Concordia Institute for Information Systems Engineering, Montreal, Canada
dssouli@ece.concordia.ca

Abstract. Scenario-driven requirement specifications are widely used to capture and represent functional requirement. More recently, the Use Case Maps language (UCM), being standardized by ITU-T as part of the User Requirements Notation (URN) has gained on popularity within the software requirements community. UCM models focus on the description of functional and behavioral requirements as well as high-level designs at the early stages of system development processes. However, timing issues are often overlooked during the initial system design and treated as non-related behavioral issues and described therefore in separate models. We believe that timing aspects must be integrated into the system model during early development stages. In this paper, we present a novel approach to describe timing constraints in UCM specifications. We describe a formal operational semantics of Timed UCM in terms of Timed Automata (TA) that can be analyzed and verified with the UPPAAL model checker tool. Our approach is illustrated using a case study of the IP Multicast Routing Protocol.

1 Introduction

The Use Case Maps language (UCM) [1] is a high level scenario based modeling technique that can be used to capture and integrate functional requirements in terms of causal scenarios representing behavioral aspects at a high level of abstraction. UCM can also provide stakeholders with guidance and reasoning about a system-wide architecture and behavior. This is being reflected by Use Case Maps being part of a new proposal to ITU-T for a User Requirements Notation (URN) [1] defining informally the abstract syntax and static semantics in Recommendation Z.152 [1]. Existing work [2,3] on formalizing the semantics of UCMs has focused on providing an operational semantics for the UCM language [2] based on Multi-Agent Abstract State Machines. This ASM model provides a concise semantics of UCM functional constructs and describes precisely the control semantics. Another formalization attempt was presented in [3], with UCM constructs being translated into the formal language LOTOS.

UCMs have been successfully used in describing real-time systems, with a particular focus on telecommunication system and services [4]. Typical characteristics of these application domains are that they include event driven behavior,

E. Gaudin, E. Najm, and R. Reed (Eds.): SDL 2007, LNCS 4745, pp. 225–241, 2007.
© Springer-Verlag Berlin Heidelberg 2007

real-time events, parallelism, and distribution. This architectural complexity often results in specifications that can contain errors and undesirable functional properties. Since the correctness of such systems depends on the right timing of operations, a visual inspection or simulation of a model provides only limited guidance in identifying these types of problems. Model checking [5] has proven to be an effective way to find such subtle errors.

In this article, we extend our ongoing research towards the construction of a formal framework for UCM to describe, simulate, analyze and verify real-time systems [2]. We believe that timing aspects must be integrated at an early stage of development to allow for a consistent analysis throughout all lifecycle phases of software product. In what follows we present a novel approach that addresses the following concrete issues:

1. The existing UCM language does not describe semantics involving time and the modeling of timing related information, such as the time required for a transition or a responsibility to complete. In this article we introduce an extension to the existing untimed UCM semantics [2], to allow for the modeling of semantics involving time to support such time related analysis of the UCM models.
2. A formal syntax and semantics in terms of Timed Automata [6] over a dense time model is presented for the timed UCM semantics.
3. Our formal semantics proposed in this paper serves as input to the timed model checker UPPAAL [7] allowing for both, the formal verification of system properties and the simulation and analysis of timed UCM specifications.

In an attempt to make this paper self-contained, we include in Sect. 2 and Sect. 3 some of the core background information relevant to this research, including an overview of the untimed Use Case Maps notation along with a scenario of a Multicast Routing Protocol. Section 4 discusses the real-time extensions to UCM. In Sect. 5, we present the syntax of the resulting timed UCM. Section 6 provides the formal semantics of *Timed UCM* in terms of Timed Automata (TA) [6] and its corresponding UPPAAL models [7]. The resulting models are optimized in Sect. 7 through the use of TA sequential composition. Section 8 describes the application of model checking to verify requirement properties. Finally, conclusions are presented in Sect. 9.

2   Related Work

In a previous work [8], we extended the UCM language with an absolute time syntax and proposed operational semantics in terms of Clocked Transition Systems (CTS) [9] over a discrete time model. In this work, we use dense-time semantics, which is more suitable for distributed systems. Existing research dealing with the addition of time support to modeling languages has taken several directions. One direction consists on focusing on the enhancement of current languages by adding new constructs and time constraints. For instance, timing constraints in variants of MSCs notations are expressed using *timers*, *delay intervals* and *timing markers* [10]. UML Real-Time profiles, such as UML SPT [11] and OMEGA-RT [12], use this approach and add features for describing a variety of timing aspects such as timing, resources, performance, schedulability, duration patterns. UML 2.0 [13] introduces a new diagram called *Timing Diagram* to allow reasoning about time and visualizing state changes over time. Alfonso et al. [14] introduced VTS, a visual language to define event-based properties such as freshness, bounded response, event correlation, etc. The underlying language is based on partial orders and supports real-time constraints in a dense time domain. However, the resulting semantics are not executable. RTGIL [15], an extension of temporal logic, has been proposed in order to enable quantification of time using bounded temporal operators, freeze quantifiers and explicit clock variables.

Another research direction is the combination of an existing notation with another formal description technique to provide better handling of timing aspects. Eshuis [16] presented a formal semantics to UML activity diagrams in terms of clocked transition systems. In [17], a formalization of UML statecharts in terms of hierarchical timed automaton (HTA) is presented. The resulting HTA is translated into a network of flat timed automata to comply with the UPPAAL format. Firley et al. [18] translated UML timed Sequence Diagrams into observers in the UPPAAL formalism allowing for formal verification using model checking. However, the presented construction only supports totally ordered sets of events.

3   Use Case Maps

A Use Case Map specification depicts scenarios as causal flows of responsibilities (operation, action, task, function, etc.) that can be superimposed on underlying structures of components. Components are generic and can represent software entities (objects, processes, databases, servers, etc.), as well as non-software entities (e.g. actors or hardware). These relationships are said to be causal because they involve concurrency, partial ordering of activities and they link causes (e.g. preconditions and triggering events) to effects (e.g. post-conditions and resulting events). Scenarios are expressed above the level of messages exchanged between components and have not necessarily to be bound to a specific underlying structure (such UCMs are called Unbound UCMs). One of the strengths of UCMs is their ability to integrate a number of scenarios together in a map-like diagram, allowing users to reason about the system architecture and behavior. A UCM specification can be further refined to a more detailed system design model such as ITU language Message Sequence Charts [19]. In the following section, we illustrate some of the basic UCM concepts based on an scenario of IP Multicast Group Membership Maintenance example in Fig. 1.

IP Multicast Protocol Group Membership Maintenance. One of the tasks of IP multicast routers is to determine the presence of receivers for a given multicast group. This allows forwarding multicast traffic only where necessary, and avoids flooding of network segments when there are no receivers interested within a given group. Group membership information between hosts and routers on local networks is exchanged through the Internet Group Management Protocol

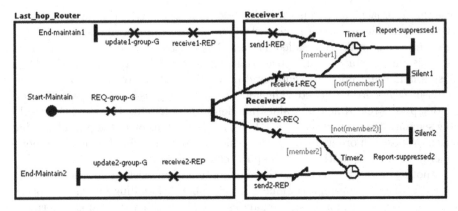

Fig. 1. IP Multicast Group Membership Maintenance

(IGMP) [20]. Hosts willing to receive traffic directed to a multicast group can send a membership *REPORT* message used by the router to enable forwarding of the requested group to the local network segment. Fig. 1 illustrates a typical scenario, where a router (e.g. *last-hop-Router*) periodically refreshes the group membership informations. This refreshing is achieved by sending membership REQUESTs as well as listening for membership REPORTSs from receivers (e.g. *Receiver1* and *Receiver2*) that are still interested in the group. Data forwarding for a group is stopped in case a request times out without any report received. In the IP-Multicast scenario shown in Fig. 1, filled circles represent start points, which captures preconditions and trigger events (start of the scenario *Start-Maintain*). End points model the resulting events, with post-conditions being illustrated as bars perpendicular to the causal paths(e.g. *End-Maintain1* and *End-Maintain2*). Concurrency and partial ordering of responsibilities are supported in UCMs through the use of AND-forks and AND-joins. The membership request (i.e. responsibility *REQ-group-G*) is received by both receivers in two parallel paths. Paths can fork as alternatives (OR-fork), in this case branches can be guarded by conditions shown between square brackets (e.g. *member1* and *not(member1)*).

In cases when the set of local receivers for a group is large, feedback storms can be avoided, by the host delaying a reply request and instead scheduling the transmission of a report (e.g. responsibility *send-report*) at a random time after the initial request. A scheduled transmission (e.g. end points *report-suppressed1* and *report-suppressed2*) is canceled if a report is received (sent by another host) before the scheduled time (e.g. timeout of the timers *Timer1* and *Timer2*).

4   Modeling Time in UCMs: Decision Points

In the context of introducing time in UCMs, the following assumptions are considered:

1. **Timed responsibility enabling.** *Initiation and termination of enabling* timing responsibilities [21] may represent a flexible and suitable choice for

UCMs. Both a lower and upper bound may be imposed on the enabling of these responsibilities. Three options can be considered (note, for illustration purposes the discrete time domain is only used):

- A responsibility R may be associated with a tuple (τ,τ'). Responsibility R is enabled (i.e. can start executing) τ units after the completion of its predecessor (will be discussed in the next bullets). This enabling is offered for τ' units and is retracted after.
- A responsibility R may be associated with a tuple $(\tau,0)$. This type of enabling is called *punctual enabling*, where the enabling retracts if the responsibility is not taken immediately.
- A responsibility R may be associated with a tuple $(\tau,\bot)$. This type of enabling is called *simple enabling*, where no upper bound is imposed on enabling. The responsibility is enabled τ units after its predecessor and never retracts. This may involve major (even infinite) system execution delays.

For simulation and verification purposes and in order to ensure a maximal progress semantics, *punctual enabling* is selected.

2. **Instantaneous (atomic) vs. durational actions.** Approaches that adopt instantaneous action semantics make the modeling more compact and easier to reason about. However, in the context of UCMs a durational semantics is adopted to allow for a more:

- Realistic description of various system requirements for a wide range of application domains, like real time system where actions take only milliseconds to business process models with actions lasting days or even weeks.
- Truly description of concurrent systems where at any given time t more than one action may be executing.

In the context of Use Case Maps, time is only consumed by responsibilities. *MinDur* and *MaxDur* denote respectively the upper and lower bound for the execution time of a responsibility. For simulation purposes, responsibilities with undefined durations are considered to take one clock tick to complete.

3. **Relative vs. absolute time.** A time constraint may be expressed using either an absolute time where the time of occurrence of a responsibility refers to the execution starting time, or a relative time where the time of occurrence of a responsibility refers to the execution of a causally preceding responsibility. In the context of UCMs, relative time is generally preferred over absolute time due to the following reasons:

- In an absolute time model context, changing the origin of time would impact all the constraints in the model.
- In UCM models containing loops the use of absolute time would not be possible because a responsibility, being part of a loop, may be traversed multiple times with different time stamps. In addition, placing an absolute time constraint on a responsibility after a loop would constrain the

number of times a loop can be traversed, which is only known at run-time. Fig. 2 illustrates the situation where the second execution of responsibility a invalidates its absolute time constraint ($MClock=x$). Furthermore, the absolute time constraint of responsibility b ($MClock=y$) will depend on how many times a is executed.

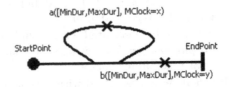

Fig. 2. Absolute time constraint in presence of UCM loop

A UCM model may have more than one start point. In such a case, an absolute time constraint is required and the user may choose the time stamp of one start point to fix the origin of time, or have an independent origin. However, special attention should be given to such decisions since it may impact the overall system constraints and behavior.

4. **Time representation and measurement.** An *interval-based* representation (in contrast to a *point-based* representation) is used to estimate the execution time of a responsibility (i.e. [MinDur, MaxDur]) and to measure the execution time of an end-to-end scenario (e.g. latency measurement).

5. **Dense vs. discrete time.** Our goal is to provide formal semantics of timed UCM in terms of timed automata to be supported by the timed model checker UPPAAL [7]. We have chosen a dense time model which will have, apart from the complexity of reasoning in the verification domain, only minor effect on the proposed semantics.

6. **Global vs. local clocks.** As stated earlier, a global and centralized clock (Master Clock: $MClock$) for measuring and increasing time globally over the system is used to trigger UCM start points. Local clocks are used (1) to measure the delay that a responsibility may have; (2) to measure the time used by a responsibility; (3) and in timers to set a duration, reset to zero and to observe for timeout.

7. **Urgency.** The concept of urgency is introduced into timed UCM semantics as follows:

   - A responsibility R which is associated with a constraint (τ,τ') is considered as *urgent* when it is enabled immediately after the execution of its predecessor construct ($\tau = 0$). Alternatively, a responsibility is considered as *delayable* when a delay is introduced ($\tau \neq 0$).
   - Except responsibilities, all other UCM constructs are considered as urgent once enabled.
   - Transitions are urgent and instantaneous. Transitions are processed as soon as they are enabled allowing for a maximal progress and can therefore be considered as *eager* according to the definition of urgency introduced in [22].

5   Syntax of Timed Use Case Maps

The assumptions discussed in the previous section are the basis for the timed Use Case Maps syntax.

Definition 1 (Timed Use Case Maps). *We assume that a timed UCM is denoted by an 8-tuple (D, H, λ, C, GVar, Bc, Bs, MClock) where:*

- *D is the UCM domain, composed of sets of typed elements. $D = SP \cup EP \cup R \cup AF \cup AJ \cup OF \cup OJ \cup Tm \cup ST$. Where SP, EP, R, AF, AJ, OF, OJ, Tm and ST are respectively the sets of Start Points, End Points, Responsibilities, AND-Fork, AND-Join, OR-Fork, OR-Join, Timers and Stubs.*
- *H is the set of edges connecting UCM constructs to each other.*
- *λ is a transition relation defined as: $\lambda = D \times H \times D$.*
- *C is the set of components (C = $\emptyset$ for unbound UCM).*
- *GVar is the set of global variables.*
- *Bc is a component binding relation defined as $Bc = D \times C$. Bc specifies which element of D is associated with which component of C. Bc is empty for unbound UCM.*
- *Bs is a stub binding relation and is defined as $Bs = ST \times IN/OUT \times SP/EP$. Bs specifies how the start and end points of the plug-in map would be connected to the path segments going into or out of the stub.*
- *MClock is the system master clock.*

The signature of timed UCM constructs (see Fig. 3) is defined as follows:

Definition 2 (Timed UCM Constructs)

- **Start Points** are of the form *SP (PreCondition-set, TriggeringEvent-set, SP-label, in, out, DL)* where the parameter *PreConditions-set* is a list of conditions that must be satisfied in order for the scenario to be enabled (if no precondition is specified, then by default it is set to true). The parameter *TriggeringEvent-set* is a list that provides the set of events that can initiate the scenario along a path. The parameter *SP-label* denotes the label of the start point. A start point should not have an incoming edge except when connected to an end point (called a waiting place) or an entry edge of a stub. The parameter *in $\in$ H* represents such incoming edge. The parameter *out $\in$ H* is the (unique) outgoing edge. *DL* is an optional absolute time delay used to introduce a delay in the start point triggering that may occur especially in the presence of more than one start point. *DL* is expressed relatively to *MClock*.
- **End Points** are of the form *EP (PostCondition-set, ResultingEvent-set, EP-label, in, out)*, where the parameter *PostConditions-set* is a list of conditions that must be satisfied once the scenario is completed. The parameter *ResultingEvent-set* is a list that gives the set of events that result from the completion of the scenario path. The parameter *EP-label* denotes the label of the end point; the parameter *in $\in$ H* is the (unique) incoming edge. End

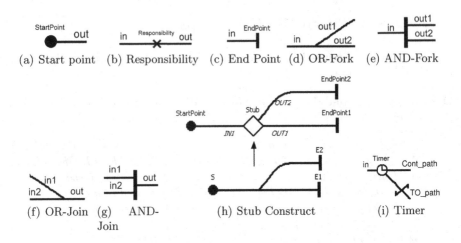

Fig. 3. UCM Constructs

points have no target edge except when connected to a start point (i.e. a waiting place) or connected to an exit edge of a stub, represented by $out \in H$. End points are not delayed.

- **Responsibilities** are of the form $Resp(in, R\text{-}label, out, [MinDur, MaxDur], DL)$ where $in \in H$ is the incoming edge, $R\text{-}label$ is the activity to be executed, and $out \in H$ is the outgoing edge. $MinDur$ and $MaxDur$ are respectively the minimum and maximum time allowed for a responsibility to complete its execution. As stated in Sect. 4, DL represents respectively a possible lower bound for the delay. As discussed earlier, we consider *punctual enabling*.
- **OR-Forks** are of the form $OR\text{-}Fork(in, [Cond_i]_{i \leq n}, [out_i]_{i \leq n})$, where in denotes the incoming edge, $[Cond_i]_{i \leq n}$ is a finite sequence of Boolean expressions, and $[out_i]_{i \leq n}$ is a sequence of outgoing edges.
- **OR-Joins** are of the form $OR\text{-}Join(\{in_i\}_{i \leq n}, out)$, where $\{in_i\}_{i \leq n}$ denotes the incoming edges, and out is the outgoing edge.
- **AND-Forks** are of the form $AND\text{-}Fork(in, \${out_i}_{i \leq n})$, where in denotes the incoming edge, and $\{out_i\}_{i \leq n}$ is a set of outgoing edges.
- **AND-Joins** are of the form $AND\text{-}Join(\{in_i\}_{i \leq n}, out)$, where $\{in_i\}_{i \leq n}$ denotes the incoming edges, and out is the outgoing edge. Time elapses in AND-Join while waiting for all incoming edges to synchronize. Such delays are conditioned by the internal execution of the system and do not represent a user requirement.
- **Timers** are of the form $Timer\ (in,\ TriggeringEvent\text{-}set,\ cont\_path,\ to\_path, TO)$. The synchronous timer is similar to a basic OR-Fork with two outgoing disjoint branches. The parameter $TriggeringEvents\text{-}set$ is the list that contains the set of events that can trigger the continuation path (i.e. $cont\_path$) and the parameter $to\_path \in H$ denotes the timeout path (marked with a crooked bar in Fig. 3(i)). TO is the timer's expiration time.
- **Stubs** have the form $Stub(\{entry_i\}_{i \leq n}, \{exit_j\}_{j \leq m}, isDynamic, [Cond_k]_{k \leq l}, [plugin_k]_{k \leq l})$ where $\{entry_i\}_{i \leq n}$ and $\{exit_j\}_{j \leq m}$ denote respectively the set

of the stub entry and exit points. *isDynamic* indicates whether the stub is dynamic or static. Dynamic stubs may contain multiple plug-ins $[plugin_k]_{k \leq l}$ whose selection can be determined at run-time according to a selection-policy specified by the sequence of Boolean expressions $[Cond_k]_{k \leq l}$. The sequence *Cond* is empty for static stubs (i.e. *isDynamic=false*). No time constraints are defined for stubs since a stub is simply a container for plug-ins and the execution of a stub is the execution of the selected plug-in.

We have added the modeling of timing as an orthogonal feature to the untimed UCM syntax presented in [2]. The untimed syntax can be restored simply by removing the duration and delay of responsibilities as well as the delay observed by start points. UCM control constructs such as OR-Fork, Or-Join, AND-Fork and AND-Join are executed without delay. No relevant user requirements may suggest such delays.

6   Formal Semantics of Timed Use Case Maps

In this section, we define the formal semantics of timed UCM models in terms of Timed Automata (TA) [6].

6.1   Timed Automata (TA)

The theory of timed automata was introduced by Alur and Dill [6]. A timed automaton is a finite-state Büchi automaton extended with a finite set of real-valued variables modeling clocks. Timed automata has been adopted in several verification tools including UPPAAL [7]. In the following section, we give the formal syntax and semantics of timed automata as defined in [23].

6.2   TA Formal Syntax and Semantics

Assume a finite set of real-valued variables C ranged over x, y etc. standing for clocks and a finite alphabet Σ ranged over by a, b etc. standing for actions.

Clock constraints. A clock constraints is a conjunctive formula of atomic constraints of the form $x \sim n$ or $x-y \sim n$ for x, y $\in$ C, $\sim \in \{\leq, <, =, >, \geq\}$ and n$\in$ℕ. A clock constraint is downward closed if $\sim \in \{\leq, <, =\}$. We use $\mathscr{B}(C)$ to denote the set of clock constraints, ranged over by g and also by D later.

Guards and Invariants. A guard is a finite conjunction over data constraints and clock constraints. An invariant is a finite conjunction over downward closed clock constraints. Both conjunction types contain additionally the constants true and false.

Assignments. A data assignment is of the form v:= A, where v$\in$V and A an arithmetic expression over V . A clock reset is of the form x:=0, where x$\in$C.

Definition 3 (Timed Automaton)
A timed automaton A is a tuple $< N, l_0, E, I >$ *where:*

- N *is a finite set of locations (or nodes),*
- $l_0 \in N$ *is the initial location*
- $E \subseteq N \times \mathscr{B}(C) \times \Sigma \times 2^C \times N$ *is the set of edges and*
- $I\colon N \to \mathscr{B}(C)$ *assigns invariants to locations*

There are two types of transitions between states: *delay transitions* (the automaton stays in a location) and *action transition* (and enabled edge is taken).

Clock assignments functions are used to track the changes of clock values. Let u, v denote such functions, and use u∈g to mean that the clock values denoted by u satisfy the guard g. For d∈ $\mathbb{R}_+$, let u+d denote the clock assignment that maps all x∈C to u(x) + d, and for r⊆C, let [r ↦0] u denote the clock assignment that maps all clocks in r to 0 and agree with u for the other clocks in C-{r}.

Definition 4 (TA Operational Semantics). *The semantics of a timed automaton is a transition system (also known as a timed transition system) where states are pairs* $< l, u >$ *and transitions are defined by the rules:*

- $\langle l,u \rangle \xrightarrow{d} \langle l, u+d \rangle$ *if* $u \in I(l)$ *and* $(u+d) \in I(l)$ *for a non-negative real d in* $\mathbb{R}_+$
- $\langle l,u \rangle \xrightarrow{a} \langle l', u' \rangle$ *if* $l \xrightarrow{g,a,r} l'$, $u \in g$, $u' = [r \mapsto 0]u$ *and* $u' \in I(l')$

6.3   The Model Checker UPPAAL

UPPAAL [7] is an integrated tool environment for modeling, validation and verification of real-time systems modeled by a network of timed automata. In addition to the timed automata features presented above, UPPAAL supports synchronization annotation of the form a!(offer) or a?(acceptance). If the transition carries such synchronization then some corresponding transition (labeled by a! or a?) of some other timed automaton has to be taken simultaneously. We refer the reader to [7] for a detailed introduction to UPPAAL.

6.4   Timed UCM Constructs in UPPAAL

As stated in Sect. 3, UCM specifications are defined above the level of messages (i.e. UCMs do not support the notion of send or receive of messages). Instead, UCMs use global variables to define different UCM execution paths. In this section, we model a timed UCM specification as a set of concurrent timed automata. Each process interacts with other processes through synchronization channels and read-write operations to global variables. Since the UPPAAL semantics does not support *maximal progress semantics*, the synchronization channels are only used to coordinate the transfer of control between UCM constructs. In what follows, we define a TA template for each timed UCM construct:

- **Start Point.** Fig. 4(a) illustrates the TA of a start point. The start point is triggered when the *PreCondition-set* is satisfied, and there occurs at least one event from the *triggeringEvent-set*, and the delay constraint is met. This is described by a conjunction of Boolean conditions attached to the transition guard: PreCondition-set ∧ triggeringEvent-set ∧ 'MClock≥DL'. The process writes into the channel *out* and the control passes to the next construct. If the start point is part of a plugin within a stub, then the start point process must synchronize with the entry edge of the stub through reading from *in* channel (see Fig. 4(b)).

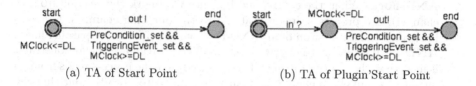

(a) TA of Start Point   (b) TA of Plugin'Start Point

Fig. 4. TA of a Start Point

Usually, a UCM describes a system and its environment in one single map. It shows the resulting interactions between the different actors and the system under design. Only for illustration purpose, Fig. 5 shows a start point that interacts with the environment through channel synchronization.

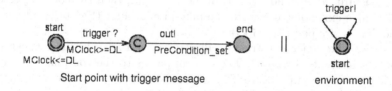

Start point with trigger message   environment

Fig. 5. Start point triggered by the environment

- **Responsibility.** Each responsibility has two local clocks: *delay* used to measure the delay that a responsibility may have and *LClock* is used to measure the duration of execution of a responsibility. The TA synchronizes with the preceding construct through the channel *in*. During this transition, local clock *delay* is initialized to *zero*. The process stays in location *wait* for *DL* (the invariant *delay* ≤ *DL* is used to model punctual enabling making the transition as *urgent* after *DL*), then start executing for an amount of time within [*MinDur, MaxDur*] interval. The location invariant *LClock* ≤ *MaxDur* is used to make the process leave the state *executing* whenever the local clock becomes greater than *MaxDur*. The control passes to the next construct after writing to *out* channel (see Fig. 6(a)). Responsibilities may have global variable assignments attached to them. These updates are attached to the transition between locations *executing* and *end*. Fig. 6(b) illustrates such a TA with assignment 'var:=x'.

- **OR-Fork.** When the control passes to the OR-Fork through reading from *in* channel, the conditions are evaluated and the control passes to the edge associated with the true condition. If more than one condition evaluates to true (i.e. nondeterministic choice), the control passes randomly to one of the outgoing edges associated to the true conditions. Fig. 6(c) illustrates the automaton associated to an OR-Fork with two outgoing edges.
- **OR-Join.** When one or many flows reach an OR-Join (i.e. through synchronization on *in* channels), the control passes to the outgoing edge through the *out* channel. Fig. 6(d) shows the automaton of OR-Join with two incoming edges.
- **AND-Fork.** When the control reaches the AND-Fork (by reading from *in* channel), the process writes repeatedly to the outgoing channels. Fig. 6(e) illustrates the automaton of an AND-Fork with two outgoing parallel flows.
- **AND-Join.** When parallel flows reach an AND-Join and the delay constraint is met, then they must be joined. It is required that the process reads from all incoming channels to enable the transition and writes into the *out* channel. The last flow arriving to the AND-Join will fire the automaton. Fig. 6(f) shows the automaton of an AND-Join with two incoming parallel flows.
- **Stub.** The stub automaton implements the binding relation between a stub and a plug-in(i.e. *Bs*), allowing for the control to pass from a stub'entry point to a start point and from a plugin end point to a stub'exit point. Fig. 6(g) illustrates the timed automaton for a stub with one entry point *entry* and one exit point *exit*.
- **End Point.** If the end point is inside a plug-in, then the control passes to the stub's exit point bound to the plug-in end point (Fig. 6(j)). Otherwise, the flow is stopped (Fig. 6(k)).
- **Timer.** The timer construct is illustrated in Fig. 6(h). The timer stays for TO in location *waiting*. The control passes to the continuation path in case an event occurs before TO. Otherwise, the control moves to the time out path (i.e. TO_path). There are situations where an action is required as soon as the timer expires (i.e. timeout event and the action are atomic). Fig. 6(i) shows a timer template with action (i.e. global variable assignment) attached to it.

A timed UCM specification is represented as a collection of timed automata where each timed UCM construct is translated into an instance process based on the underlined templates. This design solution is simple to implement and provides a great level of flexibility. However, the following shortcomings are worth noting:

- This approach is costly in terms of number of concurrent processes, number of locations and number of local clocks.
- The presented approach does not support cycles (i.e. loops). Indeed, once a construct is executed (i.e. reaches its TA end location), it cannot be executed a second time because there is no extra transition connecting its *end* location to its *start* location.

In the subsequent section, we propose an approach to reduce the number of processes considerably that also allows for the description of cycles.

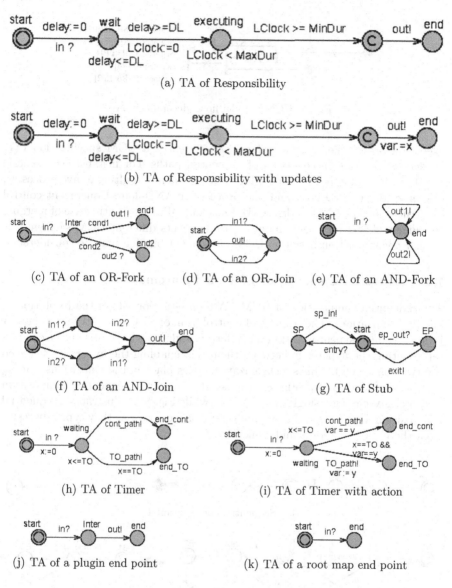

Fig. 6. TA templates of UCM constructs

7 Optimized Approach

7.1 Sequential vs. Parallel Control Flows

The transfer of control between sequential constructs occurs in a deterministic way (i.e. in complete order), while concurrent executions result in different

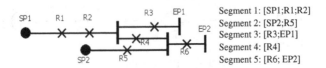

Segment 1: [SP1;R1;R2]
Segment 2: [SP2;R5]
Segment 3: [R3;EP1]
Segment 4: [R4]
Segment 5: [R6; EP2]

Fig. 7. UCM parallel flows decomposition

execution orders (i.e. partial order). Consequently, a UCM specification may be decomposed into a collection of sequential paths. For instance, the generic UCM in Fig. 7 may be decomposed into five segments resulting in five processes, one process for AND-Fork and one process for AND-Join. Concurrent control constructs such as AND-Forks, AND-Joins and OR-Joins (in the case of merging concurrent flows) represent the glue that connects different UCM segments. A further decomposition based on UCM component binding may be considered.

7.2   Sequential Composition of Timed Automata

The sequential composition of UCM TA templates consists of the resolution of all synchronizations. The transfer of control from one UCM construct to another is done through synchronization (i.e. offer(a!) and acceptance(a!)) on the channel representing the hyperedge between them (i.e. enabling the hyperedge between the two constructs). This synchronization takes place in the transitions leading to locations labeled *end*. Fig. 8(a) illustrates a generic sequential composition for processes having a single *end* location, while Fig. 8(b) illustrates a sequential composition for processes having multiple *end* locations, as they typically result from the use of OR-Forks and Timers.

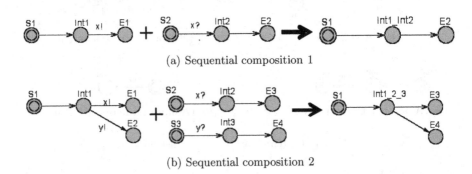

(a) Sequential composition 1

(b) Sequential composition 2

Fig. 8. TA Sequential Composition

Fig. 9 shows the result of the sequential composition for the UCM introduced in Fig. 1. Fig. 9(a) shows the timed automata of the segment composed of the start point *start-maintain* followed by responsibility *REQ-group-G*. Fig. 9(b) shows the timed automata of the segment starting at responsibility *receive-REQ*

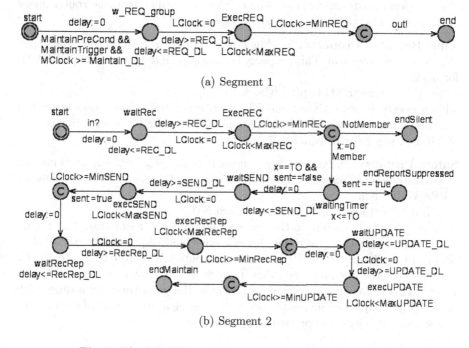

(a) Segment 1

(b) Segment 2

Fig. 9. TA of IP Multicast Group Membership Maintenance

and ends with the end points *Silent, Report-suppressed* and *End-maintain*. The later is instantiated twice, one for each receiver. The three processes are connected through an AND-Fork TA template 6(e).

8   Formal Verification

UPPAAL uses a subset of Timed Computational Tree Logic(TCTL). In this section, we verify selected properties against the model described in Fig. 1 and implemented in UPPAAL in Fig. 9. We assume that both receivers are members of the same multicast group and all responsibilities have a duration between 1 and 2 with a delay of 1. To avoid deadlock situations at *end locations*, we add a loop transition at each of the 6 *end locations* of the model in Fig. 9.

Precedence Property: *For any receiver, the sending of a report is always preceded by a reception of a query.* This property is translated into the following UPPAAL formula:

A<>(rec1.execSEND imply seg1.ExecREQ).

This property is checked to be true by the UPPAAL verifier.

Liveness Property: *In the presence of receivers, the multicast group should be updated.* This property is translated into the following formula:

E<>(rec1.execUPDATE or rec2.execUPDATE).

This property holds since one of the two receivers responds to the router query and the group is eventually updated.

Time Bounded Property: *Sending a report occurs at least 10 time units after the start of the scenario.* This property is translated into the following UPPAAL formula:

A [] (rec1.execSEND imply MClock > 10).

This property is not satisfied and UPPAAL generates an execution trace of a counter example showing that the responsibility *send-REP* may occur as soon as MClock is greater or equal to 7.

Safety Property: *In the presence of more than one receiver, only one and only one receiver should send a report.* This property is translated into the following UPPAAL formula:

A[] not (rec1.execSEND and rec2.execSEND).

This property fails leading to the generation of a counter example. This failure is due to the fact that the timer timeout event and responsibility *SEND-REP* occur in two distinct steps. Hence, timer timeouts in Receiver 1 and Receiver 2 may be triggered one after the other. In such a case, both receivers will send a report. This behavior is corrected by replacing the plain timer by a timer with action (Fig. 6(i)) which makes the action of sending a report part of the timeout transition. Therefore, the property becomes true.

9   Conclusions

In this paper, we have presented an extension to the Use Case Maps language with timing information to allow for modeling real-time systems at the early stages of a system development process. We have introduced a concise formal operational semantics for timed UCM based on Timed Automata. The resulting semantics serves as input to the timed model checker UPPAAL allowing for the formal verification of system properties. As part of our future work, we will investigate how schedulability theory can be applied to timed UCM models.

References

1. ITU-T: New draft Recommendation Z.152: URN - Use Case Map Notation (UCM). Temporary Document 3201, 27 April, ITU-T Study Group 17 (2006)
2. Hassine, J., Rilling, J., Dssouli, R.: Abstract Operational Semantics for Use Case Maps. In: Wang, F. (ed.) FORTE 2005. LNCS, vol. 3731, pp. 2–5. Springer, Heidelberg (2005)
3. Amyot, D.: Formalization of timethreads using LOTOS. Master's thesis, University of Ottawa, Ottawa, Ontario, Canada (1994)
4. Amyot, D., Logrippo, L., Buhr, R.J.A., Gray, T.: Use case maps for the capture and validation of distributed systems requirements. In: RE'99. Fourth IEEE International Symposium on Requirements Engineering, pp. 44–53. IEEE Computer Society Press, Los Alamitos (1999)

5. Clarke, J.E.M., Grumberg, O., Peled, D.A.: Model Checking. MIT Press, Cambridge (1999)
6. Alur, R., Dill, D.L.: A theory of Timed Automata. Theor. Comput. Sci. 126(2), 183–235 (1994)
7. Larsen, K.G., Pettersson, P., Yi, W.: UPPAAL in a nutshell. International Journal on Software Tools for Technology Transfer 1(1-2), 134–152 (1997)
8. Hassine, J., Rilling, J., Dssouli, R.: Timed Use Case Maps. In: Gotzhein, R., Reed, R. (eds.) SAM 2006. LNCS, vol. 4320, pp. 99–114. Springer, Heidelberg (2006)
9. Manna, Z., Pnueli, A.: Clocked transition systems. Technical report, Stanford University, Stanford, CA, USA (1996)
10. Meng-Siew, N.: Reasoning with timing constraints in message sequence charts. Master's thesis, University of Stirling, Scotland, U.K (August 1993)
11. OMG: Response to the OMG RFP for Schedulability, Performance and Time, v. 2.0. OMG document ad/2002-03-04 (March 2002)
12. Graf, S., Ober, I., Ober, I.: A real-time profile for UML. Int. J. Softw. Tools Technol. Transf. 8(2), 113–127 (2006)
13. OMG: Unified Modeling Language: Superstructure version 2.1.1, formal/2007-02-05 (February 2007)
14. Alfonso, A., Braberman, V., Kicillof, N., Olivero, A.: Visual timed event scenarios. In: ICSE '04. Proceedings of the 26th International Conference on Software Engineering, pp. 168–177. IEEE Computer Society Press, Washington, DC (2004)
15. Moser, L.E., Ramakrishna, Y.S., Kutty, G., Melliar-Smith, P.M., Dillon, L.K.: A graphical environment for the design of concurrent real-time systems. ACM Transactions on Software Engineering and Methodology 6(1), 31–79 (1997)
16. Eshuis, H.: Semantics and Verification of UML Activity Diagrams for Workflow Modelling. PhD thesis, University of Twente, Enschede, The Netherlands (2002)
17. David, A., Moller, M.O., Yi, W.: Formal verification of UML statecharts with real-time extensions. In: Kutsche, R.-D., Weber, H. (eds.) ETAPS 2002 and FASE 2002. LNCS, vol. 2306, pp. 218–232. Springer, London (2002)
18. Firley, T., Huhn, M., Diethers, K., Gehrke, T., Goltz, U.: Timed sequence diagrams and tool-based analysis A case study. In: France, R.B., Rumpe, B. (eds.) UML '99 - The Unified Modeling Language. Beyond the Standard. LNCS, vol. 1723, pp. 645–660. Springer, Heidelberg (1999)
19. ITU-T: Recommendation Z.120. Message Sequence Charts (2004)
20. Fenner, W.: Internet Group Management Protocol, IGMP version 2 (1997)
21. Bowman, H., Gomez, R.: Concurrency Theory - Calculi and Automata for Modelling Untimed and Timed Concurrent Systems. Springer, Heidelberg (2006)
22. Bornot, S., Sifakis, J., Tripakis, S.: Modeling Urgency in Timed Systems. In: de Roever, W.-P., Langmaack, H., Pnueli, A. (eds.) COMPOS 1997. LNCS, vol. 1536, pp. 103–129. Springer, Heidelberg (1998)
23. Bengtsson, J., Yi, W.: Timed automata: Semantics, algorithms and tools. In: Desel, J., Reisig, W., Rozenberg, G. (eds.) Lectures on Concurrency and Petri Nets. LNCS, vol. 3098, pp. 87–124. Springer, Heidelberg (2004)

Using Probabilist Models for Studying Realistic Systems: A Case Study of Pastry

Guillaume Châtelet, Benoit Parreaux, and Yves-Marie Quemener

France Telecom, R&D Division
2 avenue Pierre Marzin, 22300 Lannion, France
{guillaume.chatelet, benoit.parreaux,
yvesmarie.quemener}@orange-ftgroup.com

Abstract. Telecommunication services will be in the future built upon peer-to-peer protocols. This implies the need to have strong guarantees of the dependability of those protocols. One building block for such protocols are distributed hash tables (DHT in short), and Pastry is a protocol implementing distributed hash tables. We have designed a probabilist model of Pastry that enabled us to simulate it. In particular, we have studied the performance of the protocol with respect to the number of nodes. We have used for this study probabilistic model checking tools used in the RNTL project Averros. This is a significant application of academic tools to industrial concerns.

Keywords: Model checking, probabilistic models, PRISM, APMC, Pastry.

1 Introduction

One of the striking changes in the telecommunication field during the last years has been the explosion of peer-to-peer systems. Such systems deliver services, like file delivery for example, by relying upon component nodes which participate in similar roles for delivering the service. Peer-to-peer systems can be viewed as decentralized network architectures in contrast with client-server architectures where roles are sharply distinguished between clients which request the service and servers which answer the requests.

The peer-to-peer networks are today overwhelmingly used for providing file delivery services. The peer-to-peer file sharing is now universally used but telecommunication operators are envisioning to use peer-to-peer systems for delivering other services. The advantages of peer-to-peer architectures is that they provide theoretically: fault-tolerance (since all nodes play the same role, the failure of one will have few impact), scalability (again, since all nodes play the same role, it is enough to add more nodes for scaling up the service), and a lack of resource bottlenecks.

But it is difficult to guarantee the overall behaviour of peer-to-peer systems. Some special configurations could introduce overall instability. For delivering

E. Gaudin, E. Najm, and R. Reed (Eds.): SDL 2007, LNCS 4745, pp. 242–257, 2007.

more critical services using peer-to-peer systems, telecommunication operators will need to make experiments and simulations for deriving strong guarantees upon their properties. Our work takes place in this general context. We want to show how a probabilist modelling can be used in an industrial setting for designing dependable systems and obtain guarantees about performance aspects of a realistic size model.

We have studied the distributed hash table protocol called Pastry [1]. A distributed hash table (in short DHT) provides the same lookup service than a hash table but using peer-to-peer principles. Since the relevant data of the DHT is distributed between all the participating nodes, a DHT system has got to include a routing algorithm which enables to find the relevant information by hopping from node to node. Pastry is an original DHT protocol, originally designed by Rowstron and Druschel [5]. There exist open source implementations of Pastry from Microsoft Research [2]. As a DHT implementation, Pastry is a good candidate for being used as a building block for peer-to-peer services. As such, it is interesting to have guarantees upon its behaviour. We used the simulation and model-checking tools that were extended in the Averros project [1], precisely Prism [4] and APMC [3], for deriving such guarantees. Of particular interest to us, we used the possibility to model probabilistic events for analyzing the behaviour of Pastry.

In a first section, we present shortly the Pastry protocol and more precisely its routing algorithm. We then describe in the next section the choices we made during our modeling of Pastry. Our simulations are oriented towards evaluating the impact of the login/logout of the nodes on the routing performance of Pastry. The routing algorithm of Pastry is supposed to enable to route messages in a number of hops which increases as the logarithm of number of nodes. We will see that this is indeed the case.

2   A Short Presentation of Pastry

Pastry implements a distributed hash table. As such, a Pastry system is made of several identical nodes upon which the relevant hashtable information is distributed. Each Pastry node has got a Pastry identifier, which is also the hash key for its relevant information. A Pastry node also maintains a network address, which enables other nodes to communicate with it.

The most important part of Pastry is its routing algorithm. When you are performing a lookup and/or an insert in the DHT managed by Pastry, the information you have at the start is the Pastry identifier that you want to lookup or insert and a network identifier for another Pastry node. The node which is directly accessible does not have necessarily the pertinent information. This node will then have to route your request to the pertinent node. For describing this routing algorithm, we will first describe Pastry identifiers, then the routing tables that each node maintains. We will then describe the insertion and update operations and then the routing algorithm itself.

2.1 Pastry Identifiers

The addressing scheme of Pastry is based on a ring. Each node has got a position on this virtual ring according to its identifier. This identifier is attributed to the node at the initialization time. It is created using a hash function applied to node data, for instance the node's IP address. The identifier is written in base B and has a length of l digits. We can now see the virtual ring split recursively into B parts. Each digit of the node identifier corresponds to the name of a partition of the ring. There can be at maximum B^l identifiers.

For example, in the remaining of this paper, we will use a base $B = 4$ and a length $l = 8$. An example of Pastry identifier is then $i = 10322102$. The ring is divided into quadrants, and each quadrant is split itself into quadrants. For the node i, it is situated in the second quadrant of the ring (first digit of i is 1), then in the first quadrant of this quadrant (second digit of i is 0), etc.

At the initialization, we suppose that the quality of the hash function and the size of B and l is such that there is no collision with preexisting Pastry identifiers. Typical choices for B and l would be $B = 16$ and $l = 8$ to fit the most popular integer size.

2.2 Routing Tables

Internally, each Pastry node keeps updated three routing tables. A cell in those tables is a pair made of a Pastry identifier and a network address. Each time a Pastry identifier is present in one of the routing tables, it is possible to communicate directly with it, using its network address. In this case, the routing ends with a last hop.

The first routing table is called the leaf table. It contains B cells, where B is the base used for Pastry identifiers. The nodes put into that table are the neighbouring nodes, in the sense that Pastry identifiers are close. For example, for the node $s = 20322102$, we could have in the leaf table the routing data for the Pastry nodes $20322100, 20322101, 20322103$ and 20322110. Of course, in this case the four immediate neighbours of s have been created, which is not at all guaranteed. A more realistic table will contain for example the Pastry nodes $20313010, 20320013, 2322230$ and 23330010. But, it is an invariant of Pastry that the Leaf table contains the closest nodes of s with respect to the Pastry identifier. At each insertion of a new node, this insertion is realized by the closest node of the new node, which uses its own Leaf table for giving an up-to-date table to the new one. The new node will broadcast its own identity to its neighbours that will update their own Leaf tables.

The second routing table is the main routing table. It contains l lines of B cells. Each cell contains information for one representative of recursive divisions of the Pastry ring, going closer of the original identifier. The node containing the routing table will be itself its representative for its own sectors. For example, for the node $s = 20322102$, the first line of its main routing table could have nodes such as $t = 0xxxxxxx$, t will be the representative for the first quadrant; $u = 1yyyyyyy$ will be the representative for the second quadrant; s will be its own representative for the third quadrant and $v = 3zzzzzzz$ will be the representatives for the fourth quadrant. The second line will have representatives for the four subdivisions of the third quadrant. The node $s = 20322102$ is its own representative for the first division of the third quadrant, followed by, for example $w = 21aaaaaa$, $x = 22bbbbbb$, $y = 23cccccc$. Of course, this routing table can also have empty cells, with no representatives for the corresponding subdivision.

The third routing table is the network routing table. It contains Pastry identifiers whose network addresses are close, in a network sense, of the own node. It enables shortcuts in the routing algorithm. When the node has got to route a message to one node that happens to be in this network neighbours' list, it routes directly the message in one hop using this table. In our modelling of Pastry, we will not take this table into account. Since this table provides shortcuts, this means that our estimation of the routing performance of the algorithm will be an over-approximation. We will see that we nevertheless find that the order of a logarithmic performance is obtained even without this optimization.

2.3   Routing Algorithm and Table Updates

Initially, a new Pastry node has got empty routing tables. It broadcasts its Pastry identifier and it will be registered in the Pastry system by its closest network neighbour. Its network neighbours will answer to the new node with their own routing tables. This will give it first data to put in its routing table. In parallel, the closest network neighbour of the newcomer will uses the routing algorithm to register the newcomer into Pastry. It makes a routing towards the closest neighbour of the newcomer in terms of Pastry identifiers. This routing will update all the participants with the data about the newcomer. In general, each time that nodes route messages, they update their tables if they get more precise infos for filling their tables with the routing requests. As soon as routing tables are known, the routing algorithm is quite simple:

- If the identifier of the receiver is in the leaf table, the node directly sends the message to the receiver. This is a one hop routing.
- If the identifier of the receiver is not in its leaf table, the node searches in its main routing table the closest node with the receiver in terms of Pastry identifiers. This means the node with a identifier which shares the longest same prefix as the identifier of the receiver.
- In some rare cases, it may happen that the node can't find a node closest than itself in the main routing table and the receiver is nevertheless not in its leaf table. In this case, the node makes a best effort routing. It will send the message to route towards one of its referenced nodes, hoping it will be able to route better than itself. This is what we call in the following the rare case of routing.

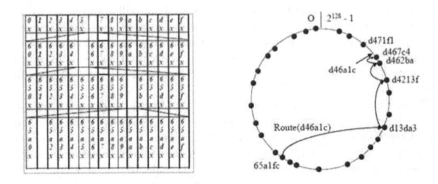

Fig. 1. A routing table and a routing example

For ensuring the termination of the routing algorithm, at each hop the distance between the receiver node and the message must decrease. Even in the rare case, the algorithm will try to route the message to a node closest to the receiver. To show that the routing algorithm works well we must show that the rare case is effectively rare.

Figure 1 shows an example of the result of the routing from node 65A1FC to node D46A1C, with an hexadecimal base and 6 digits. This example comes from [5].

3   Abstractions and the Use of Probabilist Modelling

In this paper, we developed models of Pastry in order to use them in the tools studied during the Averroès project [1]. The goal of our work is to compute the number of hops nb_hop needed to route a message, when the Pastry algorithm works with a significant number of nodes.

We could have used a classical model checking tool, developing an exact model of the behaviour of individual nodes, and trying to have an exhaustive simulation of the complete behaviour of Pastry. But such a modelling will have been impossible for a realistic number of nodes because of the well-known state explosion problem. A probabilist modelling enables properties for the whole behaviour of the system to be derived even for important sizes. In our model, the complexity of the nodes' states is abstracted by some probabilist predicates that we propose below.

Such probabilist modelling implies that we define the nb_hop function directly as a function and not as an emerging property of the individual behaviours of nodes. This makes it necessary to abstract irrelevant points for defining nb_hop. This is what we will study in this section.

3.1   Defining Distances as an Abstraction

Modelling each node with their own routing tables is not possible. The size of the model will prohibit the use of any kind of tools for a realistic number of nodes. So we need to define an abstraction of the system that will enable us to avoid to use an explicit definition of routing tables.

If we assume that the nodes are equally dispatched on the ring, we can also assume that the routing tables look sensibly the same in all the nodes. This assumption is dependent upon the quality of the hashing function used for producing the Pastry identifier at the node initialization. This leads us to assume that the routing scheme does not depend upon the Pastry identifiers of the concerned nodes but upon the distance between the sender and the receiver whatever their locations are in the ring. This is the main idea behind our modelling of Pastry. We abstract the identifiers of nodes and consider a routing in term of distances.

Consider the routing from the node $s = 20322102$ to the node $r = 32102101$. In a perfect routing scheme, s will send a message to the node in the third case of the first line of its routing table (for example, $s_1 = 30210130$). Then, this node will send the message to the node in the second case of the second line of its routing table (for example $s_2 = 32012212$). It will then continue until a node s_n will have the receiver $r = 32102101$ inside its Leaf data.

We consider this routing scheme the following way: we need to route to a node distant of 11213333, which is the distance between s and r (here $r - s$). After the first hop, the message will be in the node s_1. The distance between this node and the receiver will then be 01231311 and in the node s_2 the distance is 00023223.

By only considering the distance between nodes, we can abstract node identifiers. We also need to model the routing algorithm to use only distances:

- If the distance is small enough, the receiver should be in the Leaf list of the node. After one hop, the routing should end.
- If the distance is bigger, the algorithm will use the routing table to send the message to a node that shares the longest same prefix than the identifier of the receiver. If we consider it in terms of distance, we will say that the distance decreases by at least of one digit.
- In the rare case, the distance is unchanged. The number nb_hop is increased but the distance is not modified.

This concept of "small enough" that we just introduced implies that we need to use a probabilist modelling. If we used a traditional exact modelling and simulation, even talking in terms of distance, we will need to define exactly whether the receiver is or not close enough for being in the Leaf list. Hence, our abstraction of identifiers in terms of distances will not have been powerful enough for studying a real-size Pastry system. By defining probabilist predicates, we can abstract completely the mechanism for deciding whether a node is or is not in the Leaf list of another one.

3.2   A Predicate for Modelling Leaf Lists

According to our assumption of an homogeneous distribution of the nodes around the ring, we can compute the average distance between two nodes: $\frac{B^l}{nb\_node}$. If we note the node identifier in the base B with l digits, there are B^l identifiers so the length of the ring is B^l. If there are nb_node nodes on the ring, the average distance between two nodes is $\frac{B^l}{nb\_node}$. This allows us to define a predicate to decide whether a node a is in the $Leaf$ set of the node n: $In\_Leaf(a,n) \cong dist(a,n) < \frac{B^l}{nb\_node} \cdot \frac{L}{2}$ where L is the number of elements in the set $Leaf$.

This predicate is an approximate way to check the presence of a node in a Leaf set. We can say that sometimes, if there is a concentration of nodes in a part of the ring, the averrage distance between two nodes in this part of the ring will be less than $\frac{B^l}{nb\_node}$. Hence, the predicate may answer in this case with erroneous positive answers. On the contrary, if the node is in a part where there are less nodes in the ring, the predicate may give false negative answers. This predicate is a good first approximation of the real behaviour of the algorithm, depending upon the performance of the hashing function. We could refine it by taking into account a probabilistic distribution of nodes up the ring.

The first version of In_Leaf takes into account two nodes a and n. But, in the following, we don't take into account individual nodes. Hence, we define a predicate that is true for nodes that are situated at a distance d from each other: $In\_Leaf(d) \cong d < \frac{B^l}{nb\_node} \cdot \frac{L}{2}$.

3.3   A Predicate for Modeling Routing Tables

The Can_Route predicate is a way to model the routing table. We propose to abstract all the routing tables of all the nodes by the completeness rate of each line of the tables. We define T_i as the number of filled entries in the lines of index i of all the routing tables. This allows us to define a probabilist predicate to decide whether a node n has a routing information at the line i: $\mathbf{prob}(Can\_Route(i)) \approx \frac{T_i}{B.nb\_node}$ where $B.nb\_node$ is the number of all the entries in line i of all the routing tables. Actually, there are B entries to fill in each line of each routing table of the nb_node nodes.

This fraction represents the probability that an entry is filled in the routing table of a node. To check if a message can be routed using the line i of a routing table, we try the probability $\frac{T_i}{B.nb\_node}$. If it's a winning try, the message is routed. If it's a failed try, we face a rare case.

Once again, we assume that the completeness of the routing table lines is homogeneous. The probabilist predicate will represent the real state of the routing tables if there is an homogeneous repartition of the filled entries in the lines of routing tables.

This probabilist model of the routing table may appear a bit unrealistic but, most of the time, peer-to-peer algorithms use indeterministic systems. Actually, lots of well-known issues of distributed algorithms (like election problems or livelocks) are solved by introducing an indeterministic behavior that implies the stability of the system in time. So, introducing probabilities in the model of the specification of the Pastry algorithm looks particularly adapted to us. Moreover, classical software analysis tools are inefficient for dealing with this type of algorithm. Although they can handle a strong abstraction of the system, the result that can be expected will not reflect the complexity of the system. And if we slightly abstract the system in order to get the result we expect, the classical tools will not be able to handle the model. With a probabilist model, we get the result in a quite reasonable time, that is in agreement with the results of [9, 10] among others.

4   Models

We define two models, a reference one describing a perfect routing and a more precise probabilist one.

4.1   Reference Model

The reference model was created to compare its results to the routing table model that we present in the next subsection. This reference model gives the theoretical behaviour of a routing in the Pastry protocol. For this, we assume in this model that all the entries of the routing tables are filled and there is no rare case.

```
/* start of routing */
d = random (max_dist) ;
nb_hop = 0 ;
while (! In_Leaf(d)) {
    /* the message is always routed */
    d = d / B ;
    nb_hop ++ ;
}
/* here, the receiver is In_Leaf, this is the last hop */
nb_hop ++ ;
/* end of routing */
```

At each hop, the model follows a law in $\log_B$. This means that the distance is divided by B until it becomes less than $\frac{B^l}{nb\_node} \cdot \frac{L}{2}$. In this case, the routing node should have the receiver in its Leaf set and can route in one hop.

This model is written with no more than 10 lines of code and doesn't contain any probability. But it was useful for us as a good evaluation of the CPU usage needed to make the figures we show in the next section. It is also the reference to compare with the result of the next, more precise, model.

4.2   Routing Table Model

In this model, we introduce our abstraction of the routing tables. The algorithm becomes now probabilist.

```
/* begin of routing */
d = random (max_dist) ;
nb_hop = 0 ;
while (! In_Leaf(d)) {
   if (Can_Route(log(d))) {
    /* the message is routed */
        d = random (B^log(d)) ;
   } /* else rare case */
   nb_hop ++ ;
}
/* here, the receiver is In_Leaf, this is the last hop */
nb_hop ++ ;
/* end of routing */
```

The probabilistic predicate Can_Route returns $true$ or $false$ depending of an internal random try of the probability $\frac{T_i}{B.nb\_node}$. The log returns the logarithm in the base B. The logarithm of the distance is approximatively the line where the routing node has to search the entry to continue the routing sheme.

This code represents a routing scheme according to a number of nodes and a completeness of the routing table. We now have to model the filling of the routing tables depending upon the number of nodes in the system, since the Can_Route predicate depends upon the filling rates T_i. We use for it the array defined in the previous subsection T_i which represent the number of filled entries in the line i of the routing tables.

For each insertion of a new node, the system performs a routing from the closest node of the newcomer in terms of network distance to the closest node in terms of Pastry identifier. Let's assume that these two nodes can be any of the nodes present on the ring. The Pastry algorithm implies that all of the nodes involved in this route could update the routing table of the newcomer. But we must pay attention that not all the nodes will contribute to fill all the lines of the routing table of the newcomer. For instance, with the example proposed in the section 3.1, the node $s = 20322102$ will contribute to the first line of the routing table of $r = 32102101$, but not to the following ones, since the node s is situated in the third quadrant of the ring, and the lines of the routing table of r greater than one would need information for the fourth quadrant (where r is situated). The node $s_1 = 30210130$ would contribute for its part to the two first lines of the routing table of r.

We propose to model the update of the routing tables in the following way. During a routing scheme, at each step of the route, we keep a trace of the number of nodes that contribute to the update of each line of the newcomer. Let's call this number U_i for the line i. This number is computed by comparing the number of digits shared between the newcomer and the node.

At the end of the routing scheme, we have for each line of the newcomer the number of nodes that can possibly fill an entry. For each of those entries, we try U_i times a $Can\_Route(i)$ predicate. If there is a winning try, the entry in the newcomer is filled. In our model, we increment the number of filled entries by one. This means that we increment T_i by one. If there is no winning try, we don't modify T_i. This means that no entries are found to fill the newcomer. The difficult part is when some tries failed and there is at least one winning try. The newcomer is filled by the node that wins its try, but as the newcomer also provides its routing table to the involved node, the failed node will also be updated. To model it, we increment T_i by the number of failed tries. We call this way to update the routing table the "share" method.

We should not forget the second way to update the routing table. We have already seen that the Leaf set must be updated when a new node is inserted in the ring. But the data contained in those Leaf sets can also fill some entry in the routing tables. To model it, we try the probability that an entry in the Leaf set fills a hole in the routing table. This probability is the probability that the node has no entry; in other words, it's the probability that it can't route.

For each new data in the Leaf set, we try one $Can\_Route(i)$ with the i depending upon the average distance in the Leaf set. In case of a failed try, the entry is filled and we increment T_i. We do it $2.L$ times with L the size of the Leaf set and two times because the newcomer updates its Leaf set but an entry representing the newcomer is also added in the the Leaf set of the L closest neighbours of the newcomer. This way to update the routing table is called the "Leaf" method.

5   Result of the Model

Those two models were evaluated with two different tools: PRISM [11,12] and APMC [8,13]. Our goal is to compute the probability that a Pastry system is in a given state. A system state is defined as a tuple $(nb\_node, nb\_hop, T_1, \ldots, T_l)$. Hence, we can compute the probability that routings are made in nb_hop for a Pastry system made of nb_node nodes with routing tables filled by T_i data.

The first tool, PRISM, computes an exact probability for the system to be in a given state, whereas APMC simulates the model as many times as it is needed to get some approximate probabilities.

We study two figures that appear to us significant: the quality of the routing protocol and the routing table completeness. The model was made using identifiers written on 8 digits with a base 4 with a number of nodes up to 300.

5.1   Quality of the Routing Protocol

The quality of the routing protocol is showed by the Figs. 2 and 3. Our graphs show the following: each curve is given for a number of hops; the horizontal dimension is the number of nodes, and the vertical one is the probability.

Hence, for a given number of nodes, tracing a vertical line, each time you cross one of the curves you obtain the probability that a routing is made in the

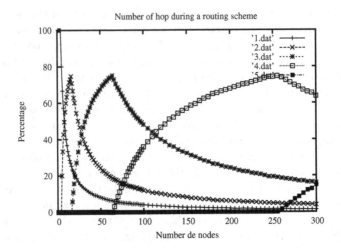

Fig. 2. Results for the reference model

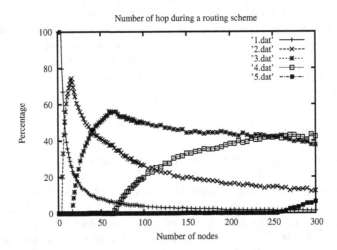

Fig. 3. Results for the routing table model

corresponding number of hops. Figure 2 shows the graphs obtained with the reference model described in Sect. 4.1, and we note for instance, that with 100 nodes, the percentage of routings done in 3 hops is 50%, the percentage of routings in 4 hops is around 35%, and it leaves 15% for routings in 1 or 2 hops.

Those first results must be compared with the results extracted from the second models defined in Sect. 4.2. Figure 3 shows the data we get from this model after simulation. We can see that the graphs decrease for the following values of node: 4, 16, 64 and 256 that correspond to the increase of $(log)_B(nb\_node)$. We show in this way that the DHT routing protocol follows a law in $(log)_B(nb\_node)$ despite the fact that there may be some holes in the routing tables of the nodes.

This is the most important result from a practical point of view, since it gives guarantees upon the behaviour of Pastry systems in the large.

We can also notice that the decrease of the curves obtained from the second model is inferior to the decrease for the first one. We may deduce that the routing is better than what we expect. For instance, for 100 nodes, the rate of routing in 4 hops is only 35% for 45% on the reference model. This can be explained because we used a really low base in our models: only 4. So the probability that, with one hop, we directly jump to the good part of the ring and save one hop is 1/4. If we used a larger base (the 16 base for instance), the difference between the two graphs should be less significant. But unfortunately, increasing the base is not a easy thing to do in our modelling choice. The limitation comes from the integer encoding in the model-checker and the dramatic influence it has in terms of model size.

5.2   Quality of the Routing Tables

Figure 4 shows the completeness rate of the routing table for different numbers of nodes and for each line of the tables. There are eight curves since we work with a length of 8. For a given number of nodes, tracing a vertical line will cross successively the 8 curves, giving the filling rate T_i for the corresponding line of the tables. The line number 8 corresponds to the more significant digit and is of course very quickly filled. The line number 6 will correspond to the lines where nodes get the information of the nodes sharing 2 digits with themselves.

We can show up to three phases in the update process of the routing tables. We recall that there is two ways of updating the routing tables and increasing the filling numbers T_i as we have seen in Sect. 4.2, the "share" method and the "Leaf" one.

1. First, the minimum for the filling rate for all curves is 25% since each node is its own representative in one of the four subdivisions of the eight lines of its own routing table.
2. The routing table begins to be updated when there are enough nodes in the ring so the probability that a node taking part in a routing enters your routing table is non zero. For instance, when there are 16 nodes, the graph 6 begins to go up. This is caused by the "share" update method.
3. The "Leaf" update method will be used to fill up the routing table when the average distance between two nodes implies that the Leaf entries for the addition of all nodes almost fill completely the line. When there are 64 nodes, the graph 6 dramatically increases.
4. The update made by sharing the routing table permits the hole in the routing tables to be filled in the last phase. The updates made following the "Leaf" method only takes place in a failed routing. When the filling is almost complete, this method is almost never used and this is the "share" method that prevails upon.

From this observation, we can deduce that the two modes of update are needed and complementary to ensure a good quality of the routing. Even if the update

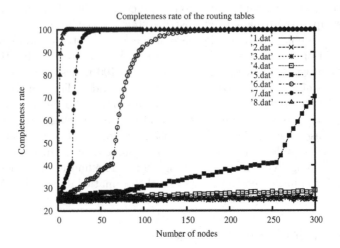

Fig. 4. Routing table completeness

made using the "Leaf" method may appear inefficient, it increases in a significant way the rate of completeness of the routing table. But this method has its limit and, around 80% of filling rate, the curves slow down. There, the second way of filling the holes, sharing the routing tables, allows the rate to reach 100% and fills the holes left by the "Leaf" method.

We can also deduce it from the model we choose. With the "Leaf" method, we increment the entry when the Can_Route try fails. This method updates the routing table when the rate of completeness is low. With the "share" method, we fill the holes when we get some winning tries. This method has a real influence when the rate is high. This observation was verified by disabling each update method in the model.

5.3   Discussion About the Results

Using two models, we have studied the behaviour of the Pastry protocol. We retain of this experiment a better understanding of this kind of algorithm, which is in line with the previous results obtained by the designers of Pastry. In particular, we confirm that the number of hops for routing is an increasing logarithmic function of the number of nodes.

The successive refinements we made to handle all the behaviours of the protocol support our belief that this kind of protocols are partially insensitive to the errors that may occur during the development of this kind of distributed application. In general, the peer-to-peer protocols that try to immunize themselves against faults are likely to present this property. For instance, the Pastry protocol can route even if the "Leaf" method of update is not implemented. The quality of this routing is degraded compared to a nominal behavior but it will still be able to route the message. Consequently, an eventual lack of accuracy of our models can be hidden despite the fact that the model behaves in the way we expect from the theory.

The same phenomenon occurs with an implementation of this kind of protocol. It may contain some errors despite the fact that the test of the application gives good results. According to this fact, validating such an application using a testing method appears a bit weak to us. A misbehaving implementation can be hidden by the fault tolerance of the system. This implies that, when there are failures, it can be first hidden by the intrinsic fault tolerance of the protocol, but, when failures will overrule the correct behaviour, it will be difficult or impossible to deduce the chain of events that originally led to failure. Such fault-tolerant systems are clearly hard to debug.

5.4   Discussion About the Tools' Performance

We have designed models of Pastry using parameters for the base B and the number of digits l of identifiers. Those parameters imply an upper bound of B^l upon the number of participating nodes in the Pastry system. A realistic size for those parameters would be $B = 16$, working in hexadecimal, and $l = 8$, working with the ANSI C integer datatype. This leads to more than 40 billion identifiers.

For our study of Pastry, we used $B = 4$ and $l = 8$. The computations for the simple model (see Sect. 4.1) took one day with PRISM and several hours with APMC. We recall that PRISM aims to compute exact probabilities whereas APMC uses a simulation to obtain results. The computations for the more realistic model failed for PRISM because of the size and took one day for APMC.

We can see here that it is possible to compute probabilistic model checking but that we had to make some abstractions for being able to use the model checking tools. The simplification which has the more influence is the use of a small base B. As we have discussed in Sect. 5.1, this implies better routing results in the routing table model than in the reference one. The probabilistic model also allows us to abstract the identifiers of the nodes and only take into account the distances. This abstraction reduces the size of the model and using model checker become possible.

6   Conclusions and Future Works

For us, this experimentation leads to several conclusions. First, even if PRISM can compute exact probabilities, this tool has difficulties for coping with realistic size of models. When the number of nodes increases, the computing time increases dramatically and we are no more able to get some results. But if we really need an exact computation of the probability, it is not possible to avoid the use of this type of tool.

The second tool, APMC, computes the probabilities using successive iterations of the model. The theory explains that, by increasing the number of iterations, we can reach an approximation of the probability as close as we want. This approach presents several advantages for us. First of all, it can handle a greater number of nodes. Secondly, we can get from the tools some partial results during the computation. So even if the computation is not completely finished, some data can be analyzed.

These two tools that we used in our experiment lead to significant results if the model analyzed fit the tools requirements. This makes us think that they probably can be used by specialists in the field of specification and abstraction to support the concept teams, but could not be used directly by those teams.

The results obtained with these tools are compatible with those provided by Microsoft. We have also shown the stability of the routing using the DHT protocol. Finally, we proved the great influence that the two kinds of update methods have to the quality of the routing.

We think that it will be really interesting to use this kind of tool to complete the result of some test or model-check inside software validation tools. This should be really adapted to the validation of distributed algorithms, in particular those that provide some fault tolerance and auto-stabilization properties. For instance, using this kind of tool, we can model check the behaviour of the Pastry nodes according to some model of the stability of the nodes. Actually, each node will be hosted by a consumer that can login and logout from the Pastry node at any time. This might be modeled also by a probabilist model. Using this model, we propose to prove that the routing protocol ensures that all the nodes can be reached from everywhere in the ring and there is no partition issues in the ring.

References

1. Averroes, Analysis and VERification for the Reliability Of Embedded Systems, RNTL, http://www-verimag.imag.fr/AVERROES/
2. Pastry, A substrate for peer-to-peer applications, Microsoft Research, http://research.microsoft.com/~antr/Pastry/
3. APMC, Approximate Probabilistic Model Checker, LRI, http://apmc.berbiqui.org/index.php/Accueil
4. PRISM, PRobabilistIc Symbolic Model checker, University of Birmingham, http://www.cs.bham.ac.uk/~dxp/prism/
5. Rowstron, A., Druschel, P.: Scalable, distributed object location and routing for large-scale peer-to-peer systems. In: Guerraoui, R. (ed.) Middleware 2001. LNCS, vol. 2218, Springer, Heidelberg (2001)
6. Castro, M., Druschel, P., Hu, Y.C., Rowstron, A.: Topology-aware routing in structured peer-to-peer overlay networks (2002)
7. Rowstron, A., Druschel, P.: Storage management and caching in PAST, a large-scale, persistent peer-to-peer storage utility. In: Prc. ACM SOSP'01, Banff, Canada, Oct (2001)
8. Hérault, T., Lassaigne, R., Magniette, F., Peyronnet, S.: Approximate Probabilistic Model Checking. In: Steffen, B., Levi, G. (eds.) VMCAI 2004. LNCS, vol. 2937, pp. 73–84. Springer, Heidelberg (2004)
9. Lassaigne, R., Peyronnet, S.: Approximate verification of probabilistic systems. In: Hermanns, H., Segala, R. (eds.) PROBMIV 2002, PAPM-PROBMIV 2002, and PAPM 2002. LNCS, vol. 2399, pp. 213–214. Springer, Heidelberg (2002)

10. Courcoubetis, C., Yannakakis, M., et al.: The complexity of probabilistic verification. Journal of the ACM 24(4), 857–907 (1995)
11. Kwiatkowska, M., Norman, G., Parker, D.: PRISM 2.0: A Tool for Probabilistic Model Checking. In: QEST'04. Proc. 1st International Conference on Quantitative Evaluation of Systems, pp. 322–323. IEEE Computer Society Press, Los Alamitos (2004)
12. Hinton, A., Kwiatkowska, M., Norman, G., Parker, D.: PRISM: A Tool for Automatic Verification of Probabilistic Systems. In: Hermanns, H., Palsberg, J. (eds.) TACAS 2006 and ETAPS 2006. LNCS, vol. 3920, pp. 441–444. Springer, Heidelberg (2006)
13. Guirado, G., Hérault, T., Lassaigne, R., Peyronnet, S.: Distribution, approximation and probabilistic model checking. In: Proc. of the 4th Parallel and Distributed Methods in Verification (PDMC 05), Lisboa, Portugal. Electronic Notes in Theor. Comp. Sci (to appear)
14. Duflot, M., Fribourg, L.: Th. Hérault, R. Lassaigne, F. Magniette, S. Messika, S. Peyronnet, Picaronny, C.: Verification of the CSMA/CD protocol using PRISM and APMC. In: AVoCS, Proc. 4th Int. Workshop on Automated Verification of Critical Systems, London, UK, September 2004, Electronic Notes in Theor. Comp. Sci. (to appear)

Opencomrtos: An Ultra-Small Network Centric Embedded RTOS Designed Using Formal Modeling

Eric Verhulst and Gjalt de Jong

Open License Society
Zavelstraat 160, B3010 Leuven, Belgium
{eric.verhuls,gjalt.dejong}@OpenLicenseSociety.org

Abstract. OpenComRTOS is one of the few Real-Time Operating Systems (RTOS) for embedded systems that was developed using formal modeling techniques. The goal was to obtain a proven trustworthy component with a clean and high performance architecture useable on a wide range of networked embedded systems. The result is a scalable communication system with real-time capabilities. Besides a rigorous formal verification of the kernel algorithms, the resulting architecture has several properties that enhance the safety and real-time properties of the RTOS. The code size in particular is very small and typically 10 times less than a typical equivalent single processor RTOS.

1   Problem Statement

Following a market research study for the European Space Agency in 2004, it was discovered that the majority of the RTOS (Real-Time Operating Systems) on the commercial as well as on open source market, cannot be verified or even certified, e.g. according to the DoD_178B or IEC61508 standards. This is due to a non-systematic software development approach, often bottom-up and with little documentation. This is remarkable as RTOS are widely used in embedded applications, often requiring properties of high reliability and safety. Similarly, software engineering is often done in a non-systematic way although well defined Systems Engineering Processes exist [3]. The software is rarely proven to be correct while formal model checkers exist. In the context of a unified systems engineering approach [4] we undertook a research project to follow a stricter methodology including formal model checking to obtain a network-centric RTOS as a trustworthy component. The availability of a network-centric runtime layer is important to support a unified semantic view of "Interacting Entities" for all activities in the Systems Engineering domain when developing a given system.

2   General Requirements for OpenComRTOS

The history for this project goes back to the early 1990's when a distributed real-time RTOS called Virtuoso (Eonic Systems) was developed for the INMOS

E. Gaudin, E. Najm, and R. Reed (Eds.): SDL 2007, LNCS 4745, pp. 258–271, 2007.

transputer. This processor had build in support for concurrency and interprocess communication and was enabled for parallel processing by way of 4 communication links. Virtuoso allowed such a network of processors to be programmed in a topology transparent way. Later on the software evolved and was ported from single chip microcontrollers to systems with over a thousand Digital Signal Processors until the technology was acquired by Wind River and after a few years removed from the market.

The motivation for the OpenComRTOS project was to use the lessons acquired from 3 generations of Virtuoso development. These lessons became part of the requirements. We list the most important ones:

Scalability: The RTOS should support a range of systems from very small single processor systems to widely distributed processing systems interconnected through external networks like the internet.

Network-centric: The above scalability requirements force data-communication to be central in the architecture, and also that the developed software is independent of the mapping onto the network topology.

Efficiency: In multi-processing systems the essence is the communication. From the RTOS point of view the challenge is to keep the latency to a minimum, while maximum performance is achieved when most of the critical code resides in the limited amount of on-chip fast memory.

Small code size: This has a double benefit: performance and less complexity with potential reduction of sources of errors and side-effects.

Trustworthy: As testing of distributed systems becomes very time consuming, it is mandatory that the system software can be trusted from the start. As errors typically occur in "corner cases", the use of formal methods was deemed necessary.

Maintainability and ease of development: The code needs to be clear and simple and facilitate the development of components such as drivers, which have often been the weak point in system software.

In the context of the Systems Engineering methodology, the use of common semantics during all activities is crucial. Hence the final goal is to be able to generate most of the implementation code from the modeling and simulation phase. Considering the use of an "Interacting Entities" paradigm, this imposes the use of a runtime environment that supports concurrency and synchronization/communication in a native way between the concurrent Entities.

3   Initial Architecture

While the above mentioned Virtuoso was a successful product, the goal was to improve on its weaknesses. The Virtuoso architecture was unique as it had two kernels inside. The lightweight nanokernel was mainly used for I/O and interprocessor communication while the microkernel provided priority based preemptive scheduling for user Tasks. This architecture was performant but very hard to port and maintain. Hence for OpenComRTOS a layered architecture was adopted but

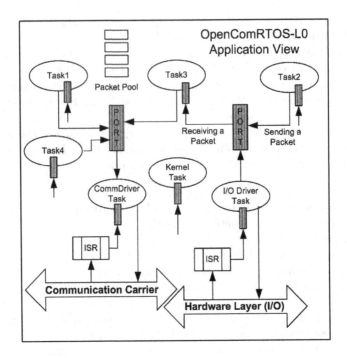

Fig. 1. OpenComRTOS-L0 view

based on semantic layering (see Fig. 1). At the lowest level the functionality is limited to priority based preemptive multitasking with Tasks exchanging standardized Packets using an intermediate entity we called Ports. Hence, Tasks can synchronise and communicate using Packets and Ports. The Packets are the essential workhorse of the system. They have header and data fields and are exclusively used for all services, rather than invoking e.g. function calls or using jump tables. Hence, it becomes straightforward to provide services that operate in a transparent way across processor boundaries. Packets are also very efficient as the kernel operation often comes down to shuffling around the packets (using handlers) between the system level datastructures.

At the next semantic level (L1) we wanted to add more traditional RTOS services like events, semaphores, queues, mailboxes, resources, etc. The concept was to achieve this using a second level of Packets whereby L0 Packets became full headers. This process is repeated for the next level L2 where we aim for support needed to address widely distributed nodes whereby the communication delay becomes substantial and the hard real-time behaviour becomes soft real-time. Such a level also requires support for mobility of code and of Entities. Finally, it was envisioned to keep the architecture simple and modular by developing the kernel as a Task as well as all drivers. All these Tasks have a 'Task input Port' for accepting Packets from other Tasks. This has some unusual consequences like the possibility to process interrupts received on one processor on another

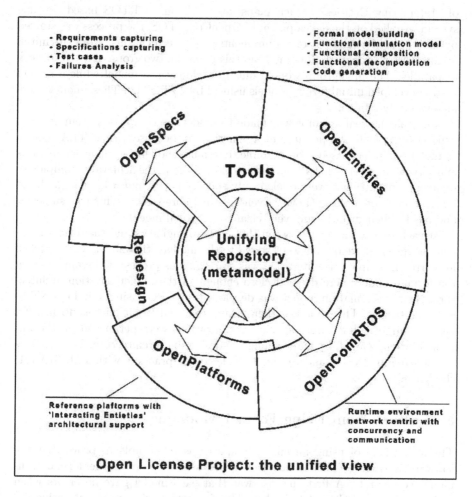

Fig. 2. Open License SE methodology

processor, the kernel having a lower priority than the drivers or even having multiple kernel Tasks on a single node.

4   Systems (and Software) Engineering Approach

The Systems Engineering approach from Open License Society (see Fig. 2) is a classical one as defined in [4] but adapted to the needs of embedded software development. It is first of all an evolutionary process using continuous iterations. In such a process, much attention was paid to an incremental development requiring regular review meetings by several of the stakeholders. On the architectural level, the system or product under development is defined under the paradigm of "Interacting Entities", which maps very well on an RTOS based runtime system. Applied on the development of OpenComRTOS, the process was started by elaborating a first set of requirements and specifications. Next an initial architecture was defined. Starting from this point on, two groups started to work in parallel. The first group worked out an architectural model while a second group developed initial formal models using TLA+/TLC [2]. These models were incrementally refined.

Note that no real attempt was made to model the complete system at once. This is first of all not possible in a generic way because formal TLA models cannot be parameterised. For example, one must model a specific set of tasks and services and very quickly the state explosion limits the achievable complexity of such models. Hence we modeled only specific parts, and a model was build for each class of services (Ports, Events, Semaphores, etc.). This was sufficient and has the benefit of having very clean, orthogonal models.

At each review meeting between the software engineers and the formal modeling engineer, more details were added to the models, the models were checked for correctness and a new iteration was started. This process was stopped when the formal models were deemed close enough to the implementation architecture. Next, a simulation model was developed on a PC (using Windows NT as a virtual target). This code was then ported to a real 16-bit microcontroller [5]. On this target a few target specific optimizations were performed on the implementation, while fully maintaining the design and architecture. The software was written in ANSI C and verified for safe coding practices with a MISRA rule checker [8].

5   Lessons from Using Formal Modeling

The initial goal of using formal techniques was to be able to prove that the software is correct. This is an often heard statement from the formal techniques community. A first surprise was that each model gave no errors when verified by the TLC model checker. This is actually due to the iterative nature of the model development process and partly its strength. From an initial rather abstract model, successive models are developed by checking them using the model checker and hence each model is correct when the model checker finds no illegal states. As such, model checkers can't proof that the software is correct. They can only proof that the formal model is correct. For a complete proof of the software the whole programming chain should be verified as well as the target hardware be modeled and verified as well. This is an unachievable result due to its complexity and the resulting state space explosion. It was nevertheless attempted in the Verisoft [6] project. The model itself would be many times larger than the software being developed. It indicates however that if we would make use of verified target processors and verified programming language compilers, the model checker becomes practical as limited to modeling the application.

Other issues were discovered in relation to the use of formal modeling. A first issue is that the TLC model checker declares every action as a critical section, whereas e.g. in the case of a RTOS, many components operate concurrently and real-time performance dictates that on a real target the critical sections are kept as short as possible. While this dictates the avoidance of shared data structures, it would be helpful to have formal model assistance that indicates the required critical sections.

The final issue is the well known problem of state space explosion. Just modeling a small OpenComRTOS application the TLC model checkers has to examine millions of states, exponentially taking more time for every Task added to the model. This also requires increasing amounts of memory and limits the model checking to subsets of the whole architecture.

6   Benefits Obtained from Using Formal Modeling

As was outlined above, the use of formal modeling was found to result in a much better architecture. This benefit is the result of the process of successive iteration and review, but also because formal models checkers provide a level of abstraction away from the implementation. In the project we found that the semantics associated with specific programming terms involuntarily influence choices made by the architecting engineer. An example was the use of both a waiting list and a buffer for a Port, which is one of the main concepts of OpenComRTOS. A waiting list is associated just with a waiting action, but one overlooks that it also provides buffering behavior. Hence, one waiting list is sufficient, resulting in a smaller and cleaner architecture. The formal modeling and abstract level has helped to introduce, define and maintain orthogonal concepts in the architecture. Orthogonality is the key to have small and safe, i.e. reliable, designs. Similarly, even if there was a short learning curve to master the mathematical notation in TLA, with hindsight this was an advantage vs. e.g. using SPIN [7] that uses a C-like syntax. The latter leads automatically to thinking in terms of an implementation code with all its details whereas the abstraction of TLA helped to think in more abstract terms. This also highlights the importance of specifying first before implementation is started.

A final observation is that using formal modeling techniques turned out to be a much more creative process than the mathematical framework suggests. TLA/TLC as such was primarily used as an architectural design tool, aiding the team in formulating the ideas and testing them in a rather abstract way. This was proven to be a team work with a lot of human interaction between the members of the team. The formal verification of the RTOS itself was basically a side-effect of building and running the models. Hence, this project has shown how a combination of team work with extensive peer-review, formal modeling support and a well defined goal can result in a "correct-by-design" product.

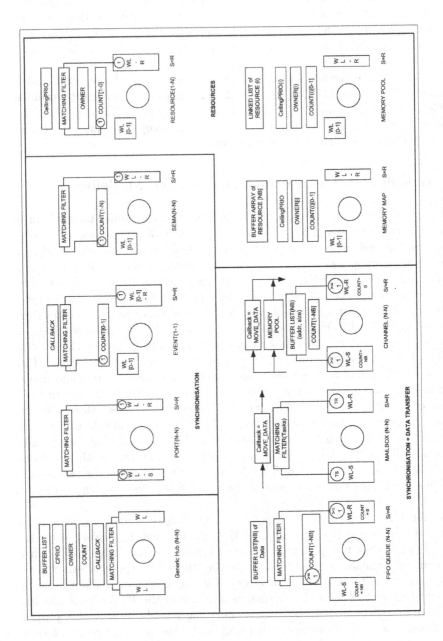

Fig. 3. L1 services derived from a generic "Hub"

7   Novelties in the Architecture

OpenComRTOS has a semantically layered architecture. At the lowest level (L0) the minimum set of Entities provides everything that is needed to build a small networked real-time application.

The Entities needed are **Tasks** (having a private function and workspace), an Interaction Entity we called an L0_Port to synchronize and communicate between the Tasks. **Ports** act like channels in the tradition of Hoare's CSP but allow multiple waiters and asynchronous communication. One of the Tasks is a kernel Task scheduling the Tasks in order of priority and managing and providing Port based services. Driver Tasks handle inter-node communication. Pre-allocated as well as dynamically allocated Packets are used as a carrier for all activities in the RTOS such as: service requests to the kernel, Port synchronization, data-communication, etc. Each Packet has a fixed size header and data payload with a user defined but global data size. This significantly simplifies the management of the Packets, in particular at the communication layer. A router function also transparently forwards Packets in order of priority between the nodes in a network.

OpenComRTOS L0 therefore is a distributed, scalable and network-centric operating systems consisting of a packet-switching communication layer with a scheduler and Port-based synchronization. This architecture has proven to be very efficient. For example, a minimum single processor kernel can have a code size of less than 1 Kbyte, with 2 Kbytes for the multi-processor version.

In the next semantic level (L1) services (see Fig. 3) and Entities were added as found in most RTOS:

Boolean events, counting semaphores, FIFO queues, resources, memory pools, mailboxes, etc. The formal modeling has allowed defining all such Entities as semantic variants of a common and generic entity type. We called this generic entity a "Hub". In addition, the formal modeling also helped to define "clean" semantics for such services whereas ad-hoc implementations often have side-effects. In Table 1 we summarise the semantics.

The services are also offered in a non-blocking variant (_NW), a blocking variant (_W), a blocking with timeout variant (_WT) and an asynchronous variant when this makes sense. All services are transparent for the topology and the network mapping of Task and kernel Entities onto this network. See Tables 1 and 2 for details on the semantics.

As the use of a single generic entity allowed a much greater reuse of code, the resulting code size is at least 10 times less than for an RTOS with a more traditional architecture. One could of course remove all such application-oriented services and just use the Hub based services. This has however the drawback that the services loose their specific semantic richness. For example resource locking clearly expresses that the Task enters a critical section in competition with other Tasks. Also erroneous runtime conditions like raising an event twice (with loss of the previous event) are easier to detect at the application level than when using a generic Hub.

Table 1. Semantics of L1 Entities

L1 Entity	Semantics
Event	Synchronisation on Boolean value. Waiting list on both sides.
Counting Semaphore	Synchronisation with counter allowing asynchronous signaling.
Port	Synchronisation with exchange of a Packet.
FIFO queue	Buffered communication of Packets. Synchronisation when queue is full or empty.
Resource	Event used to create a logical critical section. Resources have an owner Task when locked
Critical Section	Entity creating a global critical section based on locking multiple resources.
Memory Pool	Linked list of memory blocks protected with a resource
Mailbox	Synchronising entity with matching filter on Task ID. Communication happens as side-effect.
Channel	Asynchronous communication between Tasks with buffering using memory pools. Communication as a side-effect.

In the course of the formal modeling we also discovered weaknesses in the traditional way priority inheritance is implemented in most RTOS and we found a way to reduce the total blocking time. In single processor RTOS systems, this is less of an issue but in multi-processor systems, all nodes can originate service requests and resource locking is a distributed service. Hence the waiting lists can grow much longer and lower priority Tasks can block higher priority ones while waiting for the resource. This was solved by postponing the resource assignment till the rescheduling moment.

Finally, by generalization, also memory allocation has been approached like a resource locking service. In combination with the Packet Pool, this opens new possibilities for a safe and secure management of memory. For example, the OpenComRTOS architecture is free from buffer overflow by design.

For the third semantic layer (L2), we will add dynamic support like mobility of code and of kernel Entities. A potential candidate is a light weight virtual machine supporting capabilities as modeled in pi-calculus [9]. This is the subject of further investigations and will be reported in subsequent papers.

8   Inherent Safety Support

By its architecture the L0 and L1 semantic layers are all statically linked, hence an application specific image will be generated by the compiler tools. As we

Table 2. Service synchronization variant

Services variants	Synchronising Behaviour
"Single-phase" services	
_NW	Non Waiting: when the matching filter fails the Task returns with a RC_Failed
_W	Waiting: when the matching filter fails the Task waits until such events happens.
_WT	Waiting with a time-out. Waiting is limited in time defined by the time-out value.
"Two-phase" services	
_Async	Asynchronous: when the entity is compatible with it, the Task continues independently of success or failure and will resynchronize later on. This class of services is called "two-phase" services.

don't consider security risks for the moment, our concern is limited to verifying if the code is inherently safe.

A first level of safety is provided by the formal modeling approach. Each service is intensively modeled and verified with most "corner cases" detected during design time prior to writing the code.

A second level is provided by the kernel services. All services have well defined semantics. Even when asynchronously used, the services become synchronous when available resources become depleted. At such moment a Task becomes waiting allowing other Tasks to proceed and free up resources (like Packets, space in the buffers, etc.). Hence, the systems becomes "self-throttling".

A third level is provided by the data structures, mostly based on Packets. All single-phase services uses statically allocated Packets that are part of the Task context. These Packets are used for service requests, even when going across processor boundaries. They also carry the return values. For two phase services Packets must be allocated from a Packet Pool. When the Pool is empty, the system will start to throttle until Packets are released. Another specific feature of the architecture is that buffers cannot overflow. In the worst case the application programmer will not have defined enough Packets in the Pool and buffers will stop growing when all Packets are in use.

A last level is the programming environment. All Entities (at L0 and L1) are defined statically so they are generated together with all other system level datastructures by a tool and hence no Entities can be created at runtime. Of course, dynamic support at the L2 level will require extra support. However this can only be achieved reliably with hardware support e.g. to provide protected memory spaces. The same applies to the use of the stack spaces. In OpenCom-RTOS interrupts are handled on a private and separate stack so that the Task's stack spaces are not affected. On the MLX16 such a space can be protected but it is clear that such inexpensive mechanism should be a must on all embedded processors for all stack spaces. A full MMU is not only too complex and too large but it is not even needed. The kernel also has various threshold detectors and provides support for profiling, but the details are outside the scope of this paper.

9   Measurements on Real Execution Targets

We shortly summarize the results obtained. Although fully written in ANSI-C (except for the Task context switch), the kernel could be reduced to less than 1 Kbytes single processor and 2 Kbytes with multi-processor support (measured on a 16bit Melexis microcontroller). A sample application with two Tasks and two Ports required just 1230 bytes of program memory and 226 bytes of data memory (static and dynamic).

When adding L1 services (events, semaphores, resources and FIFO queues) the code increased with less than 1 kBytes. An overview in given in Table 3. All figures are for non hand optimised code written in ANSI C compiled on

Table 3. OpenComRTOS L1 code size figures

	MP FULL		SP SMALL	
	L0	L1	L0	L1
L0 Port	162		132	
Hub shared		574		400
L1 Port		4		4
Event		68		70
Sema-phore		54		54
Resource		104		104
FIFO		232		232
Resource List		184		184
Total L1 services		1220		1048
Grand Total	3150	4532	996	2104

MP Full: with router, no driver Tasks
SP Small: single processor, no router
All services: (_W,_WT,_NW,_Async)

the MLX16 16-bit microntroller. The reader will recognize first of all that the architecture has very little penalty for providing network enabled services.

A second port was undertaken to the Windows NT platform, serving as a simulator as well as host node. Further Ports are underway to MicroBlaze, SPARC and the Cell processor.

On the MLX16 microcontroller a processor specific version was developed. This version is limited to 16 Tasks and uses some processor specific instructions to reduce the overhead. Such minimal L0 RTOS could be made to fit in 904 bytes, whereas adding L1 Events, Ports and Resources only added 240 bytes to the code. Although this microcontroller runs from flash with no cache at about 6.5 Mips, the interrupt latency from a timer interrupt to the first instruction in a Task where the timer register can be read is only 52 microseconds. For a round-trip loop between two Tasks sending and receiving Packets using 2 Ports, we measured 10740 loops/second. This is about 93 microseconds for two Task switches, two L0_SendPacket and two L0_ReceivePacket services. All code, including the RTOS was compiled using the GCC compiler. The microcontroller has 4 registers.

A second version was ported on top of Windows NT and using sockets to simulate internode communication. The same test application as the one on the MLX16 could be generated for this "virtual" target by recompiling the source code and linking with the target specific libraries. This demo was transparently distributed over a number of PCs connected over a LAN. Code size figures and performance times are not really relevant for this target, but it demonstrates how a widely distributed and heterogenous network can be supported. Using this scheme an MLX16 node can read a sensor and transmit it over an UART to a "host PC" running an instance of OpenComRTOS. This PC then communicates with another PC over a VPN whereby an operator sends a control command back to the MLX16.

10 Impact on Software Quality

RTOS kernel code is typically known to be "black art" programming. This is due to the concurrent and asynchronous nature of the software, direct interfacing to the hardware, context switching and the requirement to produce not only performant but also compact code. Hence we were curious to see if the formal development path we followed would have an impact on the code quality. Therefore the code was subjected to the MISRA coding rule checker and quality software metrics of LDRA. The MISRA standard is a set of 140 rules that a program written in C should adhere to be safe. Most of these rules prevent programmers from using all the 'dirty' tricks, most often with side-effects that C allows. The source code had no problems passing this check. Also the quality of the source was very high according to the metrics generated by the LDRA tools. When the score was lower, it was due to the presence of too many comment lines or when the source file contained some in-line assembler like the context switch. The conclusion is that small optimized code doesn't need to be hand crafted provided a

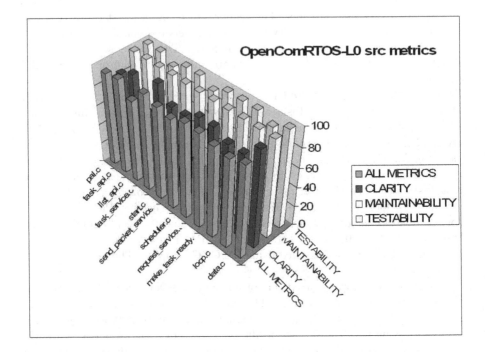

Fig. 4. Quality metrics by LDRA

lot of thought went into defining a clean architecture. The major gain is hence achieved by defining a globally optimized architecture and less from looking for punctual optimizations. The results are in Fig. 4

11 Future Developments and Research

Above we already identified the need for the model checkers to detect the minimal critical sections. Another area of research is how to maintain consistency between the formal model and the implementation. This will require that the formal model can be used as a reference and requires that the source is generated rather than written by the software engineer.

Future OpenComRTOS developments will focus on adding more safety and security properties to a SW/HW co-design pair of OpenComRTOS and processor. Formal modeling should contribute in identifying minimum architectures that still are providing safety and security in the resource constrained domain of deeply embedded systems.

Another area of interest is to find a better way to separate orthogonally the priority based scheduling from the logical behavior of the kernel Entities. For example, the use of priority inheritance supports results in this code being mixed up in the manipulation of the data structures (e.g. to sort waiting lists).

This makes the code more convoluted to read and understand while the impact is only on the timely behavior of the application.

Thirdly, OpenComRTOS will be ported to support the SDL-RT (using Real Time Developer Studio of PragmaDev). SDL type semantics map very easily on the communication based services in OpenComRTOS.

12 Conclusion

The OpenComRTOS project has shown that even for software domains often associated with 'black art' programming, formal modeling works very well. The resulting software is not only very robust and maintainable but also very performing in size and timings and inherently safer than standard implementation architectures. Its use however must be integrated with a global systems engineering approach as the process of incremental development and modeling is as important as using the formal model checker itself. The use of formal modeling has resulted in many improvements of the RTOS properties.

Acknowledgements

The OpenComRTOS project is partly funded under an IWT project for the Flemish Government in Belgium. The formal modeling activities were provided by the University of Gent.

References

1. OpenComRTOS architectural design document on:
   http://www.OpenLicenseSociety.org
2. TLA+/TLC home page:
   http://research.microsoft.com/users/lamPort/tla/tla.html
3. INCOSE: http://www.incose.org
4. Open License Society: http://www.OpenLicenseSociety.org
5. http://www.Melexis.com
6. http://www.verisoft.de
7. http://www.spin.org
8. http://www.misra.org
9. Milner, R.: Communicating and Mobile Systems: the Pi-Calculus. Cambridge University Press, Cambridge (1999)

SDL Design and Performance Evaluation
of a Mobility Management Technique
for 3GPP LTE Systems

Tae-Hyong Kim[1], Qi-Ping Yang[1], Soon-Gi Park[2], and Yeun-Seung Shin[2]

[1] School of Computer and Software Engineering,
Kumoh National Institute of Technology, Gumi, Gyeongbuk 730-701 Korea
{taehyong,saintwind}@kumoh.ac.kr
[2] Mobile Telecommunication Research Laboratory,
Electronics and Telecommunications Research Institute, Daejeon, 305-350 Korea
{yoyo,shinys}@etri.re.kr

Abstract. Using a common model for both functional verification and performance evaluation of a network protocol will reduce a considerable amount of protocol development time and cost. Although there have been several researches trying to achieve this goal, they have not been used widely yet especially in industry. This paper shows a case study in SDL design and performance evaluation of a wireless and mobile technology. In order to evaluate our mobility management technique for 3GPP LTE systems, we designed a simple 3GPP LTE system and its mobility performance system with pure SDL and Tau performance library. This paper describes our experience in pure SDL-based performance evaluation with Tau and discusses SDL design and simulation issues for more efficient performance evaluation with SDL.

1 Introduction

Formal description techniques such as the specification and description language (SDL) [1] were developed to clearly describe the specification of a network protocol syntactically and semantically. In addition to that point, they enabled us to verify the functional correctness of a protocol automatically with powerful tools supporting them such as Telelogic Tau [2]. Those tools usually provide functional simulation, validation, and code generation for the development of a reliable protocol. However, the functional correctness is just a minimal requirement of a network protocol; a crucial issue in the development of a protocol is its performance such as throughput and delays. A simulation-based evaluation with such performance parameters naturally requires a long time random simulation. Moreover it usually demands the exact consideration of the physical network environment such as noise or errors for obtaining more precise and realistic results. Those are the motivations of network-specific performance simulation tools such as OPNET [3] or ns-2 [4]. In this situation, a separate modeling and simulation is required for estimating each of functional and performance properties of a protocol.

E. Gaudin, E. Najm, and R. Reed (Eds.): SDL 2007, LNCS 4745, pp. 272–288, 2007.
© Springer-Verlag Berlin Heidelberg 2007

In order to overcome this inefficiency, there were several researches trying to design a performance model of a protocol from its functional model, especially specified in SDL. Most of them including Timed SDL [5], SPECS [6], QUEST [7], and SPEET [8] attempted to specify additional information to allow time requirements, workload modeling, and/or other performance-related information. However they have not been used widely due to their incompleteness and/or some weak points. Some of them require additional SDL syntax, which may weaken the compatibility of a model. They usually have few existing model libraries for real network protocols and environments, which may require extensive modeling work for accurate simulation. Simulation time may be very long due to their functional details. In addition, there also exists a practical difficulty that they usually use their own simulation tools whose stabilities have not been proved enough with industrial-size network protocols. The coupling of the SDL model to a well-known performance evaluation tool has also been tried and ns+SDL [9] is an impressive study where an SDL model can be used directly as an ns-2 agent.

As a part of the development project of the third generation partnership project (3GPP) long term evolution (LTE) system [10], we developed a mobility management technique with simple handover prediction for the intra evolved universal mobile telecommunication system terrestrial radio access network (E-UTRAN) mobility. A simple 3GPP LTE system with the proposed technique was designed in SDL and the functional correctness of that system was verified with Tau simulator. For performance evaluation of the proposed technique, we did not have enough time for full performance simulation with OPNET or ns-2 because that requires massive complete coding of a 3GPP LTE system. We decided to develop a performance simulation system with pure SDL and Tau's performance features before future comprehensive performance evaluation with OPNET. The above SDL-based performance tools were also considered but actually we did not feel convinced of their reliability and constant support because they are not commercial tools.

This paper presents a case study in SDL design and performance evaluation of a mobility management technique with Tau. To evaluate mobility management techniques, emulation of user mobility is necessary. SDL timers should be well managed in an SDL design and simulation with Tau where the SDL timer is the only delay source. Some other performance simulation issues are also discussed in this paper such as how to reduce the simulation time, how to manage the additional performance information skilfully in an SDL model, and how to link SDL models and simulators to other powerful performance simulation tools.

The rest of this paper is organized as follows. Section 2 introduces our mobility management technique with simple handover prediction for 3GPP LTE systems. Our SDL design of a 3GPP LTE system with the mobility management technique is explained in Sect. 3. Section 4 describes performance evaluation of the mobility management technique with the explanation of our performance simulation design. We discuss some issues on pure SDL based performance simulation with Tau in Sect. 5. Finally we conclude this paper in Sect. 6.

2   Our 3GPP LTE Mobility Management Technique

The 3G evolution project of 3GPP called long term evolution (LTE) and system architecture evolution (SAE) started in late 2004 and the standardization of their specifications was scheduled to be finished by 2007. As for the mobility of 3GPP LTE systems, the intra E-UTRAN mobility is mainly discussed at present and the intra mobility management entity (MME) / user plane entity (UPE) handover procedure was defined [11]. This section introduces our mobility management technique with simple handover prediction for the intra E-UTRAN mobility.

2.1   Handover Procedure

The standard intra E-UTRAN handover procedure is summarized as follows [11]. The source eNodeB monitors measurement reports from a user equipement (UE) and decides the handover of that UE to a new cell. It requests the eNodeB of that target cell to admit the handover of the UE, and if it receives admission from the target eNodeB, it initiates the synchronization between the UE and the target eNodeB by sending a 'Handover Command' message to the UE. Given a 'Handover Confirm' message from the UE, the target eNodeB triggers the path switching of the MME/UPE in the access gateway (aGW) with a 'UE Update' message.

Actually fast and seamless handovers are strongly required for a 3GPP LTE system because soft handovers are not available due to its orthogonal frequency division multiple access (OFDMA) technology. Our technique uses handover preparation with mobility prediction in order to achieve that goal. An outline of our intra E-UTRAN handover procedure is depicted in Fig. 1. Additional measurement reports related to the UE movements are defined for mobility prediction. The source eNodeB predicts the best handover cell with those new measurement reports and performs handover preparation with the corresponding target eNodeB. When the source eNodeB decides the best time for handover, it initiates the fast synchronization between the UE and the target eNodeB with a 'Handover Command' message. We can reduce the handover interruption time and the handover rejection rate with this technique.

2.2   Handover Prediction Technique

Mobility prediction is often expected a possible solution to fast and seamless handover with handover preparation. It is usually based on the following two technologies: time-series analysis such as the Kalman filter [12], and mobility pattern matching[13]. In spite of its usefulness, it has not appeared in the specifications of current mobile communication systems because those techniques may be somewhat complex and require more than simple change of the system.

In our technique, we use two simple prediction methods together in order to increase the accuracy of the prediction and to reduce the prediction cost as well. If we capture a nonstationary radio signal only in a short time, that part of

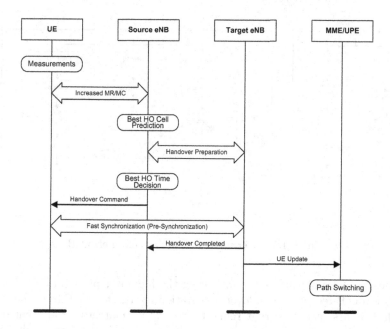

Fig. 1. Our intra E-UTRAN handover procedure (simplified version)

the signal can be considered stationary because the signal strength is related to user movements subject to the inertia. Our technique uses a simple moving average technique with a short-length window for short-term signal prediction under the assumption that the signal-to-noise ratio (SNR) is not so poor. But sometimes this simple prediction may not be adequate due to a sudden change of signal caused by exceptional non-inertial movement or strong noise. If user movements are not purely random but rather habitual, they may be estimated using past experience. We use a simple knowledge database to supplement the simple moving average for such a non-stationary but recurrent signal.

Figure 2 shows a simplified SDL-style diagram of the eNodeB's handover prediction process. An eNodeB updates the best handover candidate for a UE, denoted by b_{HO}, when it receives measurement reports from that UE. Those reports are created according to UE's reporting events including newly defined ones such as events Rn and 1D'[14]. When b_{HO} is decided, the handover preparation is performed between the source eNodeB and the target eNodeB corresponding to b_{HO}. It includes the handover admission control, and the context and radio resource information exchange for fast synchronization.

A general drawback of handover prediction is unnecessary handover due to a false alarm, therefore avoiding false alarms is a critical issue in a prediction technique. In order to achieve that goal we use a simple knowledge database (KDB) for recording the experience of false alarms. The KDB contains the false alarm information due to road-based and time-based mobility patterns of each user. An eNodeB manages the KDB and updates it when the UE movement

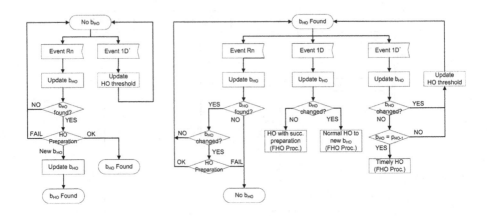

Fig. 2. Handover prediction process of an eNodeB

satisfies the false alarm condition. During the handover preparation, when the target eNodeB receives a handover preparation request for a UE from the source eNodeB, it first checks if that request information matches an element of the KDB. If yes, it refuses that request and may recommend another cell for the handover according to the KDB information. Then the source eNodeB may request the handover preparation to the new cell if recommended, or may give up handover preparation and follow the standard handover procedure.

3   Designing a 3G LTE System with the Mobility Management Technique

In designing a 3G LTE System in SDL for functional verification and performance evaluation of the mobility management technique, we used the *pure-SDL* design approach for our convenience in management [15]. With this approach, no external C-code is used and Tau's built-in ASN.1 utilities are used to encode and decode signalling messages. Our whole SDL designing process was composed of three sequential phases: basic functional design phase, mobility design phase, and performance design phase. This section covers the first two functional design phases.

3.1   SDL Design of a 3GPP LTE System

We started designing a 3GPP LTE system with the system structure and the basic signalling functions such as call processing. Figure 3 shows the package 'LTEBasicPKG' that includes three main block types for UE, eNodeB, and aGW of a 3GPP LTE system. The qualifier *virtual* was placed before the name of each block type for future redefinitions. We used two ASN.1 files for the signalling protocols, radio resource control (RRC) and radio access network application part (RANAP), and the buffer interface package is also used for ASN.1 encoding and decoding.

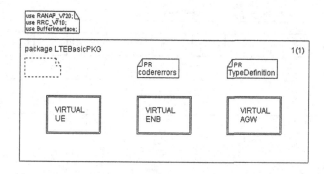

Fig. 3. Basic package for a 3GPP LTE system 'LTEBasicPKG'

When we designed each LTE node, we generally followed the present standard protocol stack [11]. As an example, the top-level first-phase design of an eNodeB is shown in Fig. 4. In that figure, the block 'SCL', indicating the signalling and control layer, is the core protocol layer which covers RRC, RANAP, etc. In the lower layer design, we mainly focused on their structure according to the existing standard specifications and did not implement their complete functions as we did in the last work [15], since the first design phase focused on the basic signalling functions. Note that two block types, 'ENB_PHY' and 'ENB_SCL' for the physical and the signalling/control layers were defined virtual for future redefinitions at the following phases. After the fist phase design, we checked the functional correctness of the system for call and multimedia broadcast multicast service (MBMS) processing with Tau simulator.

3.2   SDL Design of the Mobility Management Technique

At the second design phase, the mobility management technique was added to the 3GPP LTE system design. For better reusability and manageability, we used the inheritance and specialization in designing the mobility management technique. Fig. 5 shows the inheritance tree of our whole SDL system. 'LTEMobFTType' is a specialized system type for the mobility design, which was inherited from the basic system type, 'LTESigFTType'.

As described in Sect. 2, our mobility management technique incorporates refined measurement management in the UE side for mobility prediction and prediction-based handover preparation in the eNodeB side. In the UE side, the physical layer is the main design part at this phase which redefines the first phase design. Since there is no physical antenna that can provide the strength of receiving radio signals, we used some static signal strength data only for the functional verification at this design phase. Dynamic generation of signal strength data based on UE movements was left to the following performance simulation design. As for the eNodeB side, this design phase focuses on the signalling and control layer since no specific physical measurements of the eNodeB are used in our technique. Figure 6 shows a part of eNodeB's signalling layer design related

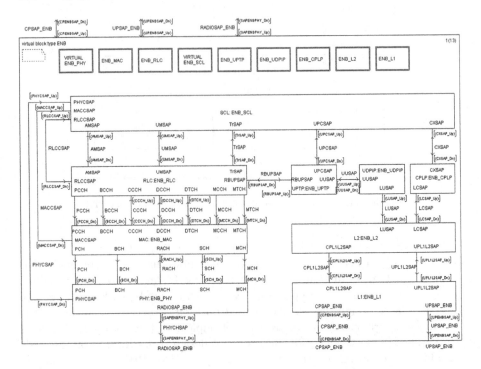

Fig. 4. Top-level struture of the basic 'ENB' block type

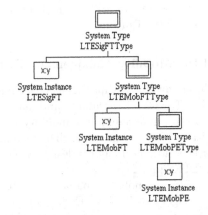

Fig. 5. Inheritance tree of the whole SDL system

to handover prediction and preparation. In this design, an eNodeB performs a handover decision based on the received measurement report according to the prediction algorithm.

For the system designed at this phase, we also checked the functional correctness of the handover procedure and handover prediction technique. The detailed results of that functional testing are omitted due to the limited space.

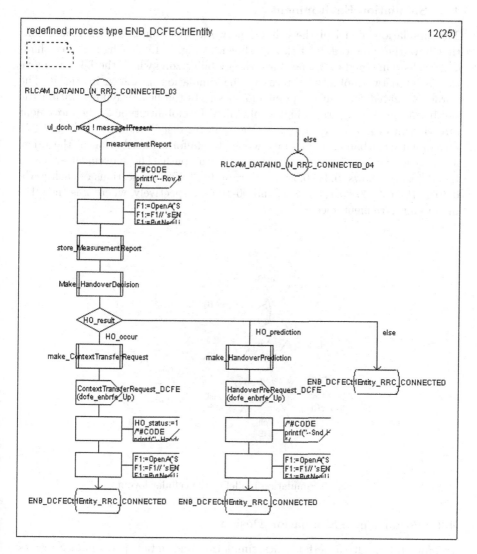

Fig. 6. Process type 'ENB_DCFECtrlEntity' redefined for handover prediction

4 Performance Evaluation of the Mobility Management Technique

For performance evaluation of our mobility management technique, we designed a simulation scenario and then constructed an SDL system for simulation with that scenario. This section describes that performance simulation design and the simulation results.

4.1   Simulation Environment

The simulation model of the cellular network area consists of 12 macro cells that have the same radius of 1km as shown in Fig. 7. In that figure three shadowed cells numbered 0, 3, and 4 are the mobility zone which the UE can move to. We used two mobility patterns in the simulation as shown in Fig. 8. The border-weighted random waypoint model selects the next waypoint within the cell border area at a certain high probability. In mobility type 2, the movement direction in degree is generated by the uniform distribution of 0, 90 and 270 for emulating urban-style mobility while the uniform distribution of the range [0, 360) in the mobility type 1. At each linear path, The movement speed of the UE is as follows: $0.3x$, $0.5x$, x, $0.5x$, and $0.3x$ for the sections of each path, 0-10%, 10-20%, 20-80%, 80-90%, and 90-100% respectively, where x is the UE's maximum movement speed.

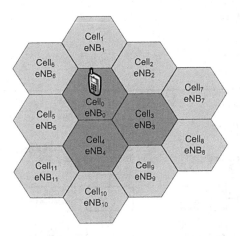

Fig. 7. Simulation model of the cellular layout

4.2   Performance Simulation Design

In order to execute a performance simulation and obtain performance results, some extra information is to be added in the functional design such as time delay or random property. We used SDL timers for all time advances and Tau performance library for queue manipulations, random number generation, and writing measurements on file. As already shown in Fig. 5, a performance model of our system was designed as an inheritance of the mobility design. Top-level structure of the performance simulation system is shown in Fig. 9.

For modeling signal broadcasting and propagation delays between LTE nodes, two extra blocks named 'RadioEnvSimulator' and 'NetworkEnvSimulator' were added in the performance model. Propagation time is calculated with the network configuration data and a time advance is realized with a corresponding SDL timer in those blocks.

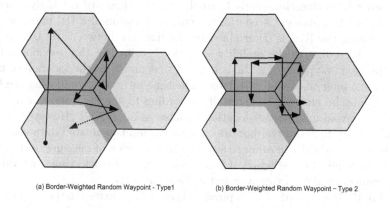

(a) Border-Weighted Random Waypoint - Type1   (b) Border-Weighted Random Waypoint – Type 2

Fig. 8. Mobility pattern for simulation

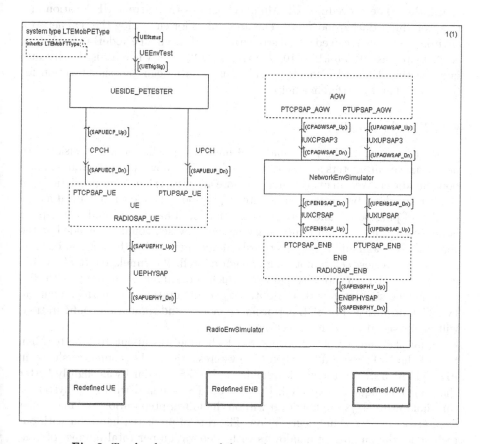

Fig. 9. Top-level structure of the performance simulation system

In order to decide the received signal strength (RSS) of a UE dynamically based on a UE movement scenario, the current location of a UE must be identified because the RSS is determined by the distance between the UE and the eNobeB. According to the mobility scenario described in the previous subsection, the next waypoint of a UE is decided first and thus the location of a UE after a time interval can be calculated. The time interval for updating the UE's location may be changed dynamically according to the UE's movement speed in order to avoid unnecessary location updates as in OPNET. However, we had to use a static time interval because some measurement-related data should be monitored periodically in order to send additional types of measurement reports related to handover prediction. Even if we used this static time interval, the performance simulation time was not so large actually.

Figure 10 shows a part of UE's physical layer design related to the UE mobility. There are four consecutive procedures to calculate the received signal strength based on UE movements: 'UE_mobility', 'Cal_Distance', 'BackgroundNoise', and 'Cal_EcNo'. The procedure 'UE_Mobility' decides the current UE location and the procedure 'BackgroudNoise' generates noises for emulating the real network environment. The received signal strength of a UE from an eNodeB i, $E_c/N_0(c_i)$, is calculated as $10 \cdot log_{10}16 - 10 \cdot 2 \cdot log_{10}(d_i/200) + n_i$, where d_i is the distance between that UE and eNodeB i, and n_i is a zero-mean gaussian function for background and interference noise.

4.3   Simulation Results

In order to examine the performance of handover prediction and decision, two performance parameters are used: the number of handovers and the rate of ping-pong handover. We can expect that the more accurate is handover prediction, the smaller are those parameters. The rate of ping-pong handover is defined as the number of ping-pong handovers per total number of handovers, and a ping-pong handover is defined as an unnecessary handover which could be avoided at the condition of maximum hysteresis threshold and after which the UE's sojourning time within a new cell is not long enough as well. We simulated 100-hour UE movements for each mobility pattern, which took about 10 minutes with Tau performance simulator with the optimized configuration on an Intel Pentium IV PC. Optimization of SDL performance models and simulation configurations will be discussed in the next section.

As for the number of handovers, our technique was about 10% better than that of the UMTS standard when the hysteresis threshold is small as shown in Fig. 11. At 5 dB hysteresis threshold, the UMTS standard was slightly better than our technique as expected. But the UMTS standard with high hysteresis threshold just delays the handover without handover preparation and may suffer from errors due to signal degradation. The rate of predicted handover with our technique, the number of handovers with preparation per total number of handovers, was about 70% for each simulation and the remaining 30% handovers had to follow the standard due to the sudden and repeated changes of the movement direction near the cell boundaries.

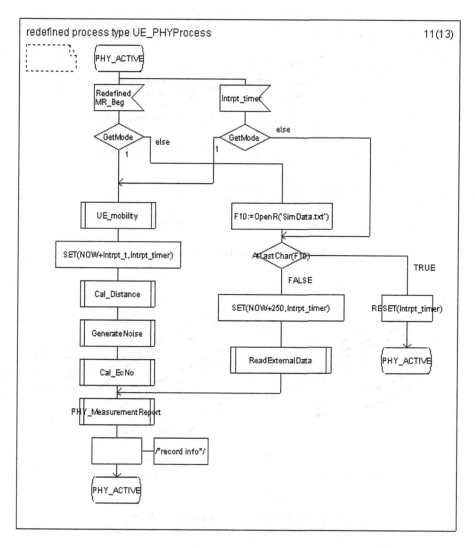

Fig. 10. Process type 'UE_PHYProcess' redefined for UE mobility

The rate of ping-pong handover shows similar results. In Fig. 12, if the sojourn time condition deciding ping-pong handover was loosened, the rate of ping-pong handover was also increased as expected. Our technique showed lower rate of ping-pong handover than that of the UMTS standard for every ping-pong handover condition except the case of 5 dB hysteresis threshold. This result shows that our technique is also useful to reduce unnecessary and ping-pong handovers owing to precise handover predictions.

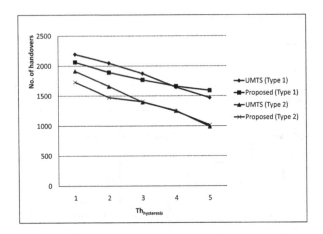

Fig. 11. The number of handovers

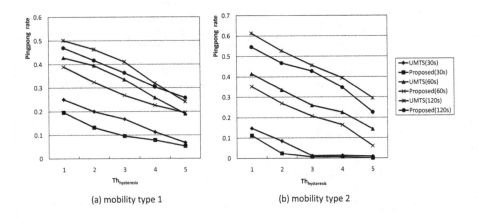

Fig. 12. The rate of ping-pong handover

5   Discussions on Pure SDL Based Performance Simulation with Tau

In this section, we discuss some SDL design and simulation issues for more efficient performance evaluation with SDL according to our experience.

5.1   How to Manage Performance Information in an SDL Model

Since functional and performance models intrinsically have distinctive goals, if we want to use a common base model for both functional and performance testing of a network protocol, we have to manage that model skillfuly for more efficient testing. If we want to perform performance evaluation of a protocol with its functional model as usual, the performance model should include some extra performance information. Functional design details which are not related to the performance, however, may reduce the efficiency of performance simulation.

We tried to handle this problem by specialization of the functional model. As described in Sect. 4.2, we redefined the SDL design for functional verification of the mobility technique to obtain a performance evaluation model. In the aspect of manageability, this approach can be a good solution. In order to use two models with higher manageability and reusability, sectioning functional details properly and hiding the details of each section with a procedure call is recommended in functional modeling. Otherwise a change of functional design may require a corresponding change in the performance model. As for the efficiency of the performance model, functional details which are not relevant to the system performance should be masked in the performance model by redefining transitions. Sometimes a process or a block may not be necessary for performance evaluation but removing a structural element is not allowed in SDL type inheritance. A possible practical solution is to add extra channels for detouring those structural elements with additional gate definitions and corresponding signal matching. Such a manual filtering process may be generalized and automated by analyzing the control flow of the functional model related to the performance measures.

5.2 How to Reduce the Performance Simulation Time

Another main issue of pure SDL-based performance simulation is how to reduce the simulation time. Since we already had a short discussion on the inefficiency of performance simulation due to unnecessary functional details, we mainly handle the problems due to SDL simulators which were not designed optimally for performance simulation in this subsection.

Event-based performance simulation tools such as OPNET usually have sophisticated memory management techniques for efficient handling of the event queues and performance measurement data. As for the Tau performance simulator, it is basically identical to the original SDL simulator except that it does not contain the monitor system in order to increase the simulation speed. For handling simulation information, it only provides some I/O functions for recording measurements on file. The user should decide how to collect simulation information and performance statistics with those functions. Since accessing a file takes a considerable amount of time, file writing should be designed minimally for reducing the simulation time. Using a so-called RAM disk [16] for such a measurement file is a good practical method for simulation time reduction. We also need to turn off printing on screen user simulation information for monitoring for the same purpose. Actually we could increase the execution speed about ten times with those optimizations.

5.3 How to Link to Other Performance Simulation Tools

Even though pure SDL-based performance models are well designed and SDL performance simulators are well managed, pure SDL-based performance

simulation of a network protocol may not be a complete substitute for performance simulation with powerful network-specific performance tools such as
OPNET. One of the main reasons is that those tools have huge existing model
libraries for real communication protocols, networks, and related technologies. It
would be very inefficient to design a large number of models additionally in SDL
for performance evaluation of a certain technique. Therefore, it is a very important issue how to link SDL models and/or SDL simulators to such a powerful
tool. There have been already several studies such as ns+SDL and they can be
categorized into two classes: tool coupling and model mapping. Since OPNET
is our main network performance tool, here we discuss the way to link our SDL
models and Tau simulator to OPNET.

Actually we have already used an indirect tool coupling with OPNET in
our performance design by allowing OPNET's measurement data to be used
in an SDL model. That example is shown in Fig. 10. In order to obtain more
realistic signal strength data with actual noises, we made an option to use signal
strength data produced by OPNET (modified UMTS library) with the same
network and mobility configurations as the SDL simulation. There have been
no meaningful differences between the simulation results of the two different
measurement methods. Model mapping of an SDL model to an OPNET model
is an interesting issue because both their designs are based on the same EFSM
model. Actually there was already an initial study about this issue [17]. But
this issue still leaves open because that initial work did not show systematical
mapping details.

6   Concluding Remarks

For estimating the properties of a network protocol, using a common model for
both functional verification and performance evaluation of a network protocol
will reduce a considerable amount of protocol development time and cost. There
have been several researches trying to achieve this goal but they have not been
used widely yet especially in industry due to their incompleteness and/or some
weak points. This paper showed a case study in SDL design and performance
evaluation of a wireless and mobile technology. In order to evaluate our mobility
management technique for 3GPP LTE systems, we designed a simple 3GPP LTE
system and its mobility performance system with pure SDL and Tau performance
library. We described our experience in designing those systems and performance
evaluation with Tau and discussed some SDL design and simulation issues for
more efficient performance evaluation with SDL.

This paper focused on mobility modeling and simulation with time resource
handling in SDL but we also have experience in SDL performance engineering
of other network performance features such as modeling of physical channels
with unreliability and queuing systems with limited buffering and computing
resources. Most of such performance features can be designed in simple SDL
models with some design skills. We are building some SDL model libraries for
easier network performance design in SDL.

In order to make SDL-based performance simulation used extensively and considered as an acceptable performance evaluation method in academia and industry of the networking area, a lot of success stories should happen with various network technologies. Tool venders' active support may be required for more efficient performance evaluation with SDL such as extending performance features, improving performance simulators, and providing predesigned protocol/network models.

As we discussed before, SDL-based performance simulation of a network protocol may not be a complete substitute for performance simulation with powerful network-specific performance tools. Therefore, there should be also continual studies on linking SDL models and simulators to those powerful performance tools such as OPNET or *ns*-2. We have started to develop a model conversion system from an SDL model to a corresponding OPNET model using systematical mapping algorithms. Even if that conversion is not complete, it would be a valuable help to the users which want to use OPNET for comprehensive performance evaluation of a certain network technology after functional verification with its SDL model.

Acknowledgements

This work was supported by the Korea Research Foundation Grant funded by the Korean Government (MOEHRD, Basic Research Promotion Fund) (KRF-2006-331-D00471) and by the IT R&D program of MIC/IITA, [2005-S-404-23, Research and development on 3G long-term evolution access system].

References

1. ITU, Recommendation Z.100, Specification and Description Language (SDL). ITU, Geneva (August 2002)
2. Telelogic AB Inc., Telelogic TAU SDL Suite, See http://www.telelogic.com
3. OPNET Technology Inc., OPNET Modeler, See http://www.opnet.com
4. Information Science Institute, University of Southern California, The Network Simulator ns-2, See http://www.isi.edu/nsnam/ns
5. Bause, F., Buchholz, P.: Qualitative and Quantitative Analysis of Timed SDL Specifications. In: Kommunikation in Verteilten Systemen, Reihe Informatik aktuell, pp. 486–500. Springer, Heidelberg (1993)
6. Bütow, M., Mestern, M., Schapiro, C., Kritzinger, P.S.: Performance Modelling with the Formal Specification language SDL. In: FORTE IX/PSTV XVI, Chapman & Hall, Sydney (1996)
7. Diefenbruch, M., Heck, E., Hintelmann, J., Müller-Clostermann, B.: Performance Evaluation of SDL Systems Adjunct by Queuing Models. In: SDL '95 with MSC in CASE, Elsevier, Amsterdam (1995)
8. Steppler, M.: Performance Analysis of Communication Systems Formally Specified in SDL. In: WOSP'98. Proc. of First Int'l Workshop on Software and Performance (1998)

9. Kuhn, T., Geraldy, A., Gotzhein, R., Rothländer, F.: ns+SDL – The Network Simulator for SDL Systems. In: Prinz, A., Reed, R., Reed, J. (eds.) SDL 2005. LNCS, vol. 3530, pp. 103–116. Springer, Heidelberg (2005)

10. 3GPP, UTRA-UTRAN Long Term Evolution (LTE) and 3GPP System Architecture Evolution (SAE), See http://www.3gpp.org/Highlights/LTE/LTE.htm

11. 3GPP, E-UTRA and E-UTRAN; Radio Interface Protocol Aspects. TR 25.813 V.7.1.0, 9 (2006)

12. Welch, G., et al.: An Introduction to the Kalman Filter. University of North Carolina TR 95-041, UNC (2002)

13. Michaelis, S., et al.: Comparison of User Mobility Pattern Prediction Algorithms to increase Handover Trigger Accuracy. IEEE VTC 2006-Spring, Melbourne (2006)

14. Kim, T.-H., Yang, Q., Lee, J.-H., Park, S.-G., Shin, Y.-S.: A Mobility Management Technique with Simple handover Prediction for 3G LTE Systems. IEEE VTC 2007-Fall, Baltimore (2007)

15. Kim, T.-H., Kim, J.-W., Yang, Q.-P., Lee, J.-H., Park, S.-G., Shin, Y.-S.: SDL Design of a Radio Resource Control Protocol for 3G Evolution Systems with Two Different Approaches. In: Gotzhein, R., Reed, R. (eds.) SAM 2006. LNCS, vol. 4320, pp. 166–182. Springer, Heidelberg (2006)

16. Wikipedia Foundation, Inc., RAM disk. Wikipedia, the free encyclopedia, http://en.wikipedia.org/wiki/RAM_disk

17. Martins, J., Hubaux, J.-P., Saydam, T., Znatny, S.: Integrating Performance Evaluation and Formal Spefication. In: ICCE' 96. Proc. of Int'l Conf. on Communications, IEEE Computer Society Press, Los Alamitos (1996)

Author Index

Lecture Notes in Computer Science

Sublibrary 5: Computer Communication Networks and Telecommunications

For information about Vols. 1– 4373
please contact your bookseller or Springer

Vol. 4026: P.B. Gibbons, T. Abdelzaher, J. Aspnes, R. Rao (Eds.), Distributed Computing in Sensor Systems. XIV, 566 pages. 2006.

Vol. 4003: Y. Koucheryavy, J. Harju, V.B. Iversen (Eds.), Next Generation Teletraffic and Wired/Wireless Advanced Networking. XVI, 582 pages. 2006.

Vol. 3996: A. Keller, J.-P. Martin-Flatin (Eds.), Self-Managed Networks, Systems, and Services. X, 185 pages. 2006.

Vol. 3976: F. Boavida, T. Plagemann, B. Stiller, C. Westphal, E. Monteiro (Eds.), NETWORKING 2006. Networking Technologies, Services, and Protocols; Performance of Computer and Communication Networks; Mobile and Wireless Communications Systems. XXVI, 1276 pages. 2006.

Vol. 3970: T. Braun, G. Carle, S. Fahmy, Y. Koucheryavy (Eds.), Wired/Wireless Internet Communications. XIV, 350 pages. 2006.

Vol. 3964: M.Ü. Uyar, A.Y. Duale, M.A. Fecko (Eds.), Testing of Communicating Systems. XI, 373 pages. 2006.

Vol. 3961: I. Chong, K. Kawahara (Eds.), Information Networking. XV, 998 pages. 2006.

Vol. 3912: G.J. Minden, K.L. Calvert, M. Solarski, M. Yamamoto (Eds.), Active Networks. VIII, 217 pages. 2007.

Vol. 3883: M. Cesana, L. Fratta (Eds.), Wireless Systems and Network Architectures in Next Generation Internet. IX, 281 pages. 2006.

Vol. 3868: K. Römer, H. Karl, F. Mattern (Eds.), Wireless Sensor Networks. XI, 342 pages. 2006.

Vol. 3854: I. Stavrakakis, M. Smirnov (Eds.), Autonomic Communication. XIII, 303 pages. 2006.

Vol. 3813: R. Molva, G. Tsudik, D. Westhoff (Eds.), Security and Privacy in Ad-hoc and Sensor Networks. VIII, 219 pages. 2005.

Vol. 3462: R. Boutaba, K.C. Almeroth, R. Puigjaner, S. Shen, J.P. Black (Eds.), NETWORKING 2005. XXX, 1483 pages. 2005.